IMAGES
of America

WAUWATOSA

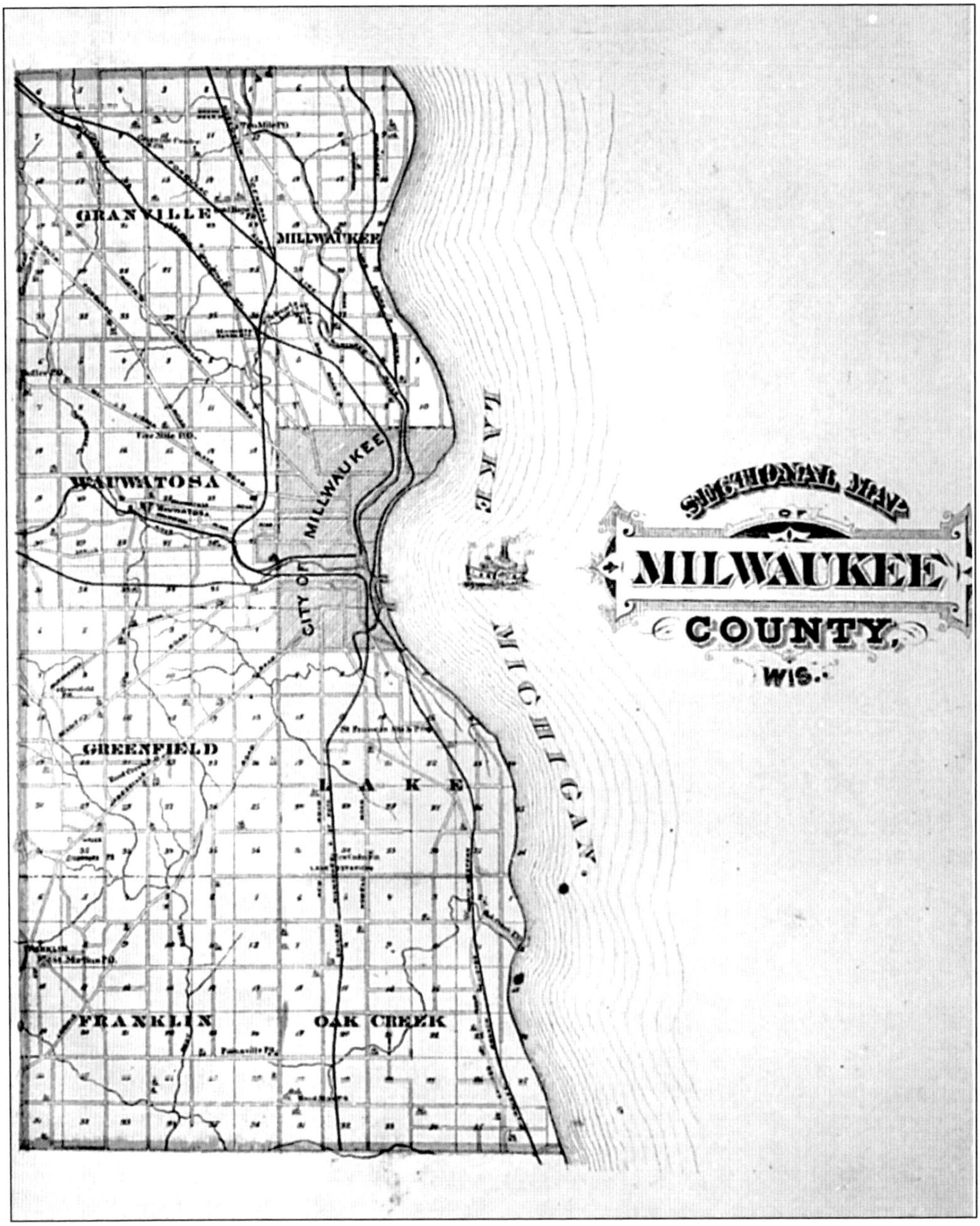

This map of Milwaukee County is from the *Illustrated Historical Atlas of Milwaukee County, Wisconsin, 1876*. The boundaries of Milwaukee County were formed in 1846 and have not been changed to the present day. Within the county were seven townships created by a federal land survey; one became Wauwatosa. First the territorial and then the state legislature assigned governmental authority to these townships, which were then referred to as towns. Wauwatosa, before it incorporated as a village in 1892, existed within the Town of Wauwatosa for nearly 60 years. (WHS Map Collection.)

Cover Photo: Wauwatosa Steam Laundry in the Village can also be seen on page 16.

IMAGES
of America

WAUWATOSA

Wauwatosa Historical Society

ARCADIA
PUBLISHING

ISBN 978-0-7385-3232-5

Published by Arcadia Publishing
Charleston, South Carolina

Printed in the United States of America

Library of Congress Catalog Card Number: 2003116542

For all general information contact Arcadia Publishing at:
Telephone 843-853-2070
Fax 843-853-0044
E-mail sales@arcadiapublishing.com
For customer service and orders:
Toll-Free 1-888-313-2665

Visit us on the Internet at www.arcadiapublishing.com

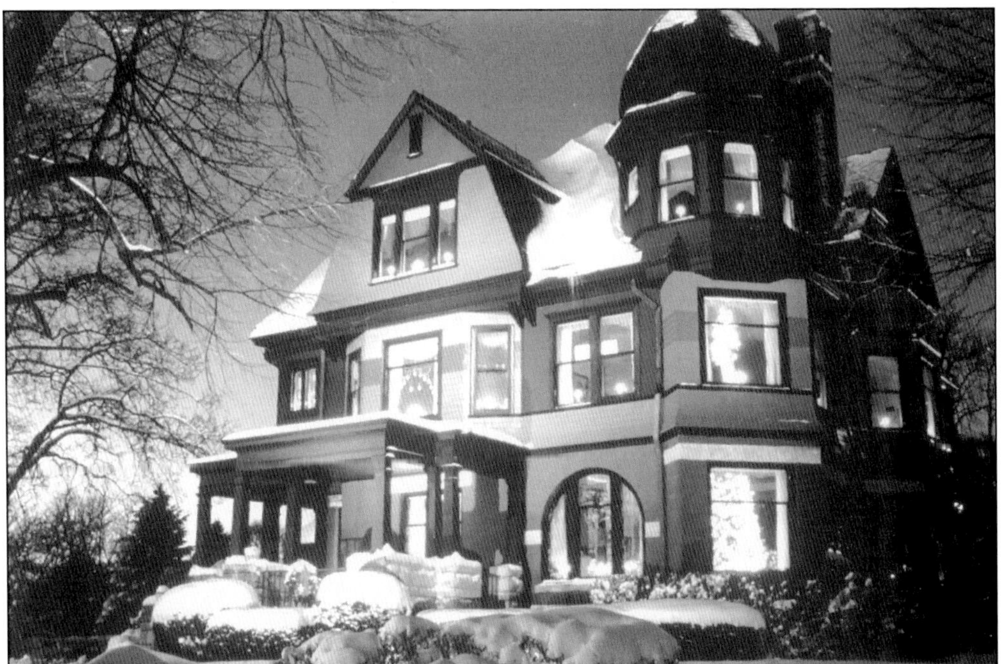

This 1890 Queen Anne residence at 7406 Hillcrest Drive is the headquarters of the Wauwatosa Historical Society. For nearly 100 years, only two families lived here and its present name, the Kneeland-Walker House, honors those occupants. The house is now a model for historic preservation and a center for society and community events. The society restored the exterior to its original five-color paint scheme, seen in this 1990s image, and interior refurbishing has returned the residence to period splendor. In summer its one-and-a-half acre Victorian gardens are profuse with color. (Photo by Lawrence A. Michael, WHS Photo 757.)

Contents

Acknowledgments		6
Introduction		7
1.	Prologue to Prosperity: The Village	9
2.	Commercial Spread	27
3.	For the Common Good	41
4.	Health and Human Services	49
5.	Educating the People	59
6.	Our Faith Grows Deep	73
7.	Voluntary Organizations	81
8.	People, Pleasures, and Pastimes	89
9.	A City of Homes	103
10.	A Changing Landscape: Post-World War II	119

ACKNOWLEDGMENTS

Without the leadership of Judith A. Simonsen, this book would not have been possible. The Wauwatosa Historical Society is sincerely grateful for her guidance, her expertise in historic documentation, and the many hours Judy spent as chair of this project. She and the society's president, Jim Vint, served as historical editors. We also thank the many people who assisted in research tasks, especially our caption writers, who worked with historical records and publications and conducted interviews: Barbara Benton, Dan Jones, Patricia A. Martens, Judith A. Simonsen, Kay Tierney, Jim Vint, David M. Vogel, and Raymond J. White. We are indebted to Carolyn Dressler for scanning many of the photos; to Anne Bingham, copy editor; to Rachael VerDuin for transcribing; to Kathie Vint, reader; and to the society's executive director, Janel Ruzicka, for her layout work.

Much of the information in this publication was compiled from these sources: *Historic Wauwatosa*, the newsletter of the Wauwatosa Historical Society; *The Wauwatosa Story*, 1985 Revised Edition; *Sketches of Wauwatosa*, compiled by Elizabeth V. Foley, 1932; *Reminiscences of the Early History of Wauwatosa*, by Emma Clapp Watner, 1902; *City of Wauwatosa 100th Anniversary 1835–1935*; and *Trading Post to Metropolis: Milwaukee County's First 150 Years*, edited by Ralph M. Aderman, 1987.

With this book, the Wauwatosa Historical Society seeks to present a panorama of our community's past through historic photographs, rather than an all–inclusive history of our city. The images are primarily from the society's collection, and we thank the generous individuals and families who donated these photographs. Our hope is that this time capsule of people, places, and events will entice our readers to learn more about Wauwatosa history through the resources at the Wauwatosa Historical Society research library and the Wauwatosa Public Library, as well as from other sources of local history.

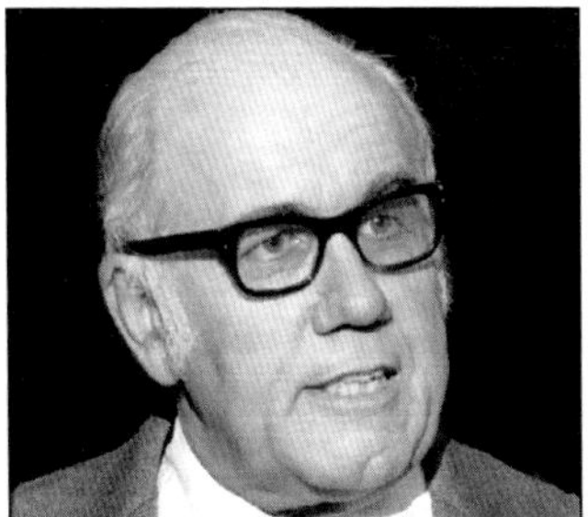

Dr. Frederick I. Olson (1916–2003)
This book is dedicated to Dr. Olson, Professor Emeritus of History, the University of Wisconsin-Milwaukee. A native and life-long resident of Wauwatosa, he loved his hometown and its history. Many of his writings were used for research for this book. Fred was a steadfast supporter of the Wauwatosa Historical Society and promoted the dissemination of the history of our community and preservation of its material culture. (Courtesy of Jane Olson.)

INTRODUCTION

Native Americans first lived in the wilderness that would become Wauwatosa, hunting in the lush forests and fishing in the Menomonee River. Shortly after the federal government entered into treaties with the Menomonee and Potawatomi Indians in the 1830s, this area was surveyed in preparation for land sales by the United States government.

For nearly 60 years, unincorporated Wauwatosa existed within the Town of Wauwatosa. The town, established in 1840, was a governmental entity contiguous with the federal land survey of the Township of Wauwatosa. This six-mile-square area was bounded on the east by Twenty-seventh Street, the west by 124th Street, the south by Greenfield Avenue, and the north by Hampton Avenue. The first recorded town meeting occurred in 1842. Wauwatosa incorporated as a village in 1892, followed by designation as a fourth class city in 1897.

Wauwatosa is unique among the 18 suburbs of the City of Milwaukee. It is not the largest in area (it is third, with 13.1 square miles) or in population (it is second, with 47,271 residents as of the 2000 census). It was the first Milwaukee County settlement in the 1830s, apart from the settlement that became the City of Milwaukee.

Charles Hart, the founder of Wauwatosa, arrived in Milwaukee in 1835 and learned that five miles to the west there was a prime spot for settlement. He erected a log house on approximately the southwest corner of Harwood and Wauwatosa Avenues. Hart first built a sawmill around 1838 to convert the abundant supply of hardwood trees into lumber for building construction. Later he built a gristmill and millpond. This early settlement became known as Hart's Mills. Thomas B. Hart joined his brother Charles in 1837. Their work to exploit the power of the Menomonee River formed the nucleus of a small community that would grow by serving travelers and local farmers. Reflecting the origin of the early Yankee and New York pioneers, a village reminiscent of New England's, complete with a commons, emerged in the hilly crossroads at the Menomonee River. It became Wauwatosa in approximately 1841, the name's origin is obscure.

Education and religion were of primary importance, and the pioneers established schools, churches, and voluntary organizations. Joined by Germans and some Irish, these early settlers would mold the community. The early home of Oliver Damon and his son Lowell, built from 1844 to 1846, is the city's oldest surviving residence, preserved today as a museum. The Little Red Store in the Village, constructed in 1854, is the oldest surviving commercial structure and is now owned by the City of Wauwatosa.

Several early developments spurred Wauwatosa growth. Transportation links from Milwaukee and extending beyond Wauwatosa were significant. In 1838, the federal government built the United States Road (present Harwood Avenue) and by 1851 both a railroad and a toll road, the

Watertown Plank Road, passed through the Village. The Milwaukee County Board's decision in 1852 to establish a county poor farm near the Village on the plank road brought Wauwatosa attention from the entire county. After the Civil War, the National Soldier's Home and the Wisconsin State Fair Park were established in the Town of Wauwatosa. Industries included two breweries, a pickle factory, and several limestone quarries, as well as the farms throughout the Town of Wauwatosa. A catastrophic fire in 1895 devastated a large portion of the commercial area in the Village, but also provided an incentive for new growth and commercial spread.

Known as the "City of Homes," Wauwatosa has a diverse housing stock, with numerous Victorian-era residences and a variety of twentieth century architectural styles. By the 1930s, Wauwatosa had the character of a bedroom suburb, and it was the second city in the state to adopt a zoning ordinance. In 1931, a major street renaming and renumbering occurred in Wauwatosa. Throughout this book, current names and numbers are used; structures no longer extant will not carry an address.

Wauwatosa values its built environment and in 1975 established the Wauwatosa Landmark Commission, presently the Wauwatosa Historic Preservation Commission. Currently there are 18 Wauwatosa buildings and districts listed in the National and State Registers of Historic Places, and 17 designated as official local historic landmarks.

For more than a century after its settlement in 1835, Wauwatosa was the quintessential and largest residential suburb in the county. One of the greatest strengths of the Wauwatosa Historical Society's photographic collection is the number of images that record the changes in the Village over 100 years. Today, the original Village remains the cherished heart of the community.

Wauwatosa was transformed in the post-World War II era when the city acquired eight-and-one-half square miles of the old Town of Wauwatosa and tripled its size. Wauwatosa became a major center for commercial, office building, and industrial development. Citizens value the 2,000-plus acres of parks and recreational land within the city limits. Public and parochial schools offer quality education—more than 85 percent of high school graduates go on to higher education. Wauwatosa is welcoming to business and industry as well as to institutions and families. Its population reflects a multicultural background. With an emphasis on keeping a friendly, small-town feel within a bustling urban setting, Wauwatosa values its traditions while providing an environment where all can live, grow, and prosper.

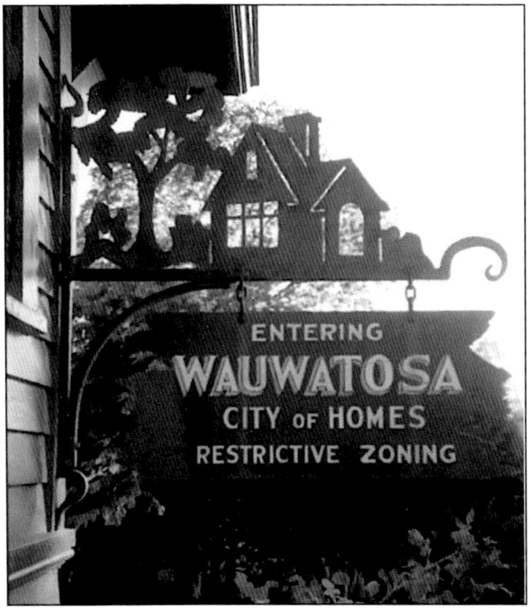

For decades, welcome signs like this greeted people as they entered the city of Wauwatosa. (Photo by James Ruzicka, WHS Artifact Collection and Photo 708.)

One

PROLOGUE TO PROSPERITY

THE VILLAGE

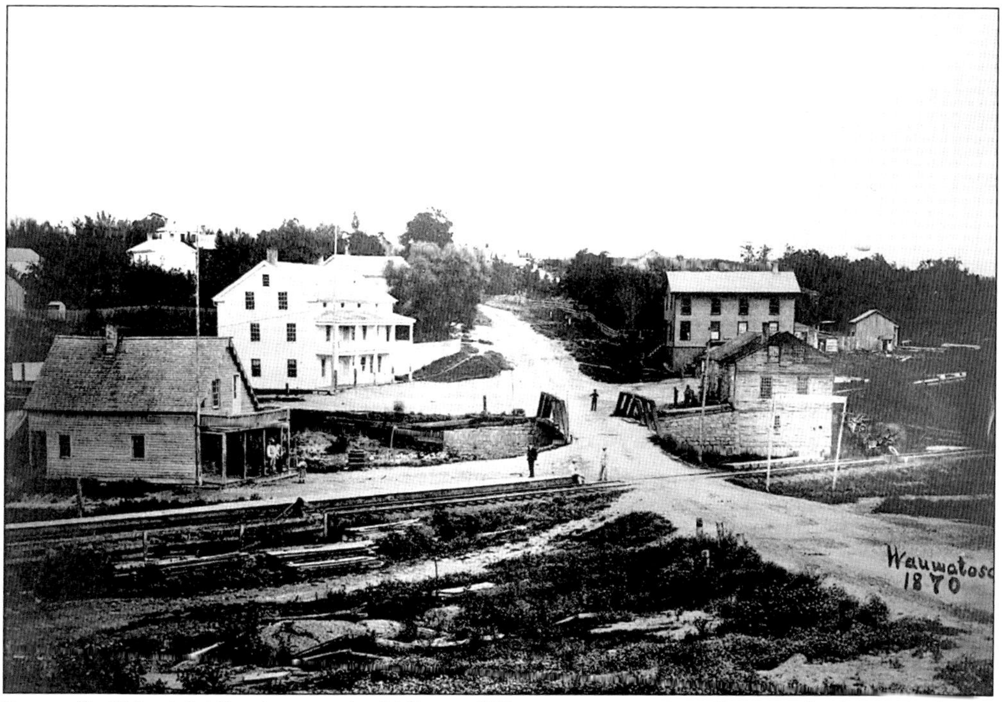

First called Hart's Mills, this was the Village of Wauwatosa in 1870. The view looks up the broad United States Road, renamed Main Street and later Harwood Avenue. In the foreground, along the single railroad track, are wooden platforms for passengers. The first railroad in the state arrived here from Milwaukee in 1850 and extended to Waukesha in 1851. Across the tracks on the left is one of the oldest surviving structures in the city, built in 1854, and today called the Little Red Store because it wore a coat of red paint for over a century. Uses of this modest building at the time of this photograph included a general store, rail depot, and post office. The two-story frame inn beyond the Red Store was the Wauwatosa House. The Dearsley Tavern stands across the street on the right. Alongside the wooden bridge spanning the Menomonee River is Wesson's Wagon Shop. (WHS Photo 402.)

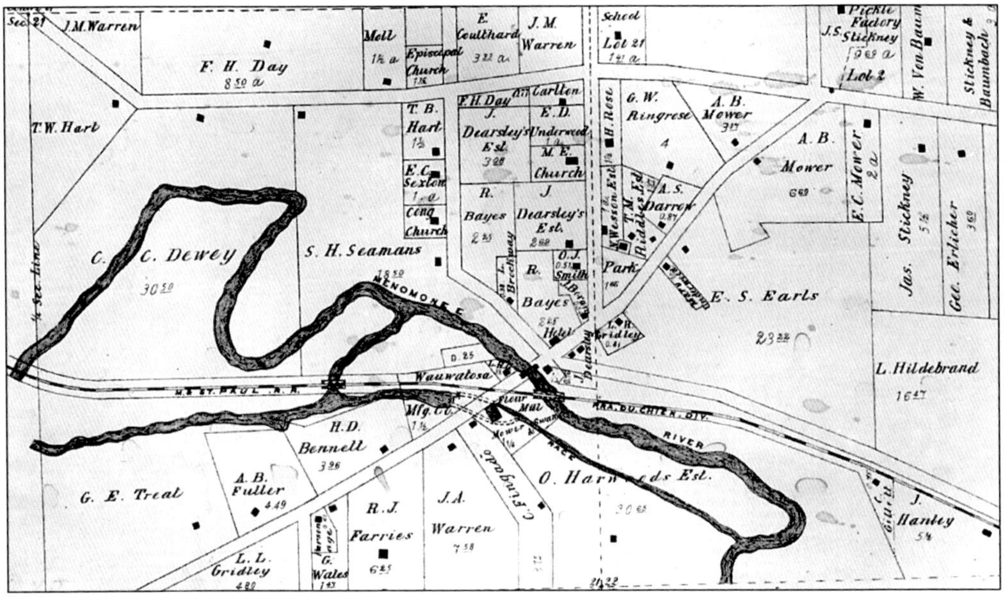

Names of Yankee and New York settlers predominate in this 1876 plat map of the Village. The first was Charles Hart, who arrived in 1835 and in 1838 built a sawmill adjacent to the Menomonee River that provided power. Hart then built a gristmill in 1841 and a millpond that greatly improved waterpower for the new mill. The millpond, millrace, spillway, and overflow are linked to the river south of the railroad track. The settlement was first called Hart's Mills because of these operations. (WHS Map Collection.)

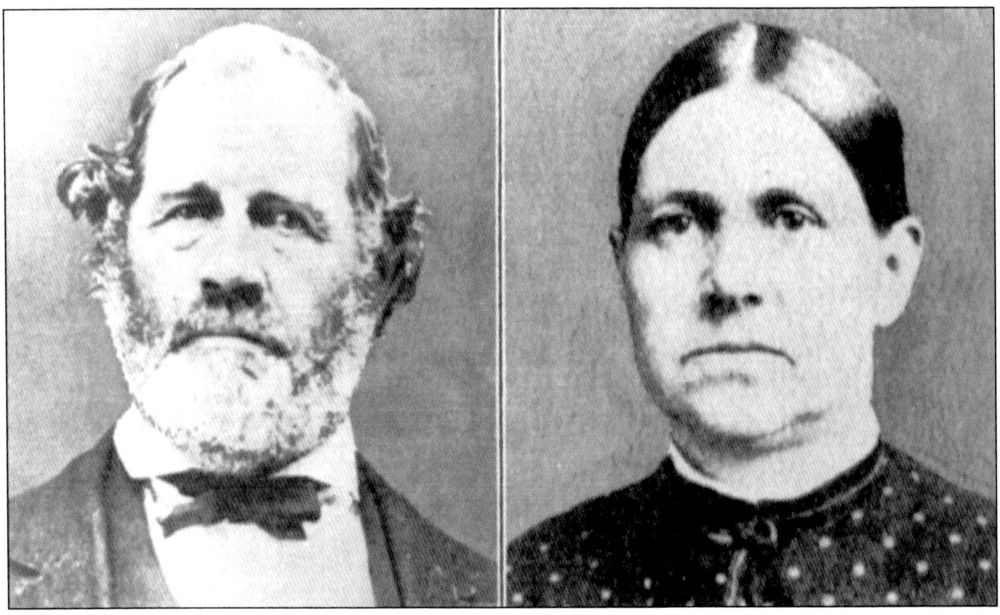

These are early photographs of first settler Charles Hart (1807–1880) and his second wife, Hannah Caroline Leland Hart (1824–1878). Hart arrived in 1835 by way of central New York State, having left his birthplace in Connecticut with his family in search of greater opportunity. Hart's brother, Thomas Benjamin Hart, joined him in 1837. In the early years, the brothers operated the mills together. (WHS Photo 711.)

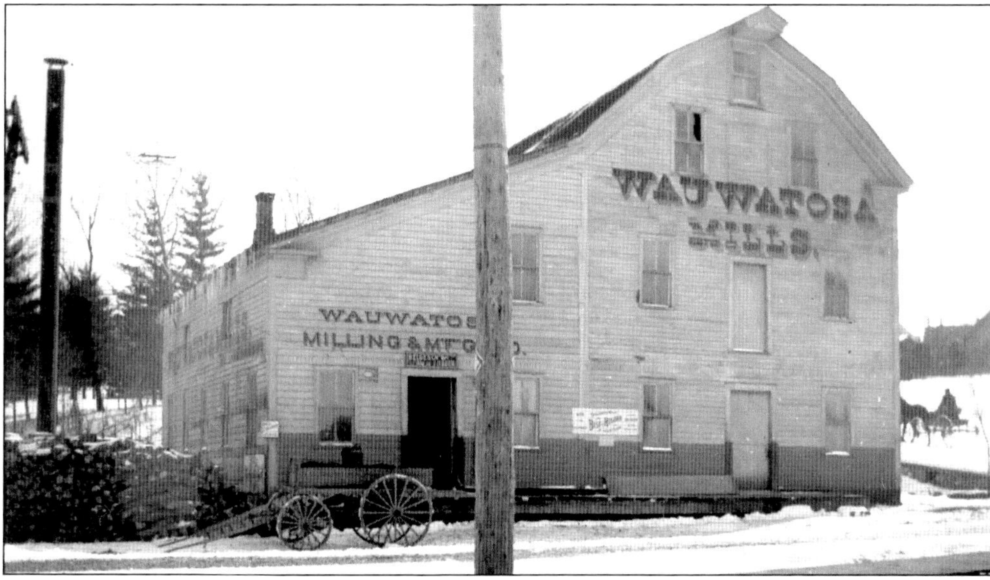

Hart's gristmill remained a going concern well into the twentieth century. At the time of this photo, approximately 1897, the business was known as Wauwatosa Milling and Manufacturing Company. By 1886, the mill had been purchased by Oscar Helgesen and Jerome H. Pitcher, whose names appear on the sign above the doorway at the left. Icicles hang from the roof at the left in this wintry scene. (WHS Photo 458.)

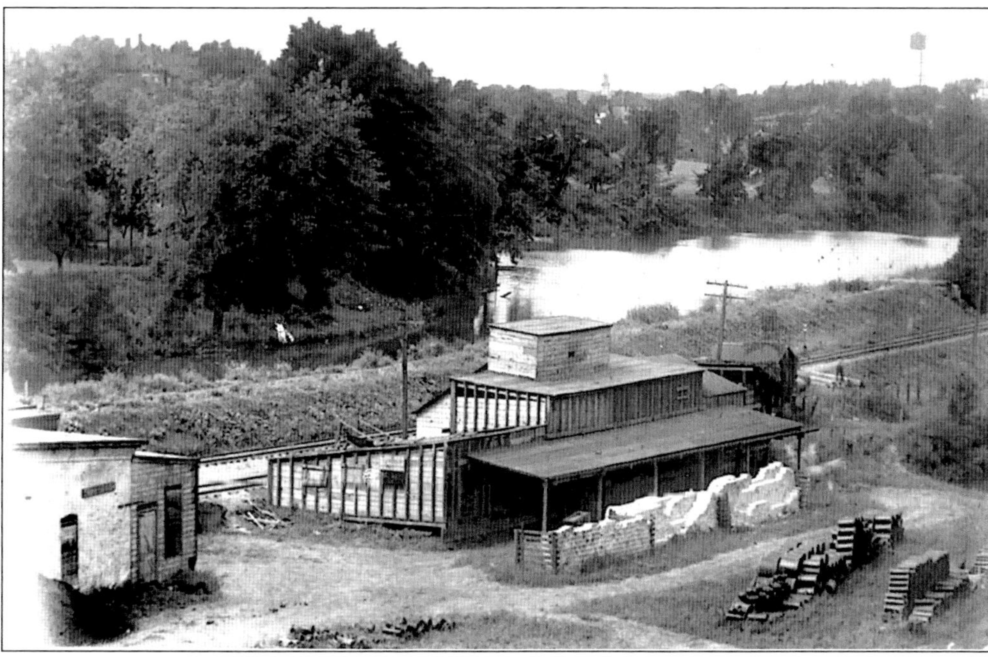

The millpond dominated low terrain west of the mills. A levee, perhaps a remnant of the Milwaukee to Watertown Plank Road, protected the railroad tracks, the Red Store, and the storage yards and sheds of the W.B. Morse Coal and Fuel Company (later Wauwatosa Fuel and Supply), seen in the foreground. Beyond the pond, the insane asylum tower and a water tower on the grounds of the county poor farm are visible. (WHS Photo 249.)

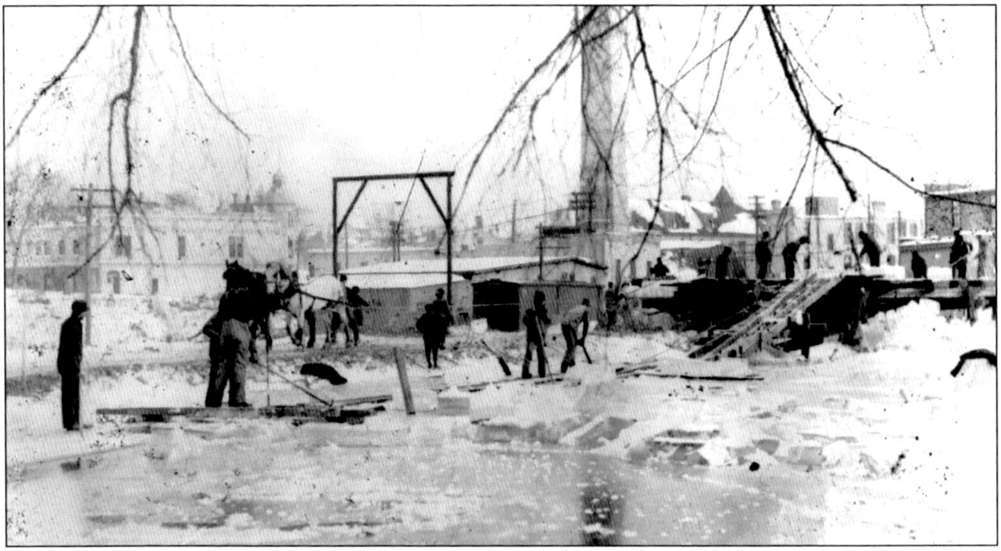

Before the days of electric refrigeration, cooling in summer depended on a good harvest of ice in the winter. The millpond provided an ideal place to cut large slabs with the help of many workers, large saws, and a team of horses. The tall chimney of the power plant is seen, along with the new brick Dittmar hardware store at the left, in this image from approximately 1900. (WHS Photo LGP 900.)

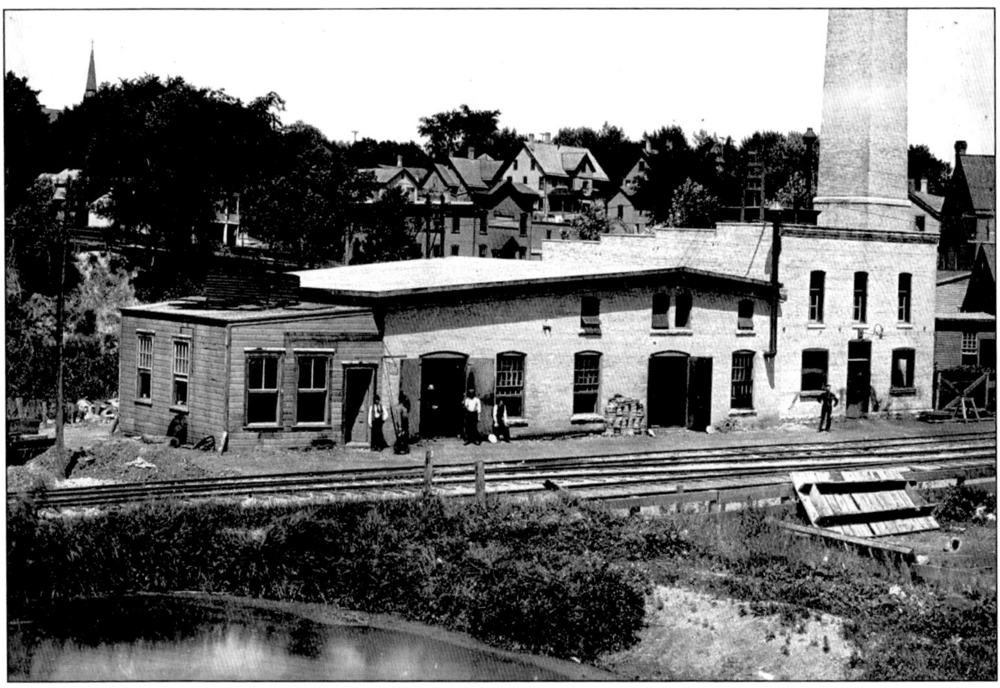

One of the earliest brick buildings in the heart of Wauwatosa was this power-generating plant, dating from about 1888. It was situated across the railroad tracks from the millpond. The wood frame addition on the left served as the office. Extensions at the back of the Red Store are visible at the right; the millpond is in the foreground. Wood structures, visible beyond the power plant, were characteristic of most buildings in the Village well into the 1890s. (WHS Photo 712.)

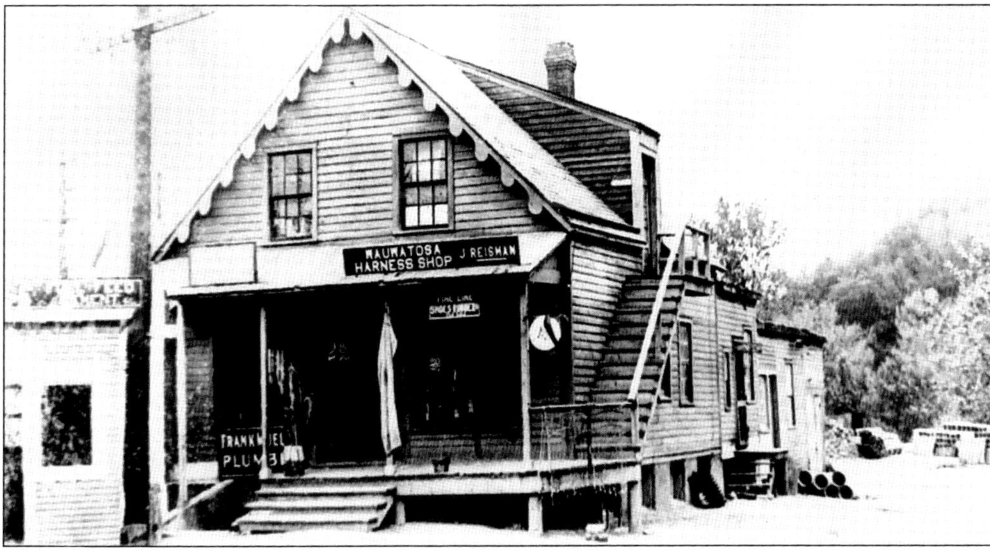

At least four separate businesses were operating in the Red Store at the time of this photo, including a plumber and J. Reisman's Wauwatosa Harness Shop. Signs advertising two other businesses are not legible. On the photo, a hand-written note indicates the store was once a depot and also served as a post office in the 1870s. At the left, between the railroad track and the store, was Morse's Fuel Feed and Cement business. (Courtesy of Milwaukee County Historical Society.)

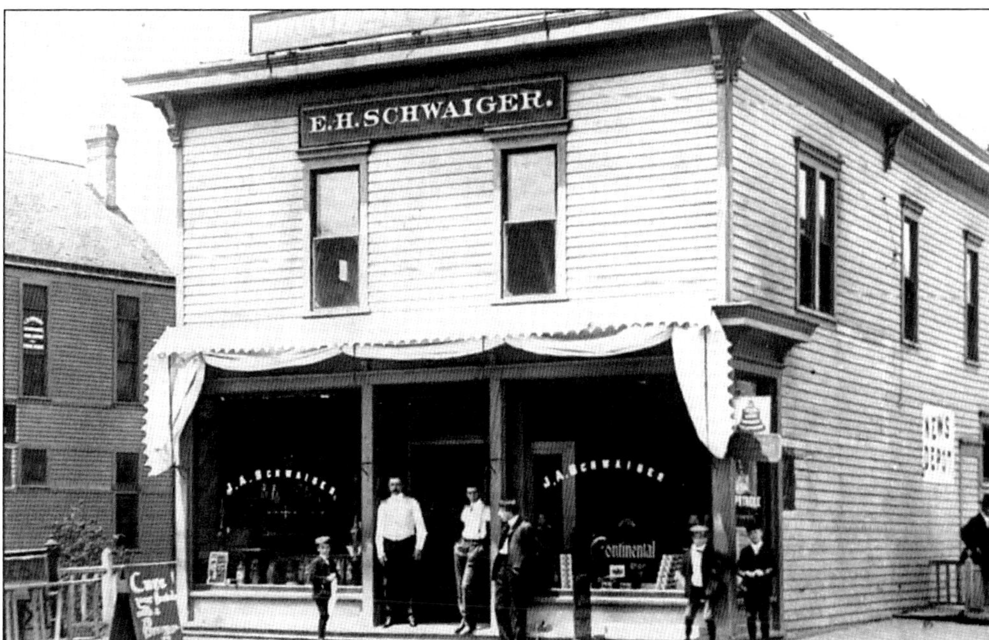

Early directories show that Edward H. Schwaiger and Dr. Melanchton Fisk owned the drug and medicine shop on this site. By 1902, Jerome A. Schwaiger had joined Edward in operating this drugstore and news depot at the southwest corner of State Street and Harwood Avenue. Few wood frame buildings remained in the Village when this photo was taken in approximately 1904. (Courtesy of Milwaukee County Historical Society.)

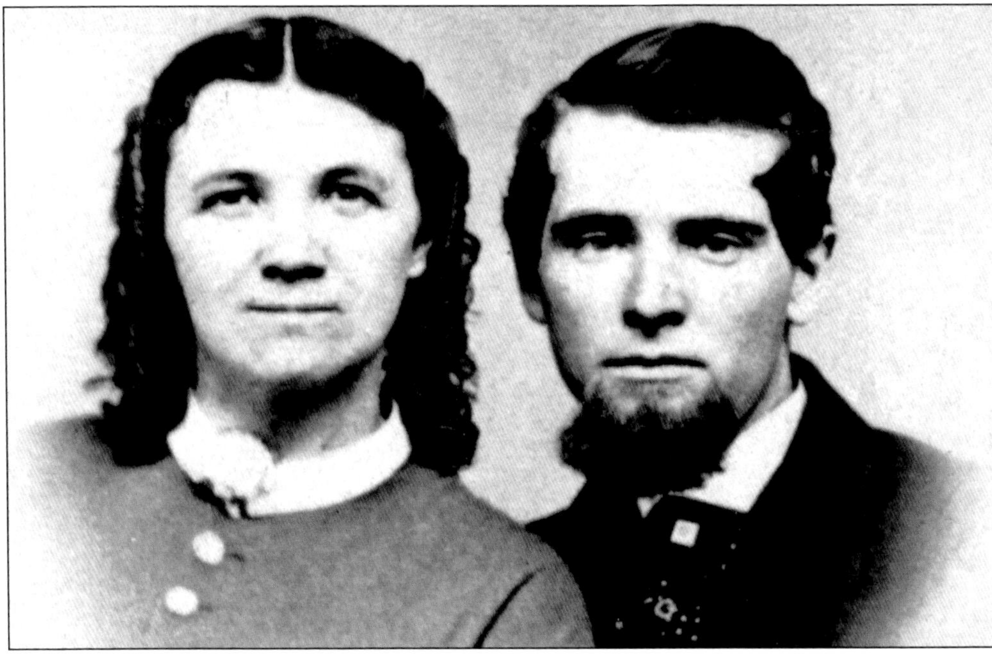

Construction of a number of toll roads made of wood planks throughout Milwaukee County generated numerous inns along their routes. The Wauwatosa House served travelers using the Milwaukee to Watertown Plank Road that reached Wauwatosa in 1849. The first proprietor of the hotel (see page 9) was P.J. Shumway. His daughter, Merry, and her husband, Mr. Smith, are captured here in an unusual informal Victorian photograph. (WHS Photo 713.)

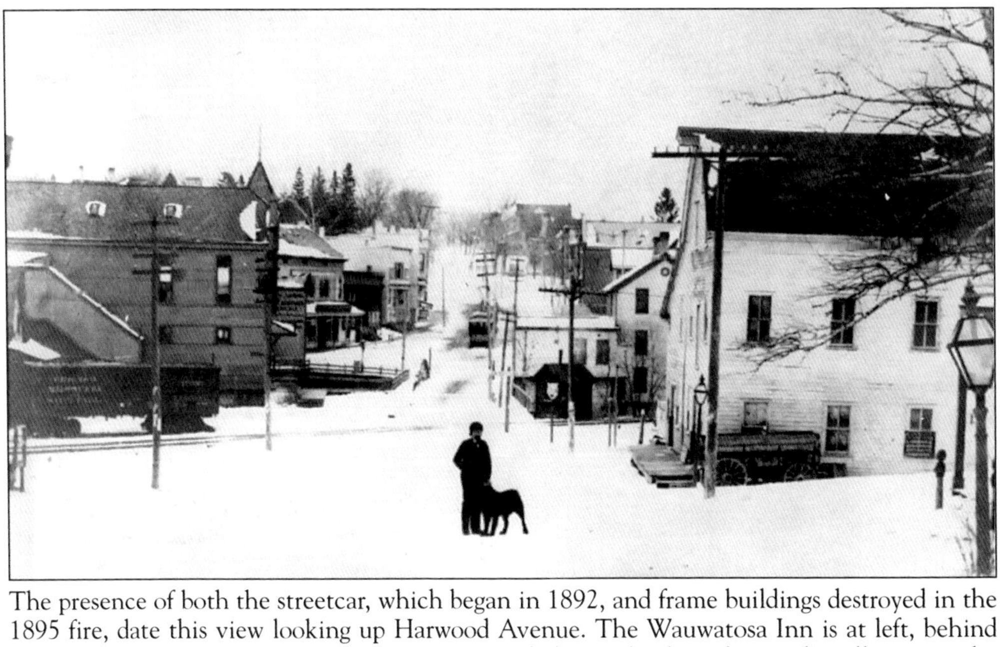

The presence of both the streetcar, which began in 1892, and frame buildings destroyed in the 1895 fire, date this view looking up Harwood Avenue. The Wauwatosa Inn is at left, behind the boxcar. At right is the gristmill. Note the gaslight, at the far right, used to illuminate the streets. Arthur Fingado, son of Wauwatosa's first butcher, is believed to be the man with his dog in the snowy street. (WHS Photo 430.)

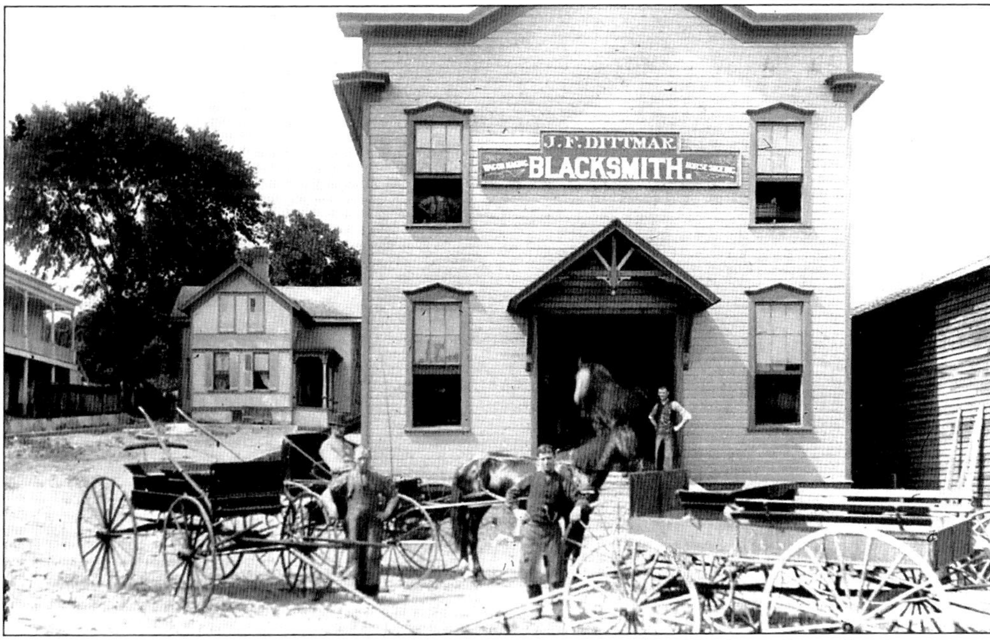

J.F. Dittmar operated his shop in the Village. He may be the blacksmith, in leather apron, standing at the shop doorway with a carefully placed horse. Another man looks out from the left window on the second floor. Patrons seeking shoeing for their horses pose attentively in the foreground with their wagons. Partly visible on the left is the "Bird's Nest" house on lower Church Street, built by Dr. F.H. Day. (Courtesy of Milwaukee County Historical Society.)

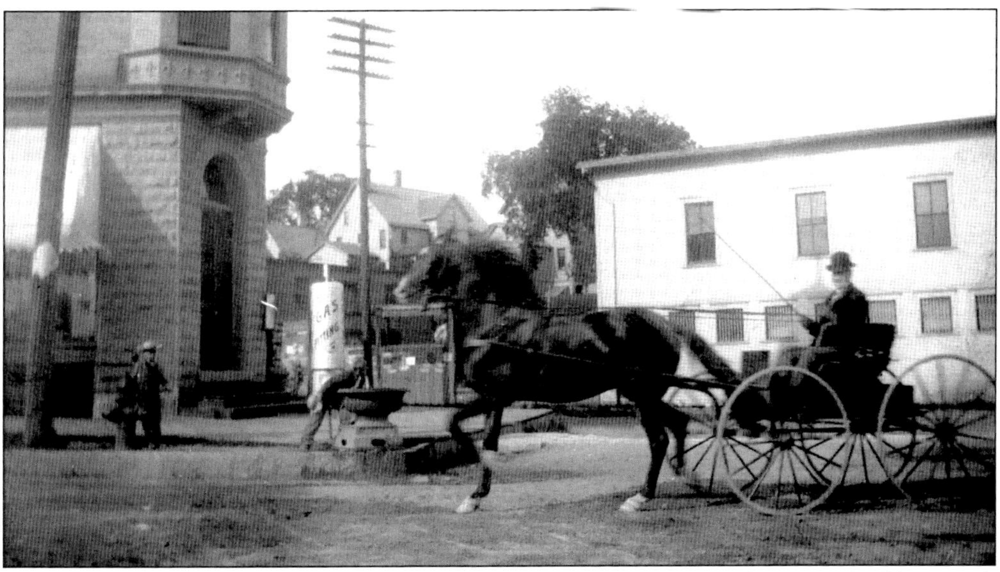

In later years Dittmar's blacksmith shop was replaced by the substantial Dittmar building, with its Wauwatosa limestone entryway, at left. A hardware store has occupied the ground floor of this building since its construction in 1897. Near the entrance, a young boy stands alongside a fire hydrant. Another boy samples water from the drinking fountain and horse trough while a horse-drawn carriage moves past. At the right is the back of the Lefeber Bros. first store. This photo was taken in approximately 1904. (WHS Photo 460.)

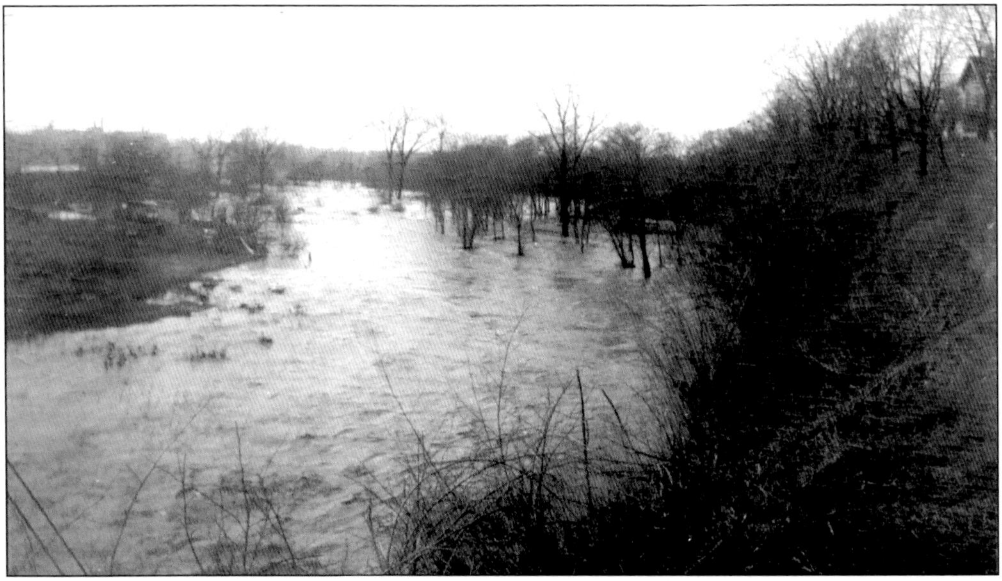

Spring thaws often brought rising waters along the Menomonee River and flooding to the Village area. The Milwaukee and Watertown Plank Road was built alongside the river course in 1849, originally passing through low land often reclaimed by the river. After several years of springtime distress, operators of the road rerouted it to higher terrain following the United States Road, now Harwood Avenue. (WHS Photo 579.)

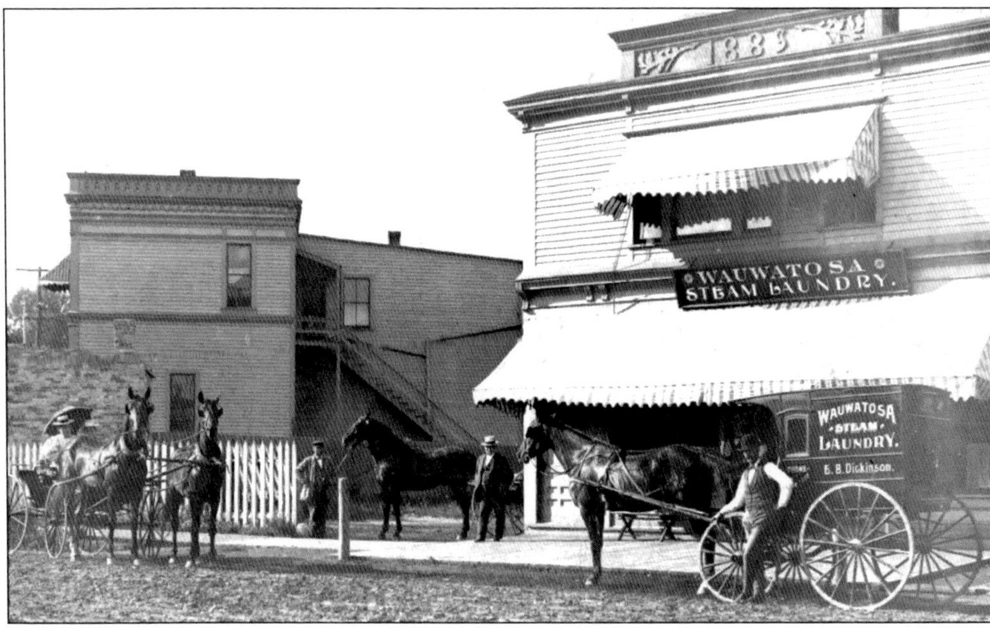

A horse and driver pose with the delivery van for the Wauwatosa Steam Laundry owned by B.B. Dickinson. The building, dated 1889, is believed to have been located near the corner of State Street and Seventy-fifth Street. The person in the three-piece suit, at the corner of the laundry, is Morton Casperson. The two-story frame building, left, was also built in 1889 and provides a glimpse of commercial development at that time. Note the typical striped awnings on both buildings. (WHS Photo 464.)

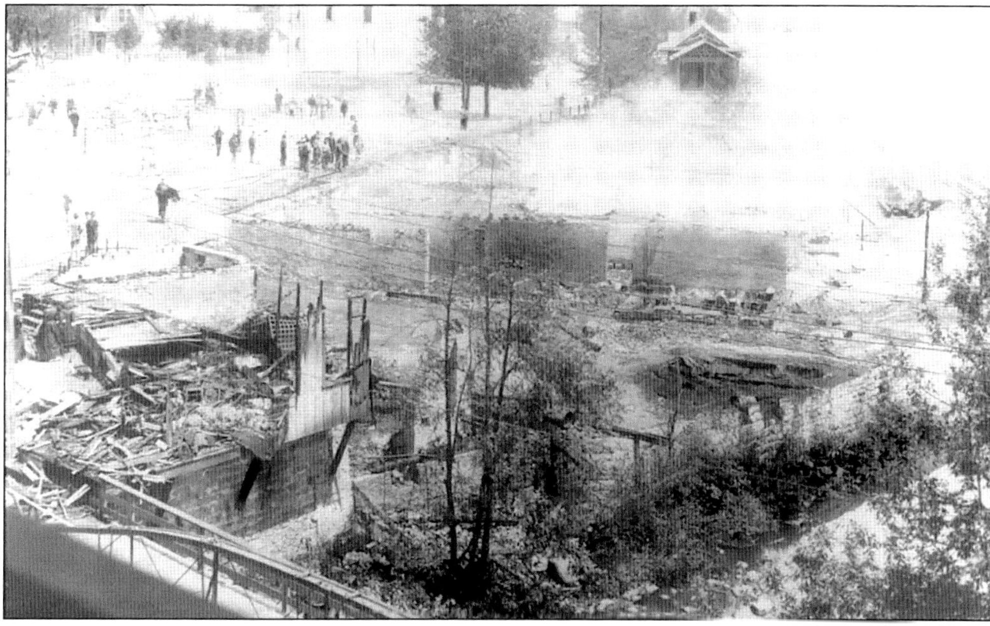

A devastating fire on the morning of July 10, 1895, destroyed 13 wood-frame buildings and damaged a number of others in the eastern half of the Village business district. The railroad depot (*looking east, above*) escaped the flames, but little else remains of buildings or the goods they contained. Believed to an "incendiary plot" (arson), the fire spread rapidly at six o'clock in the morning. Firefighting was hampered because the millpond's water level was low—perhaps someone had tampered with the millpond's dike gate. Fresh breezes hastened the spread of flames. The fire scene shows buildings across Harwood Avenue, which escaped the devastation (*looking west, below*). As a result of the fire, the Village of Wauwatosa established a fire department, ordered that buildings in the business area must be brick or stone, and incorporated as a city so as to be able to issue bonds for redevelopment of the area. (Courtesy of Milwaukee County Historical Society and WHS Photo 410.)

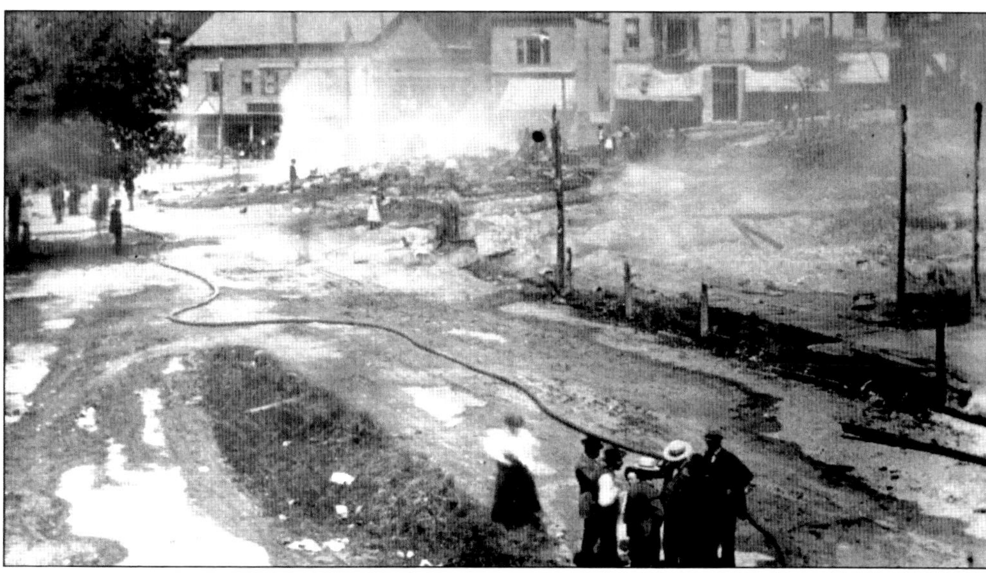

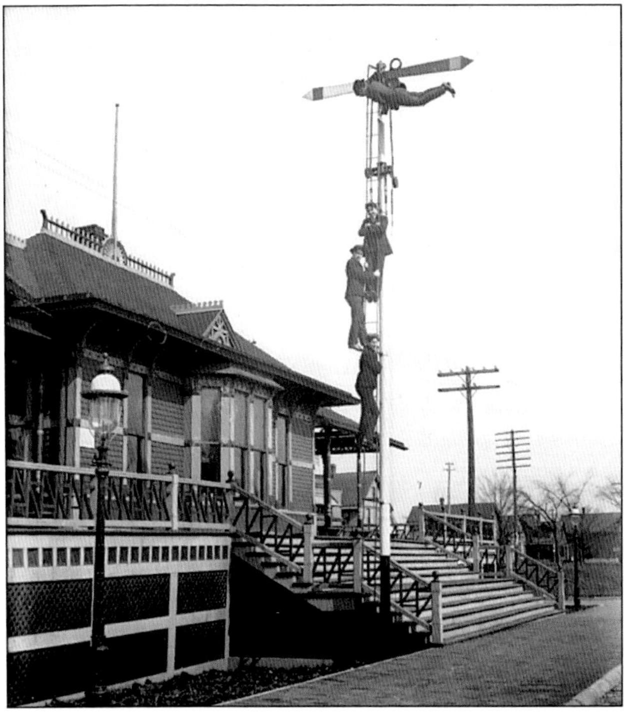

The Victorian Stick-style depot of the Chicago, Milwaukee, and St. Paul Railroad was built in 1880. It was saved from the 1895 fire by a grassy lot to its west. Here, young men pose on the signal tower in 1903. The Victorian penchant for contrasting paint colors to emphasize decorative details is evident here. In 1945 the depot was demolished and replaced by a functional red brick structure in the prairie style. (WHS Photo LGP 204.)

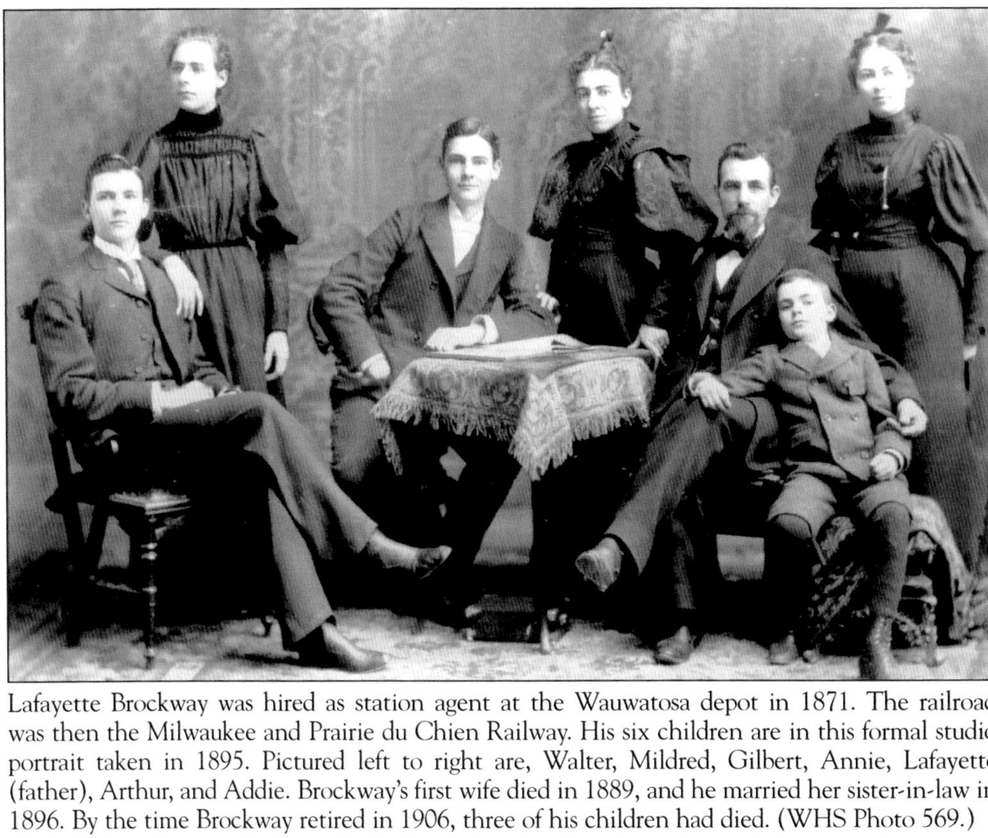

Lafayette Brockway was hired as station agent at the Wauwatosa depot in 1871. The railroad was then the Milwaukee and Prairie du Chien Railway. His six children are in this formal studio portrait taken in 1895. Pictured left to right are, Walter, Mildred, Gilbert, Annie, Lafayette (father), Arthur, and Addie. Brockway's first wife died in 1889, and he married her sister-in-law in 1896. By the time Brockway retired in 1906, three of his children had died. (WHS Photo 569.)

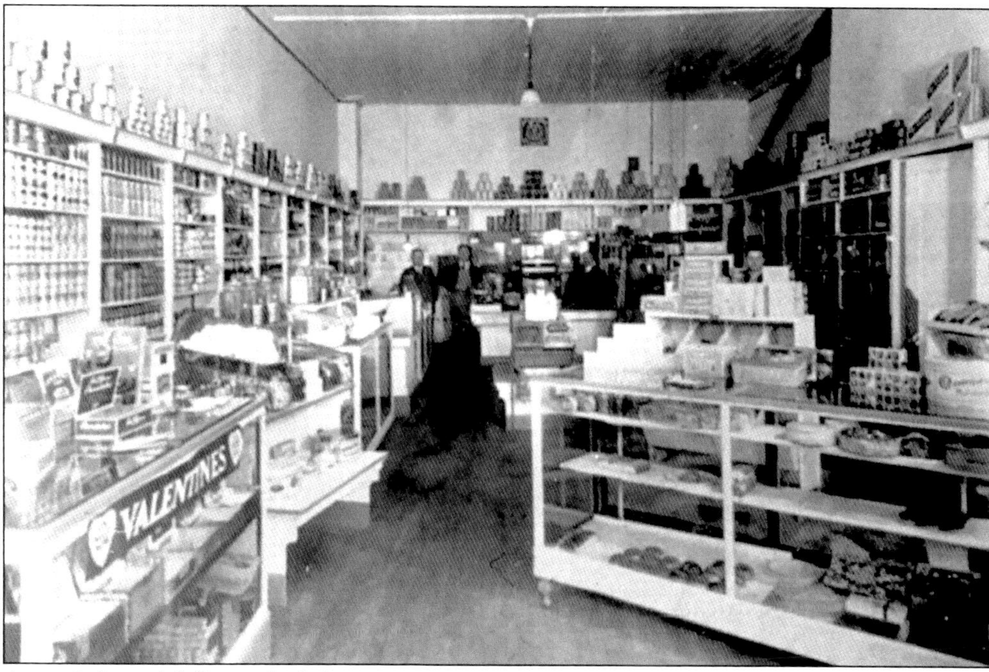

An orderly and fully stocked Garvens' Grocery Store stood on Harwood Avenue. At the rear of the store stand Edwin Garvens, his son Arvine, and his brother Otto. The display case at left offers Valentine candies. Baked goods are visible in the case on the right. Otto and Edwin started their careers as clerks at Lefeber's store. Later they opened this shop just a few doors up the street. (WHS Photo 454.)

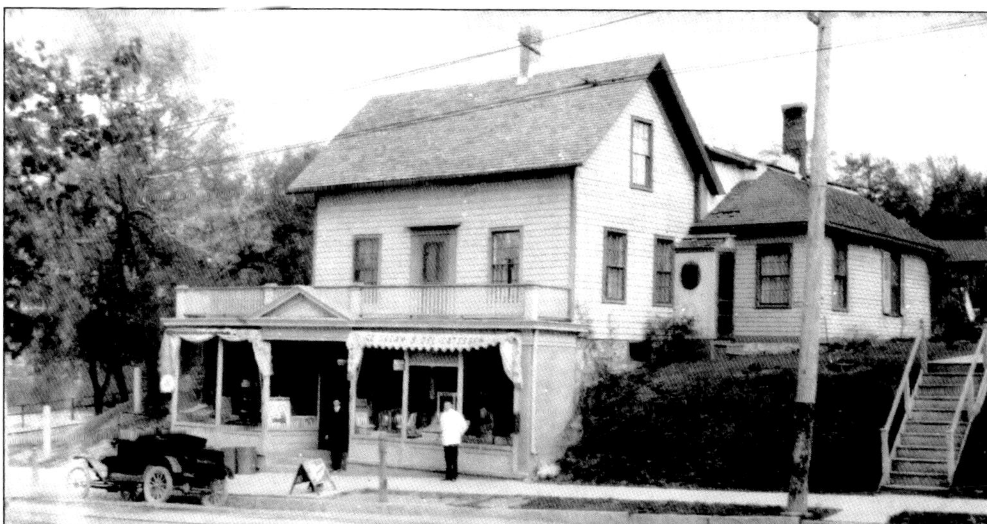

Charles Fingado, Wauwatosa's first butcher, operated the Pioneer Meat Market in the basement of this house, at 7751 Harwood Avenue, from the late 1860s until his death in 1901. His son Arthur carried on the business until 1913, when he sold it to Adolph Becker, who opened this delicatessen and later expanded the business into a full grocery store. A hitching post and an open-topped car reflect the gradual change from horse-drawn conveyances to the automobile. (WHS Postcard 629.)

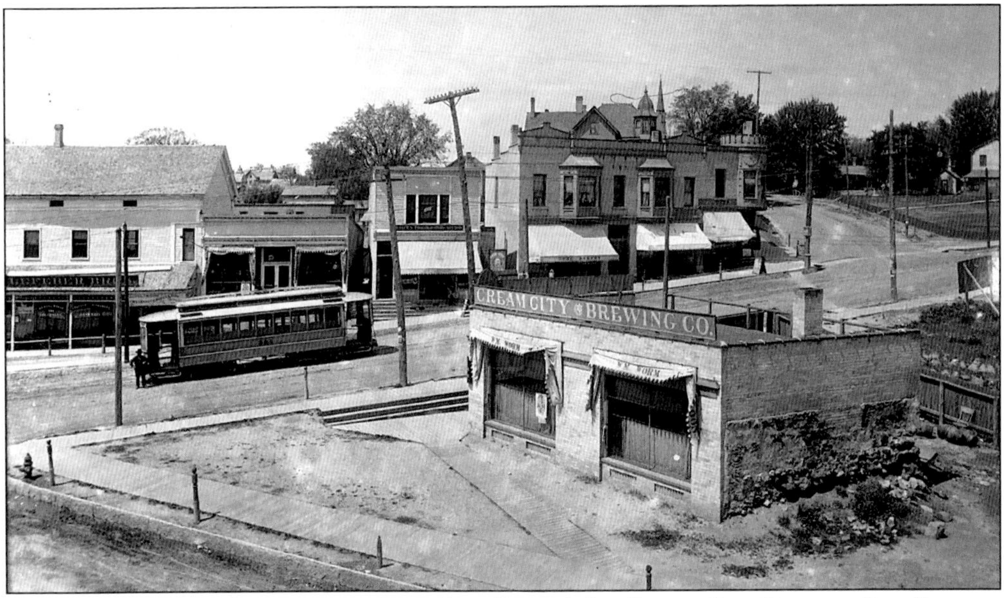

Following the 1895 fire, new wooden sidewalks and the Cream City Brewing Co. illustrate early efforts to rebuild. The Walnut Street and National Avenue streetcar, named for its route through the City of Milwaukee, is stopped at the end of the line in this 1898 photo. Behind it, buildings untouched by the fire are visible. The most important of these are the Lefeber Bros. store at the left and the Greenwood Block, later Streff Advertising, which remains today, on the corner. (WHS Photo 436.)

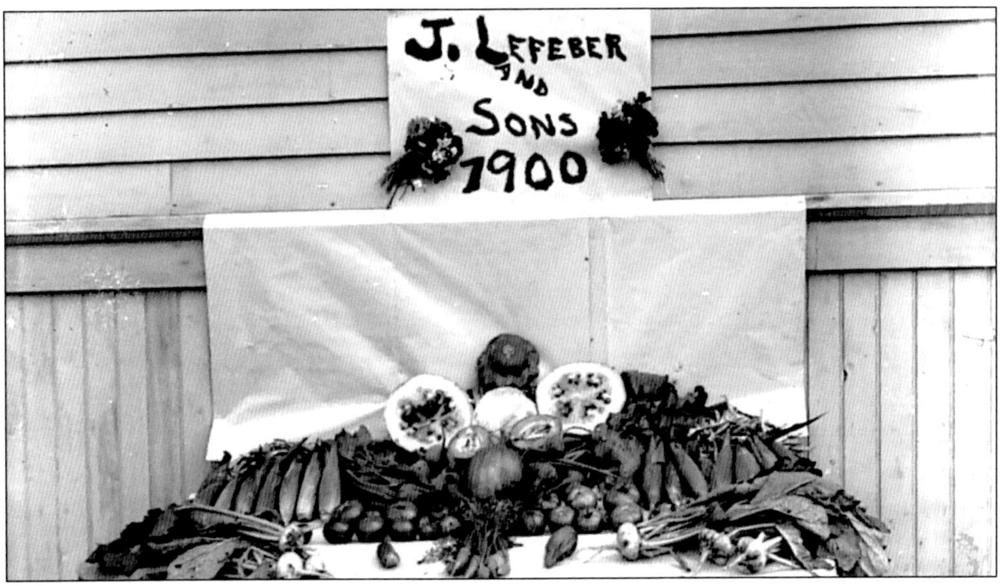

In 1886, the Lefeber Bros. store moved into the former hotel, The Wauwatosa House. James, Abraham, and Joseph Lefeber were its proprietors, specializing in farm implements and general merchandise. In this photograph, August 1900, a carefully arranged display may have been an advertisement for Lefeber's. This photo is from a large collection of glass plate negatives. The photos were taken by several Lefeber family members at the turn of the nineteenth century and later donated to the Wauwatosa Historical Society. (WHS Photo LGP 25.)

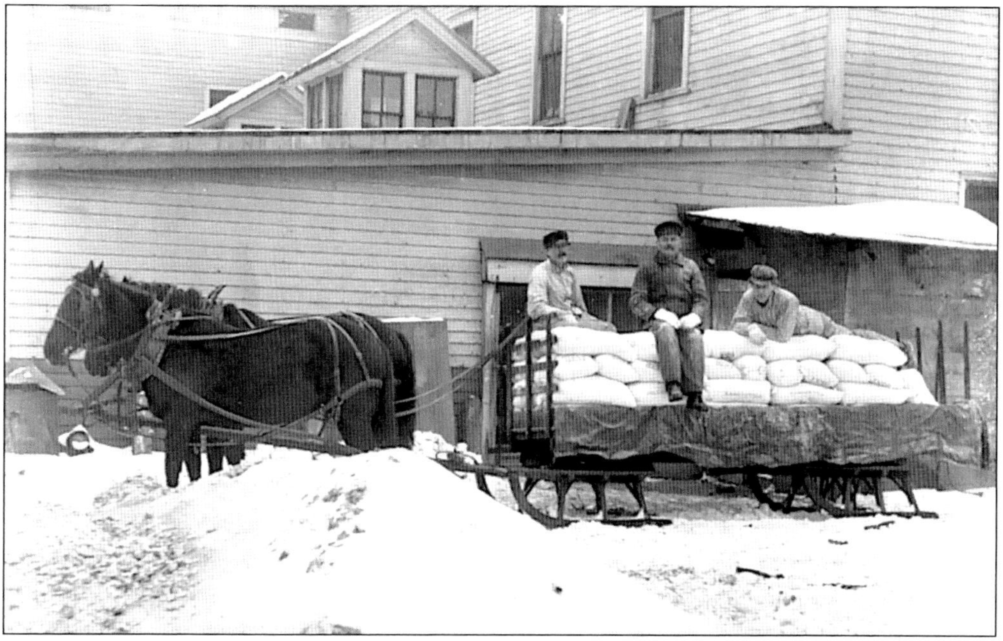

Workers pose atop sacks of flour behind the Lefeber Bros. store in a photograph taken in January 1905. Snow covers the ground and the flour is loaded on a large sleigh with runners. A notation accompanying the glass plate negative indicates "Pillsbury Flour, carload of 165 barrels, argo finish." Photographs printed from glass plates reproduce well, providing extraordinarily crisp details. (WHS Photo LGP 434.)

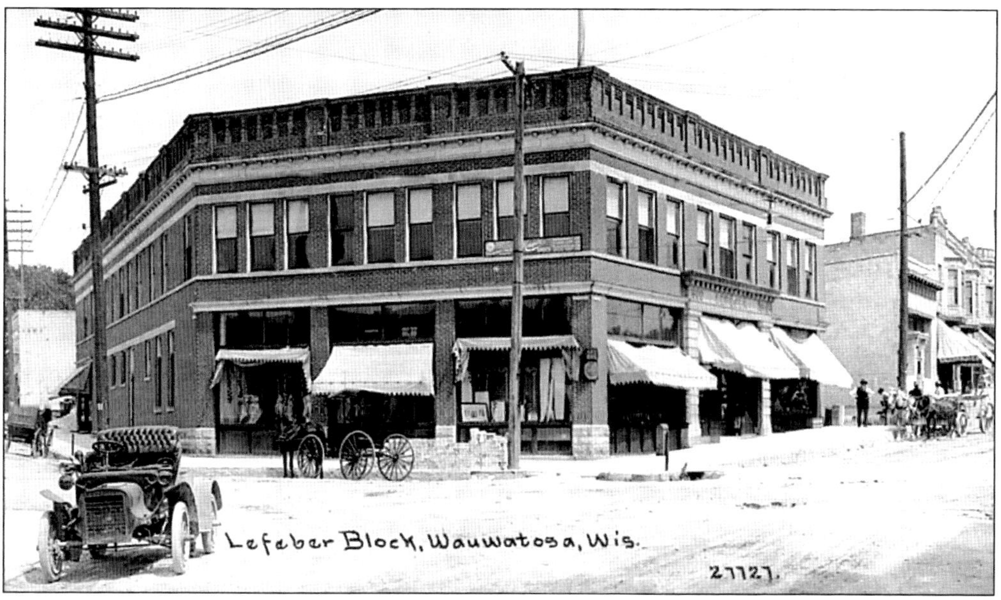

A new home for Lefeber Bros., a red brick building dated 1906, marked the coming of age of the Village business district. Lefeber's would soon be known as a department store and as the anchor of a thriving commercial area. The development, two miles to the west, of the Mayfair Mall shopping center in the late 1950s led to a decline in business in the Village. Lefeber's closed in 1958 and was destroyed by fire in 1964. (WHS Postcard 624.)

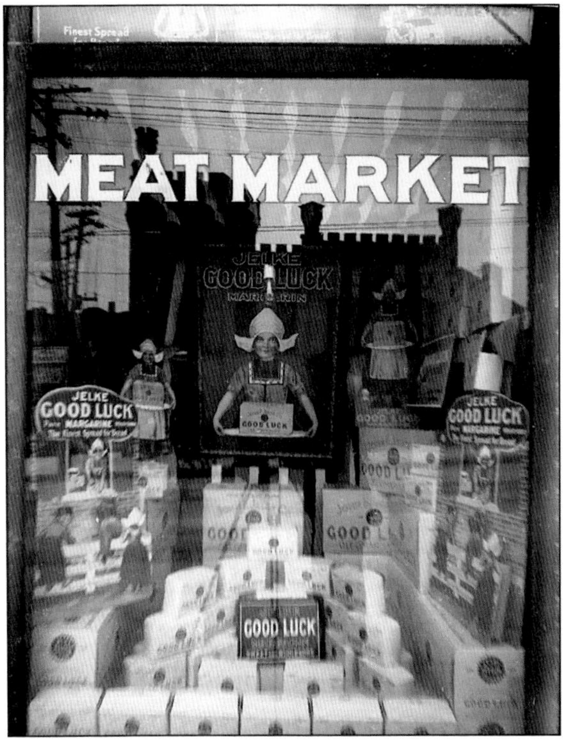

A display window in the new Lefeber's advertises the meat market and shows a carefully arranged display of products featuring Jelke Good Luck Margarine. A local newspaper in 1910 noted, "Lefeber Bros. have installed a new coffee grinder run by an electric motor. It's a dandy." The more interesting feature of this photograph is the reflection in the window of the Pabst Saloon across the street, with its medieval tower and ornamental features. (WHS Photo LGP 901.)

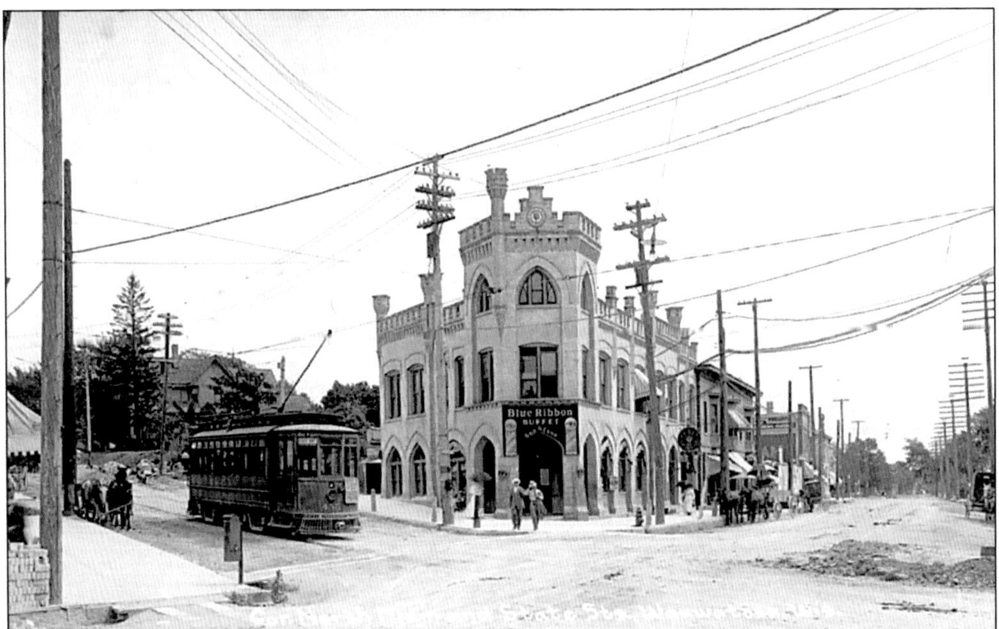

The Pabst Brewing Company constructed this post-fire, brick saloon in the style of a medieval castle in 1899, on the site of the early Dearsley's Tavern. The sign over the door promotes the Blue Ribbon Buffet. The view down State Street (to the right) shows a number of the buildings that replaced those lost in the fire. To the left of the saloon building, still is use today, reconstruction has not begun in this image from about 1905. (WHS Postcard 626.)

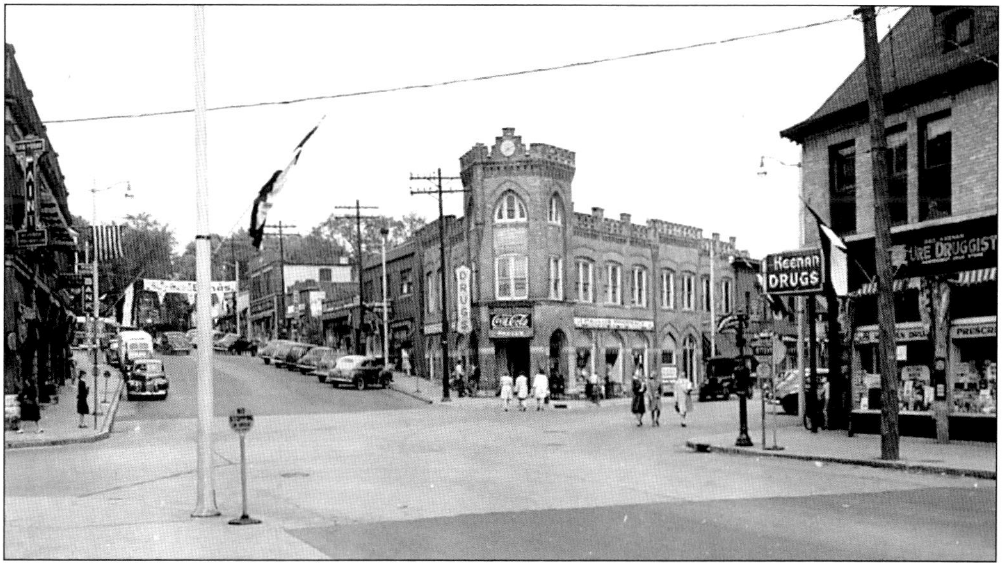

The former Pabst Saloon stands at the point of a fully developed business district. Since the earlier photograph (see page 22), it has lost the stylized turrets on the roof, and the Pabst emblem at the top of the tower has been chiseled away. This view from about 1944 looks up Harwood Avenue, with Lefeber's Department Store on the left and Keenan Drugs on the right. Innovative angle parking on the right side of Harwood Avenue accommodates the growing number of automobiles. (WHS Postcard 628.)

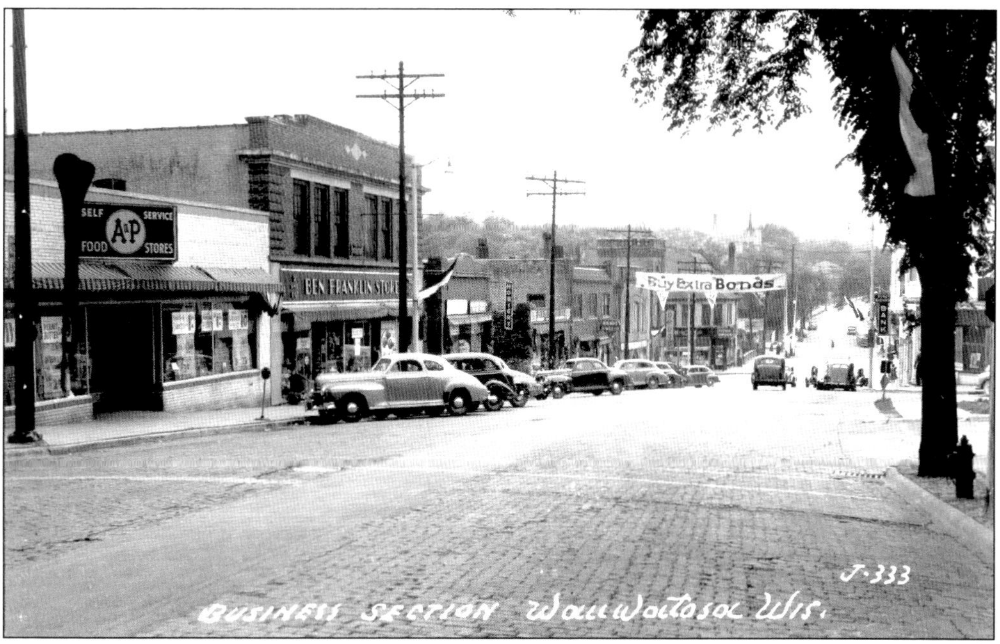

This view, from the upper end of the business district, looks down Harwood Avenue to the southwest (the photo above looks up the avenue). Both were taken about the same time during World War II. Note the banner urging "Buy Extra Bonds." Chain stores such as the A&P Food Stores and the Ben Franklin Store have gained a foothold in this important market. The streetcar tracks are paved over—the line was closed in 1933. (Courtesy of Len Borkowski.)

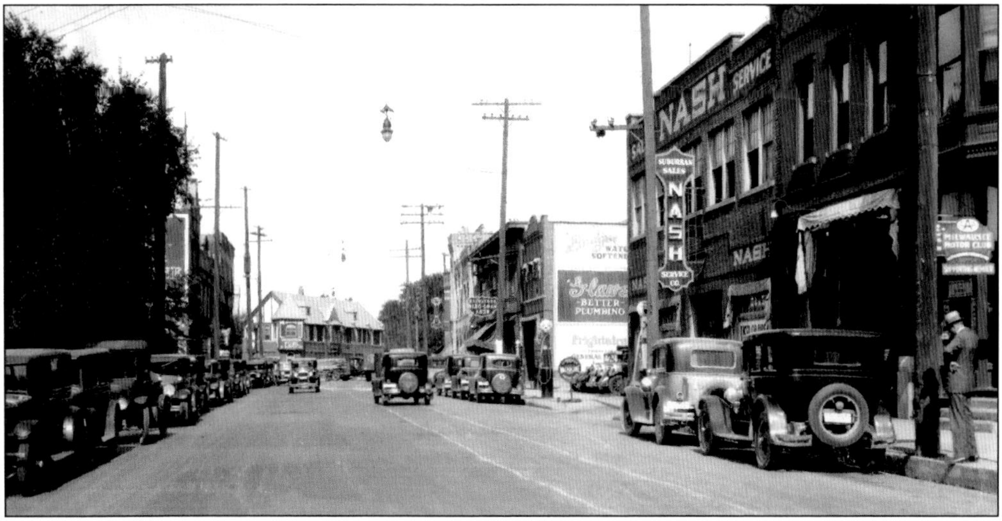

A bustling life, centered on the automobile, has emerged by the late 1920s, as seen in this view to the west on State Street. A Nash car dealership is to the right, and a sign on the post says, "AAA Milwaukee Motor Club, Supporting Member." A gasoline pump stands at the curb, just beyond the dealership. In 1915 a local paper boasted, "State St. is nearly finished, giving Wauwatosa one of the best and longest asphalt roads in the county." (Courtesy of Frederick I. Olson.)

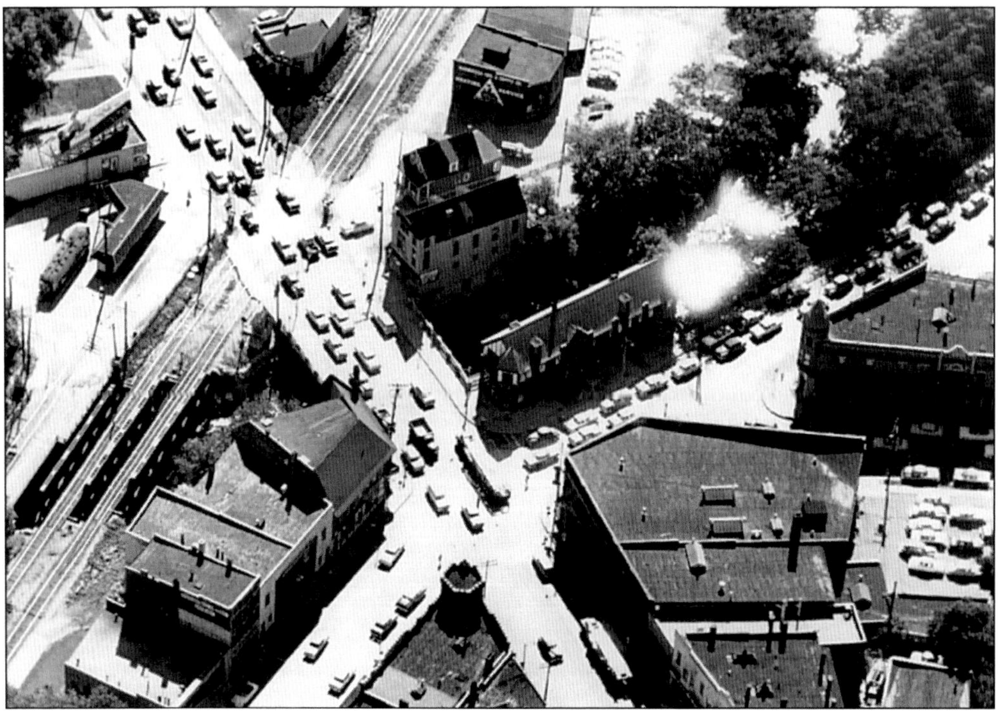

An aerial photograph from the early 1950s gives a dramatic view of the Village. Harwood Avenue passes from top left to lower right. State Street runs parallel to the railroad tracks, lower left. Traffic congestion is apparent. In a few years, several buildings seen here were removed to provide parking even as the business district began to decline. Major redevelopment efforts began in the 1970s. (WHS Photo 287.)

As the prosperity of the community grew, three substantial banks operated in the Village business district. In 1907, the First National Bank of Wauwatosa opened. Established in 1920, the Wauwatosa State Bank used advertising in a 1926 city directory to promote business, highlighting the image of substance and strength in the bank's building on State Street. In 1921, the Wauwatosa Savings and Loan was founded. All three institutions continue today under new names. (WHS Book Collection.)

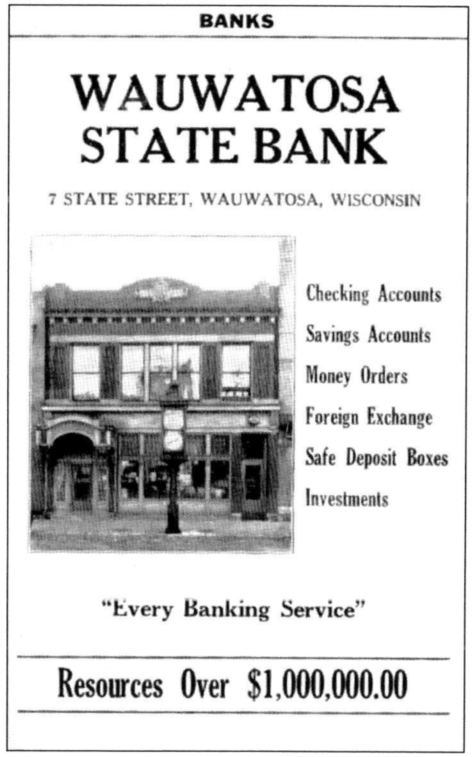

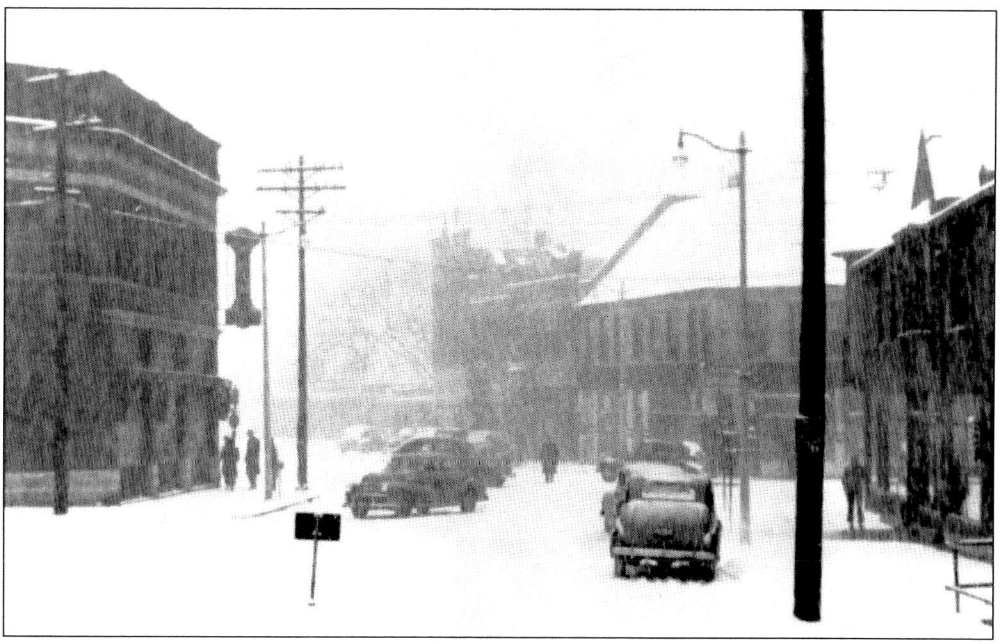

Snow slows traffic at Harwood and State in about 1947. The Wauwatosa State Bank is in the center of this scene and Lefeber's Store is at the left. Viewers will see great similarities from this vantage point today, except for Lefeber's, demolished after a 1964 fire. A new structure of similar proportions was built on that vacant site in 2001. Other buildings have been changed or adapted to new uses, including restaurants and offices. (WHS Photo 465.)

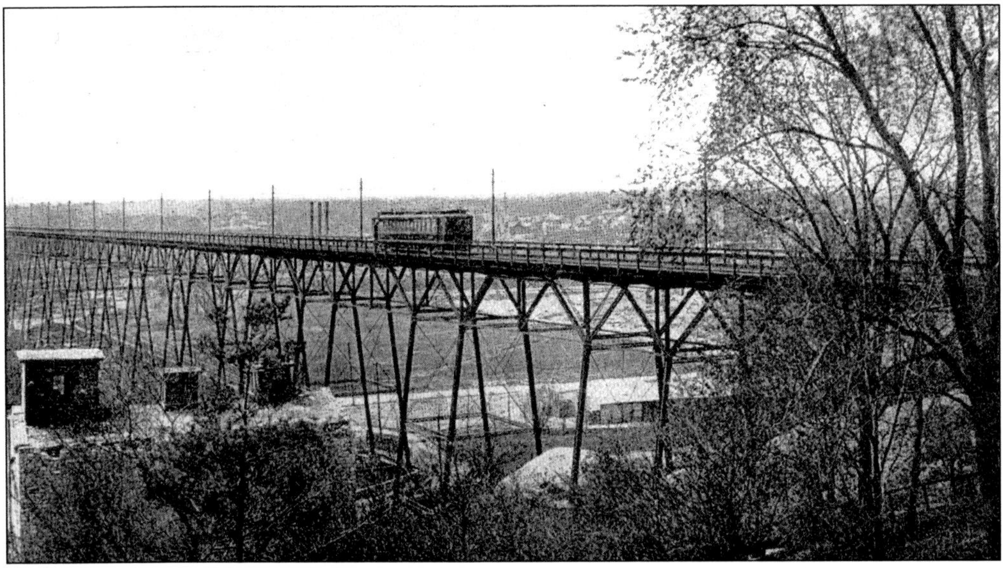

Milwaukee's Wells Street car line crossed the wide Menomonee River Valley on a precarious trestle, the streetcars rocking and clattering as they went. Development of Wauwatosa as a suburb was fostered by the convenience of a streetcar commute to Milwaukee, offering an attractive alternative to those able to afford to live outside the central city. (Courtesy of Len Borkowski.)

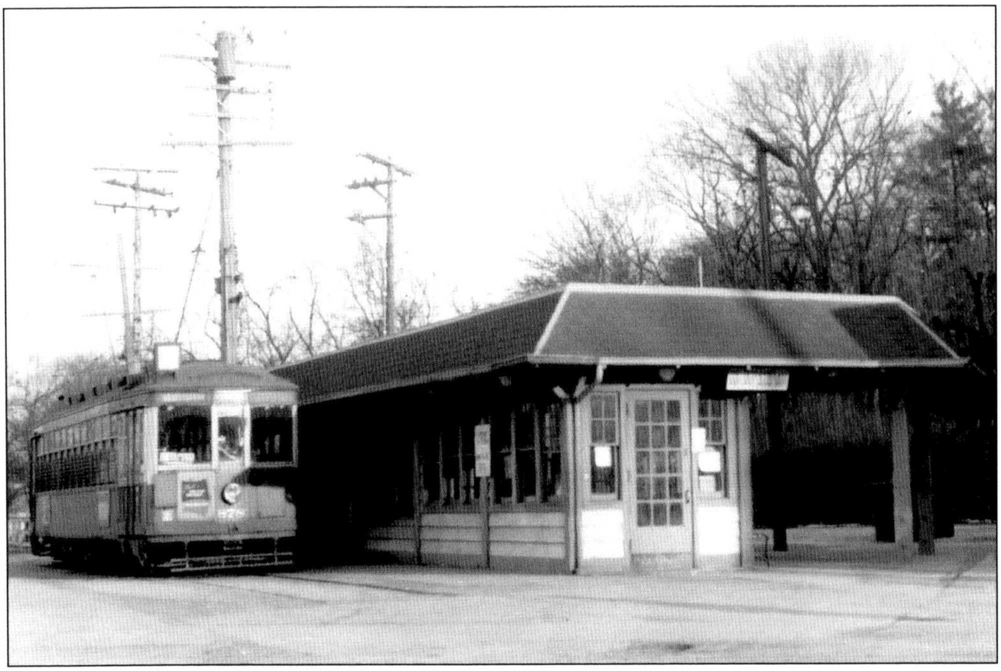

Car 878 running on the Wells Street #10 line stops in 1957 at the Harwood terminal in the Village. Between 1899 and 1936, the streetcar route had extended west to the County Institutions. In 1958, the streetcar era ended and the terminal was no longer needed. In a community where growth had been tightly linked to the plank roads, railroad, and local mass transit, now freeways and dispersed growth catered to the automobile. Increased personal mobility brought dramatic changes in the character of the original Village. (WHS Photo 563.)

Two

COMMERCIAL SPREAD

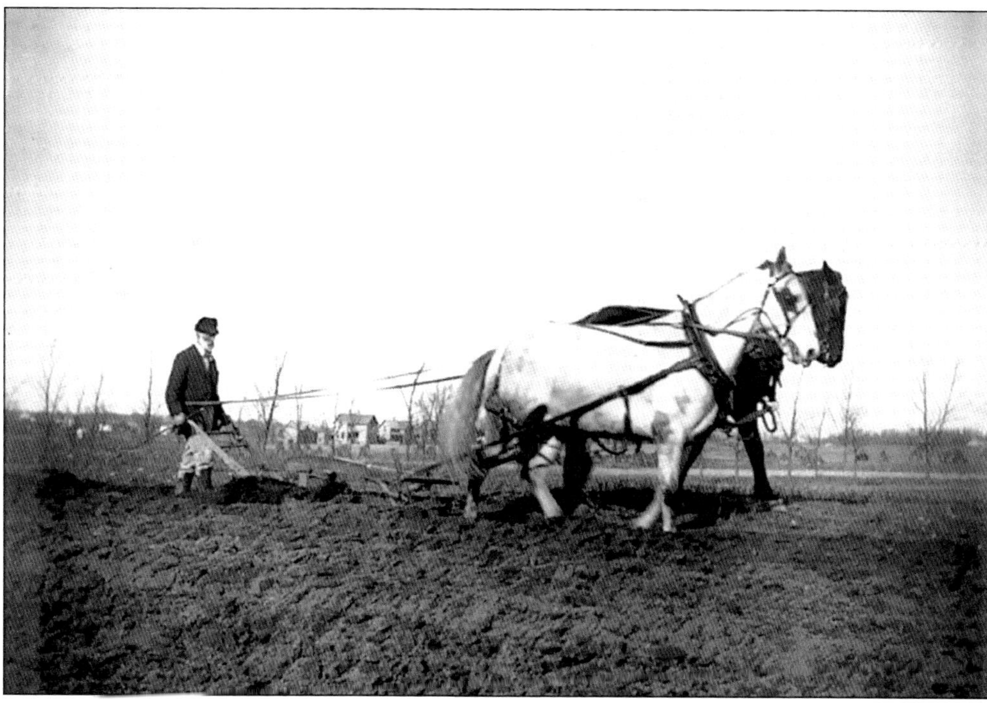

Much of the original 36-square-mile Township of Wauwatosa was used for farming until after World War II. Because of the township's proximity to Milwaukee, wheat was an early crop. However, by the late 1870s local farmers shifted from wheat and grains to cash crops that could be sold in the city, such as fruits and vegetables, and pigs and chickens. In the early years, the sawmill and gristmill in the Village served their needs, as did the plank roads that provided access from the hinterlands to Milwaukee. In this undated photo, a Wauwatosa farmer identified as Tom Richards guides a horse-drawn plow, a labor-intensive task. As the city grew, commercial areas beyond the Village emerged, principally along North Avenue and at Sixty-eighth and Wells Streets. Annexations after World War II spurred a commercial, industrial, and residential explosion and changed the face of the community. (WHS Photo LGP 512.)

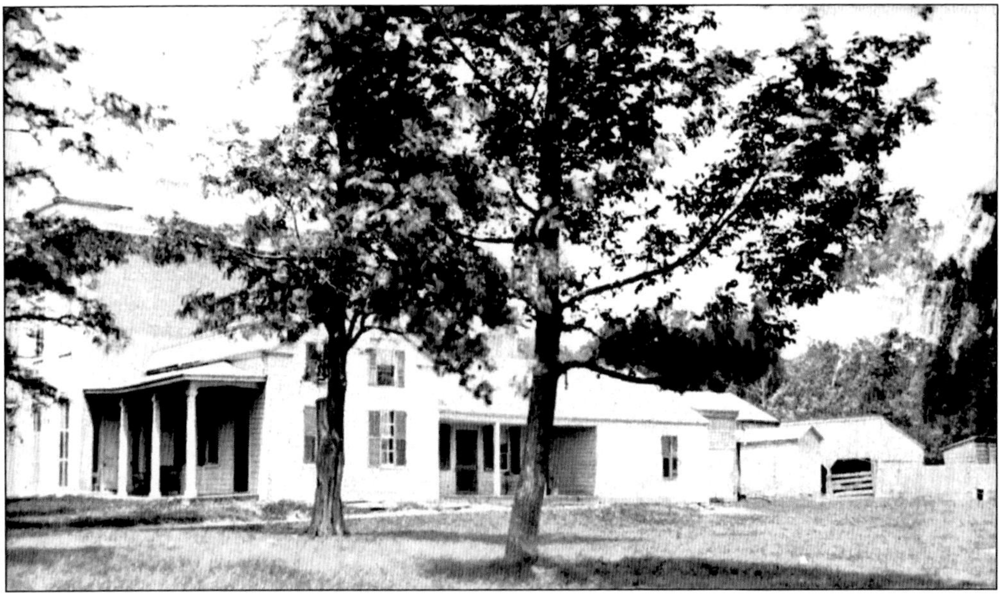

One of Milwaukee's first merchants, New Yorker Allen O.T. Breed, owned a dry goods shop from 1835 to 1839 on present North Water Street, south of East Wisconsin Avenue. He then bought 235 acres in the Town of Wauwatosa at two dollars an acre, and took up farming. Breed's Greek Revival farmhouse was north of Vliet Street, in what today is Washington Park in Milwaukee. In 1842, he became the first treasurer of the Town of Wauwatosa. Allen Breed died in 1875. (WHS Photo 717.)

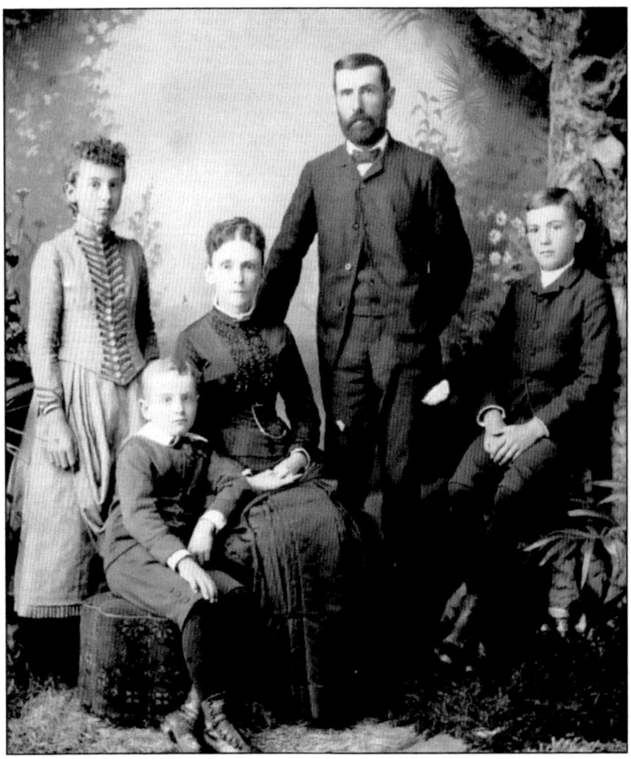

Charles A. Breed, son of Allen O.T. Breed, continued the family farm. He moved to Wauwatosa in 1891 and served on the first common council in 1897. This portrait, c. 1887, shows Charles; his wife Marion (married in 1873); and children Allen Albert, Ruby Louise, and George Louis—two other children died young. Ruby Louise married Augustus Gregg in 1899 at the First Congregational Church, receiving one of the first marriage licenses issued by Milwaukee County under a new license law. (WHS Photo 714.)

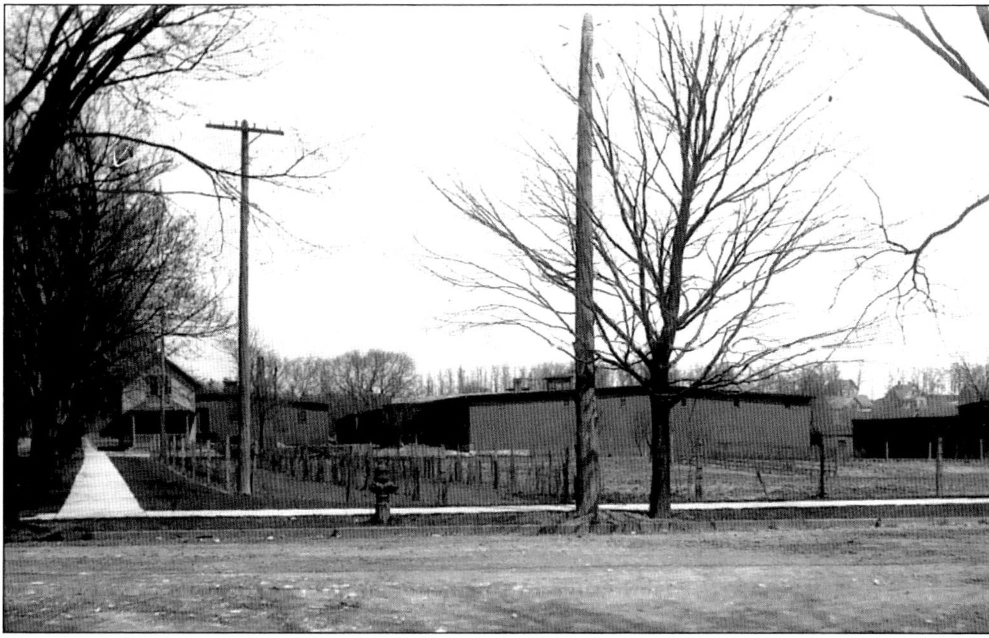

The name of Stickney was synonymous with pickles from the 1870s to the early 1900s. The Milwaukee Pickle Company occupied the area from Hillcrest Drive to Milwaukee Avenue, between Seventy-first and Seventy-third Streets. This 1899 view (*above*) looks to the northeast from Milwaukee Avenue. James Stickney and his son Charles were the proprietors; their business produced vinegar and cider as well as pickles. A recognized authority, James Stickney spoke to the Farmer's Institute on special crops in 1883. During the 1880s, Stickney contracted with farmers in Palmyra for cucumbers, even opening a branch office there in 1890. Nearby Yale Place was known as Pickle Alley. The factory became too smelly for neighbors and was razed in 1912. Charles Stickney (*right*), son of James Stickney, married Julia Fisher. Her father, Charles Thompson Fisher, a prominent farmer, owned property at North Avenue and Mayfair Road. (Courtesy of Milwaukee County Historical Society and WHS Mss. 112.)

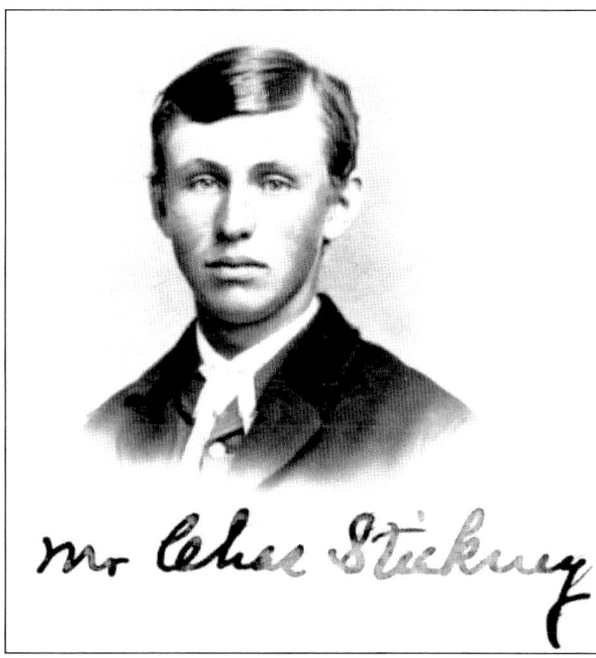

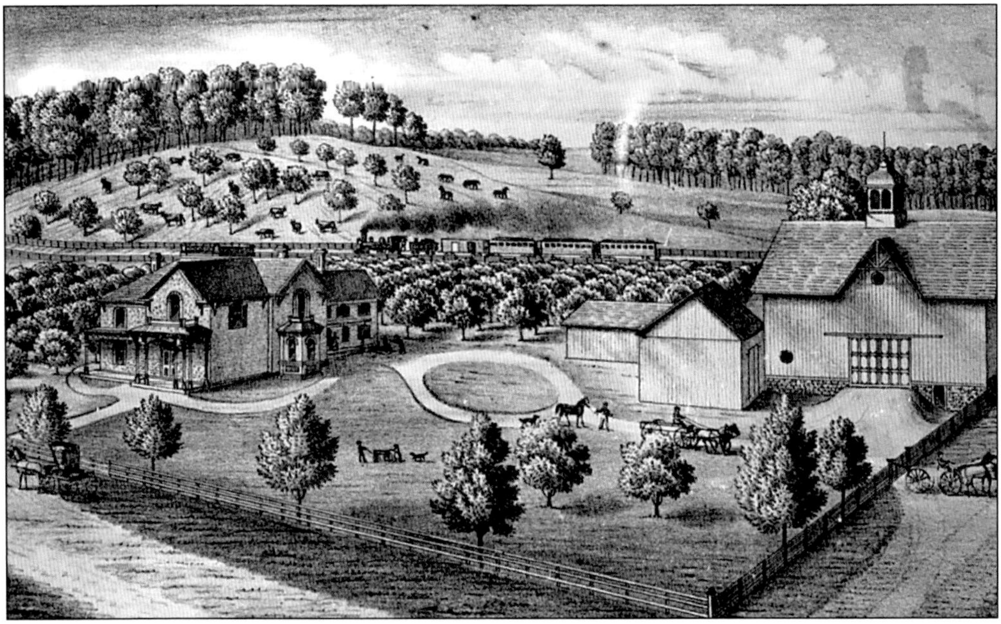

William I. Fisher developed this farm at Mayfair Road and North Avenue, building a creek-driven sawmill, a frame house, and barns. He died in 1851 at age 37, when his only son, Charles Thompson Fisher, was five years old. Charles married Nancy Swan, daughter of Nathaniel and Hannah Gilbert Swan. Charles had an active political career, serving as town treasurer, Milwaukee County Board chairman, state senator, and on several Governor's special commissions. He is buried in Wauwatosa Cemetery. (WHS Photo 76.)

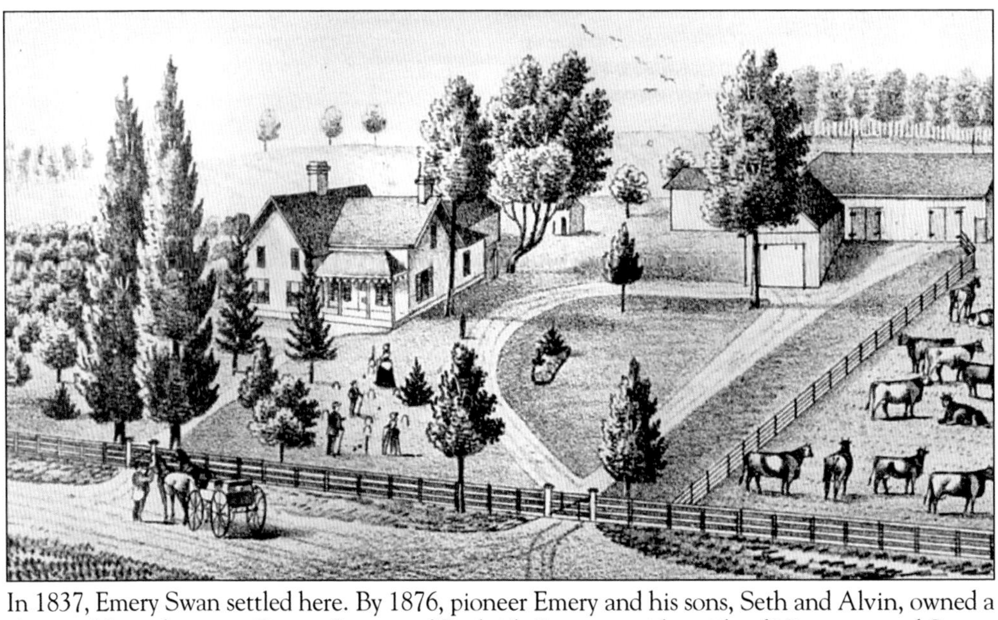

In 1837, Emery Swan settled here. By 1876, pioneer Emery and his sons, Seth and Alvin, owned a cluster of farms between Center Street and Burleigh Street on either side of Ninety-second Street. The father had 80 acres, Alvin 20 acres, and Seth 100 acres. Emery's eldest son, Nathaniel, farmed 123 acres at the northeast corner of Burleigh Street and Mayfair Road. This lithographic view of Seth's farm is from 1876. Seth's daughter Bertha sold the farm in 1936. (WHS Photo 87.)

Seth Barber Swan, born in 1829, married Maria M. Moore, born in 1832. The Wauwatosa Historical Society is fortunate to have in their collections two portraits of the couple. They are fine examples of Victorian professional photographic styles. To the right is a solemn Civil War era photo, c. 1865, with Maria in a dress with a large hoop skirt, the fashion of the day. Both are seated, with no background features, just a book on the table between them. (WHS Mss. 112.)

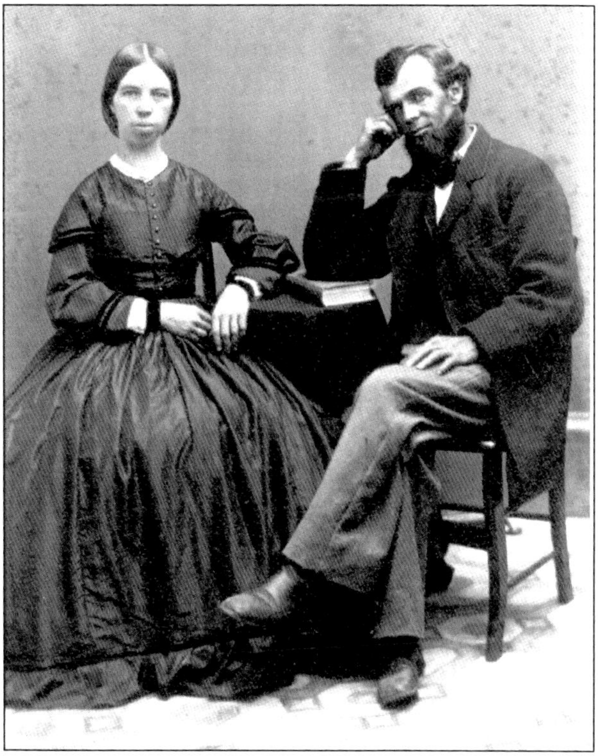

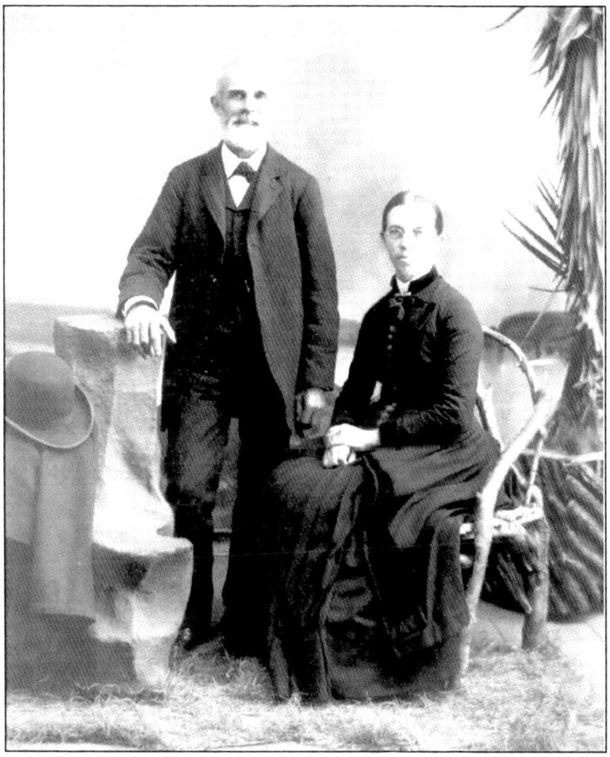

In the image to the left, c. 1890s, their positions have changed, with Seth standing and even with a slight smile on his face. The photographer created a tropical atmosphere with a scenic mural and props not typical of Wauwatosa or Milwaukee. The Swans had five children, yet only two, Bertha and Clarence, survived to adulthood. Bertha was born in 1860 and died in 1954. She lived on the family farm until 1936. Clarence, born in 1865, died in 1942. (WHS Mss. 112.)

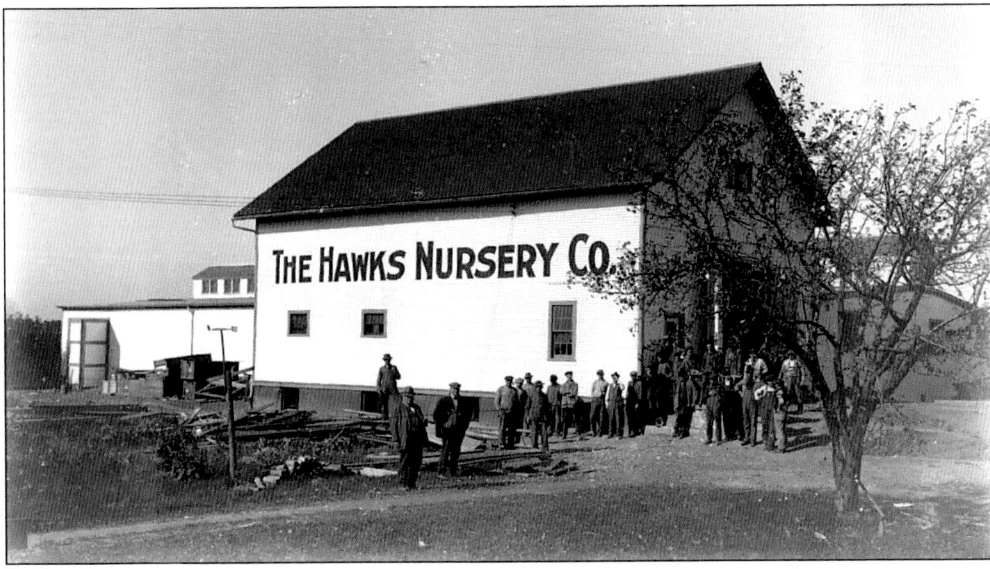

In 1875, Charles Hawks Sr. became a founder of Hawks Nursery in Rochester, N.Y. Agents traveled the country selling fruit and shade trees. They began a Wauwatosa operation in the 1890s. In the 1920s, Charles Hawks Sr. and Jr. moved here and purchased land at 122nd Street and Watertown Plank Road—the business site today. In the 1930s, the firm's emphasis shifted to ornamental landscaping. This photo, *c.* 1923, is believed to show the northeast corner of Mayfair Road and Burleigh Street. (WHS Photo LGP 902.)

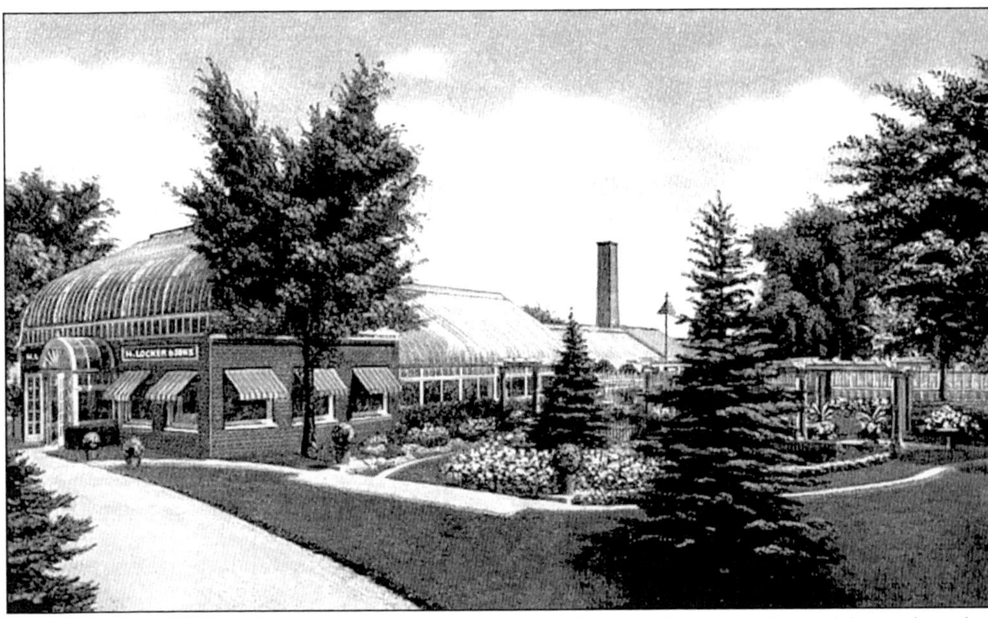

Hugo Locker and his two sons, Alfred and Arthur, purchased a farm in 1911 and formed Locker & Sons. They located their Wauwatosa store at 9125 West North Avenue and advertised as the "Sweet Pea King of Milwaukee," because they grew cut flowers for distribution to wholesalers in Milwaukee and statewide. The demand for funeral flowers, due to the 1919 flu epidemic, spurred expansion, and a semi-steel conservatory was built north of the 1911 greenhouses. Family ownership ended in the 1990s. (WHS Postcard 645.)

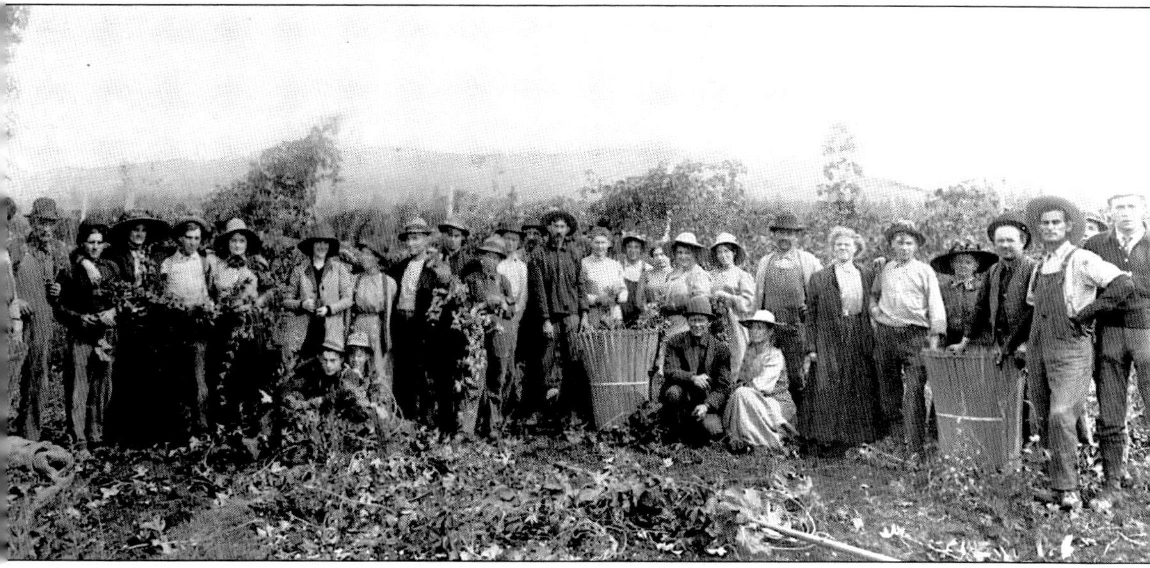

In the 1870s, the Phillip Best Brewery purchased 780 acres in an area bounded by North Avenue and Milwaukee Avenue, and Sixtieth and Sixty-eighth Streets, except for a few tiny parcels. The brewery used the farm to grow hops for beer production and to raise Percheron draft horses to pull wagons (*below*). Frederick Pabst succeeded his father-in-law, Phillip Best, as brewery president, and in 1889 the business name became the Pabst Brewing Company. Hops pickers pose for this undated picture (*above*). Note the wide-top baskets used to protect the delicate hops as they were harvested. The plants, grown on tall poles, can be seen in rows behind the workers. Pabst maintained a rural retreat at the farm, which was linked to Milwaukee by streetcar when Pabst helped create the Milwaukee & Wauwatosa Rapid Transit Co., which ran on Pabst Avenue, now Lloyd, to the Village. A portion of the farm is today the Washington Highlands subdivision. (Courtesy of Milwaukee County Historical Society.)

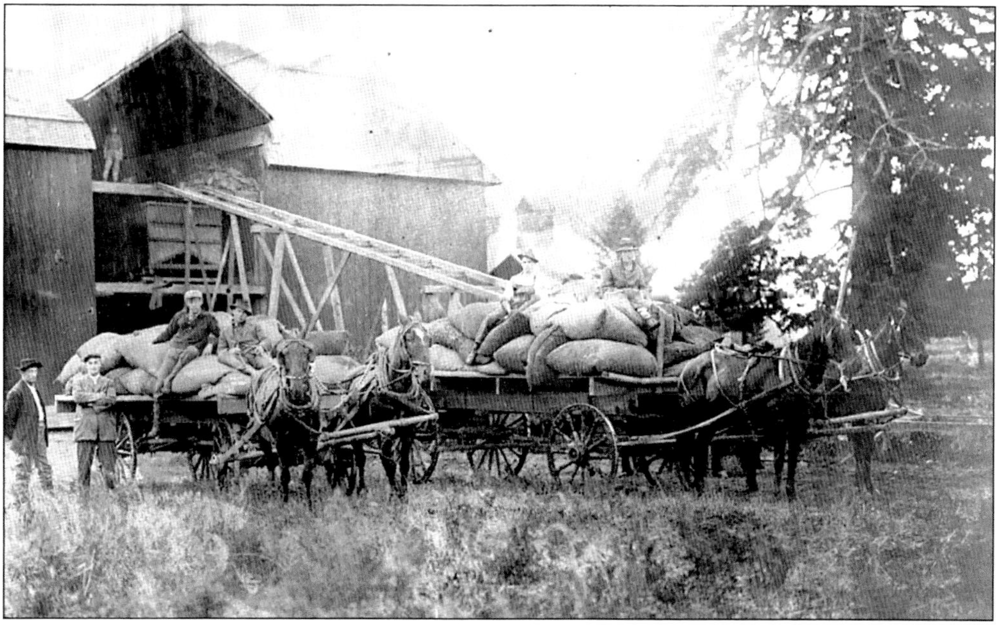

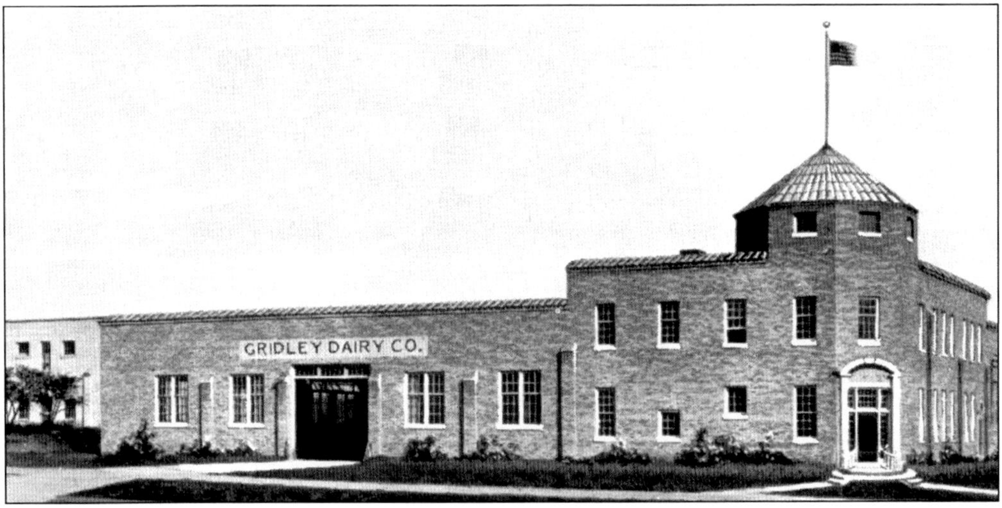

Today it is St. Pius X Catholic Church and school, but this building, built in 1925 at 2504 Wauwatosa Avenue, began as a major distribution plant for the Gridley Dairy Company. Their barn stabled up to 56 horses for milk wagons. Sold to the Borden chain in 1929, the Gridley name disappeared in 1953. In 1944, Borden sold this property, retaining a dairy office. First used as the Don Bosco Youth Center in 1952, the site became the home of the St. Pius X Parish. Leander L. Gridley founded his dairy in 1873 and retired in 1894. His son, Leander V., continued the business, consolidating with four other small plants in 1903 to form the Gridley Dairy Company. Employees of the Gridley Dairy Company, (*below*) and their families enjoy an outing, possibly at Waukesha Beach, *c.* 1900. They traveled on the Milwaukee Electric Railway and Light Company interurban route from Milwaukee to Waukesha. (Courtesy of St. Pius X Parish and WHS Postcard 707–1.)

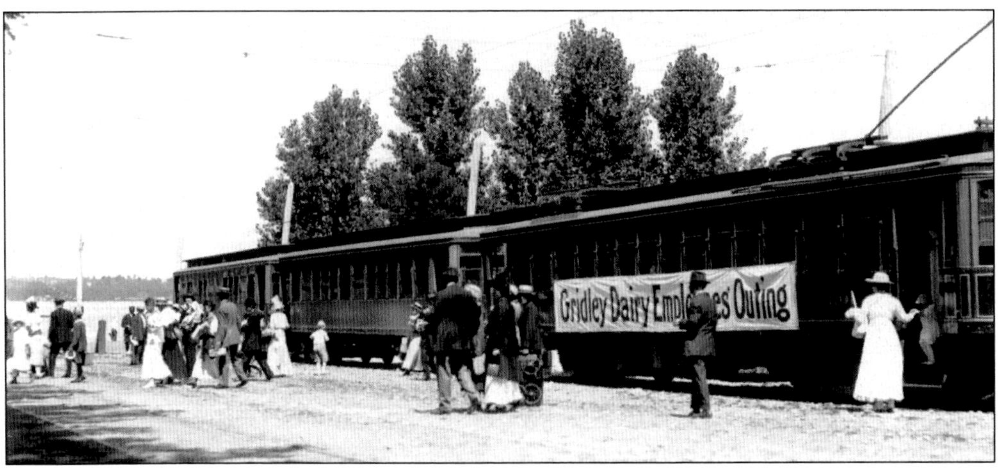

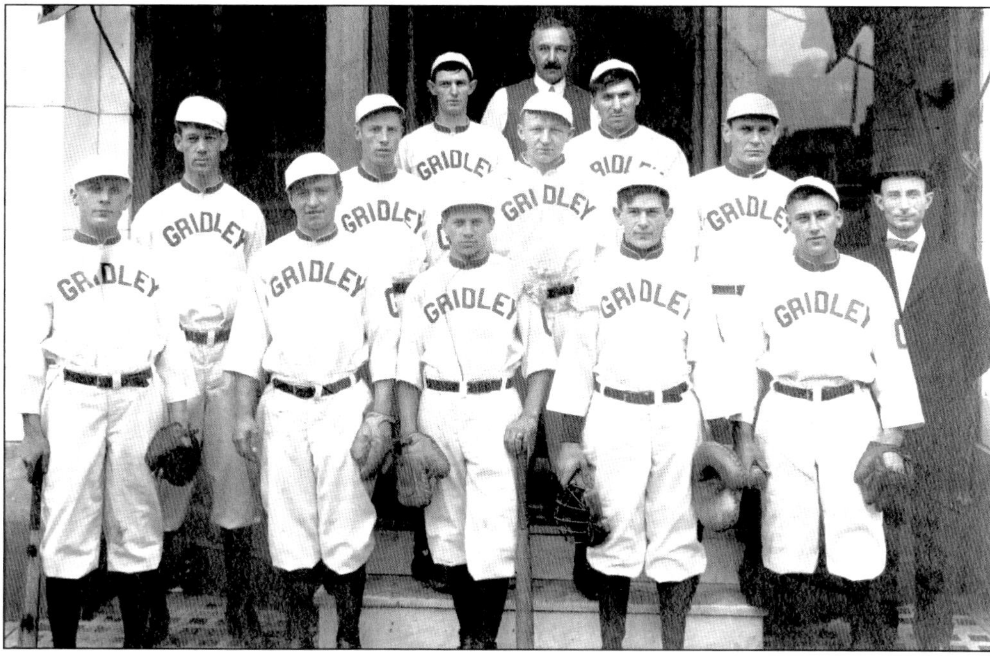

The Gridley Dairy Company promoted its products with newspaper and billboard advertising throughout Milwaukee County. The company and its employees could further spread the Gridley name as they celebrated the national pastime of baseball. (WHS Photo 754.)

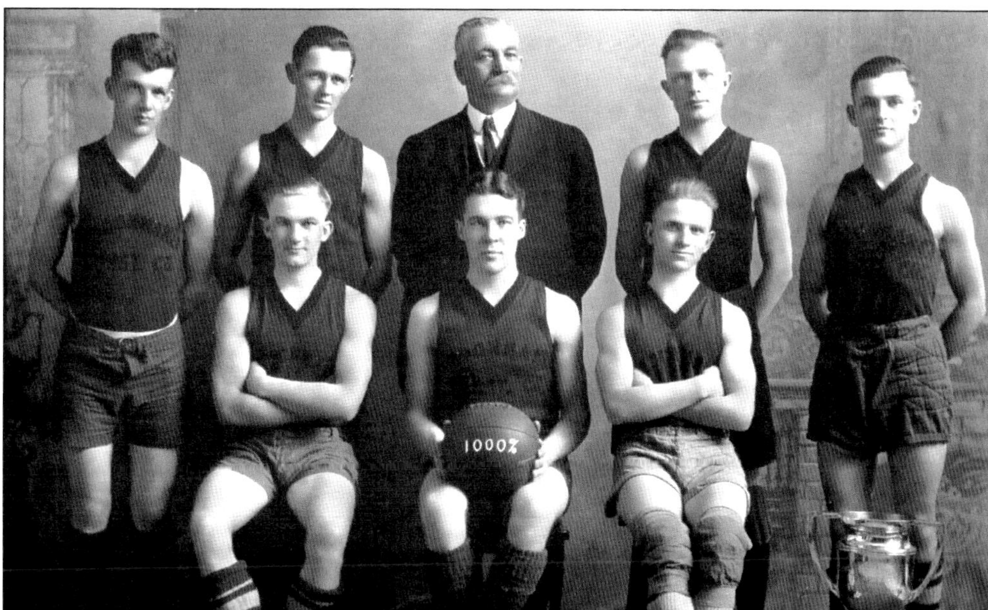

The Wauwatosa Commercial League was organized in 1919 and this 1921 team won the league championship. Basketball fans could come to the Wauwatosa High School gym on Thursday nights and see at least three basketball games. Admission "to witness the fray" was 10¢. Team sponsors included Schoonmaker Construction Co., Kuhnmuench Drugs, Rubel Rexall Drugs, Hawks Nursery, and the First National Bank of Wauwatosa. (WHS Photo 753.)

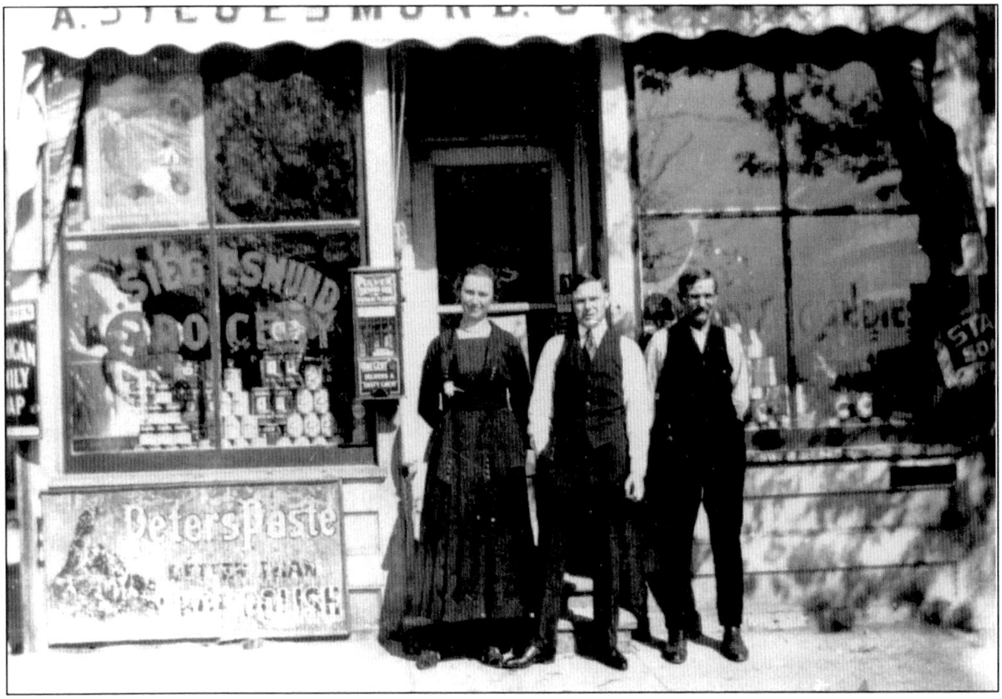

Mr. and Mrs. Albert Siegesmund and his father, John Siegesmund, are in front of the Siegesmund Grocery store located at 1386 North Seventy-second Street. John immigrated here in 1880, married Ida in 1882, and in approximately 1886 built this two-story building for his grocery store, with living quarters upstairs. Members of the family continued the business until 1941, when competition from larger stores, such as the A&P and National Tea, proved too great as customers gained mobility with their automobiles. (WHS Photo 758.)

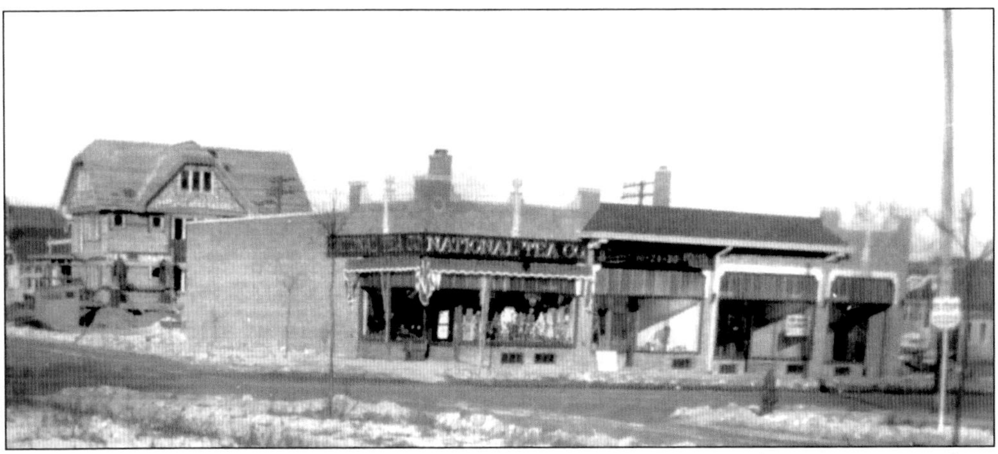

In 1927, the National Tea grocery at 6926 West North Avenue was under construction, along with a house at 2318 North Seventieth Street. Competition intensified in 1938 when the Great Atlantic & Pacific Tea Co. opened across the street, next to separate fruit and meat markets. By 1941, when A&P opened a modern supermarket at 7326 West North Avenue, the National Tea store closed. Other businesses occupied the site, the scene of a major fire that destroyed half the building in 1993. (WHS Photo 482.)

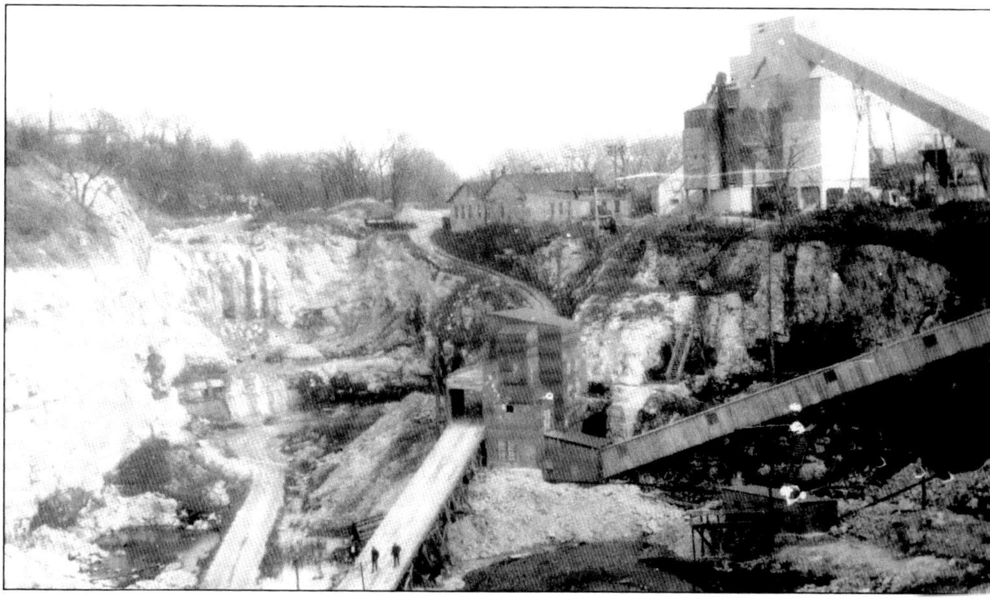

Quarrying lime for mortar and limestone used in construction were significant nineteenth century industries at several sites in Wauwatosa. John Schoonmaker began producing lime at the northeast corner of North Sixty-eighth and West State Streets in the late 1850s. After 1910, G.D. Francey took over the business, producing crushed stone used as aggregate in concrete. In this 1934 photo (*above*) the crusher building is visible in the center. The quarry closed in 1950. The site was later filled in and has been occupied since 1972 by a supermarket. Early geologists described the 400-million-year-old Silurian rocks at the site as part of a huge fossil reef, the first to be recognized in North America, suggesting that Wauwatosa once was part of a shallow tropical ocean. The Schoonmaker Reef received National Historic Landmark designation in 1998. The Schoonmaker family's Greek Revival house (*below*) was built above their quarry. John is standing at the right. (WHS Photo 584 and Courtesy of Caroline Schoonmaker Timmerman.)

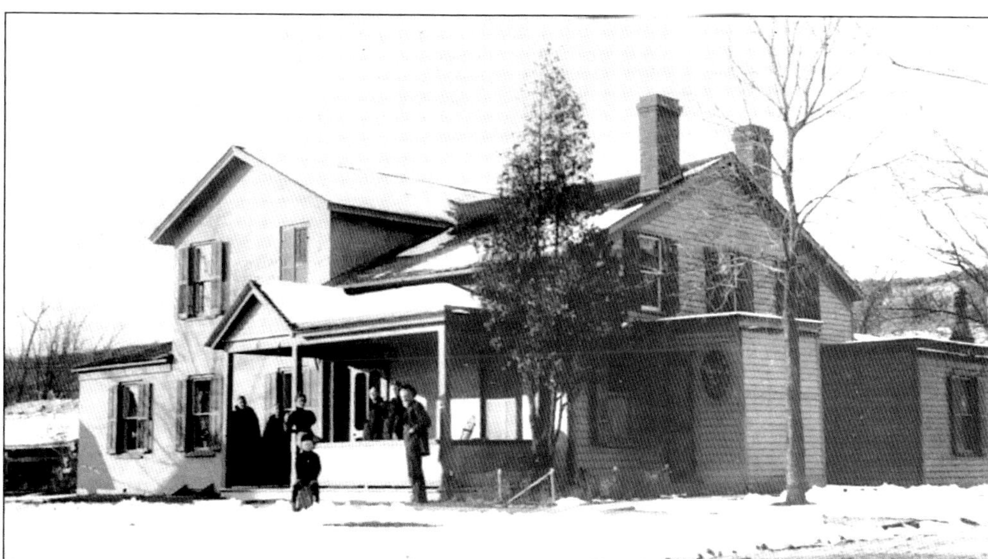

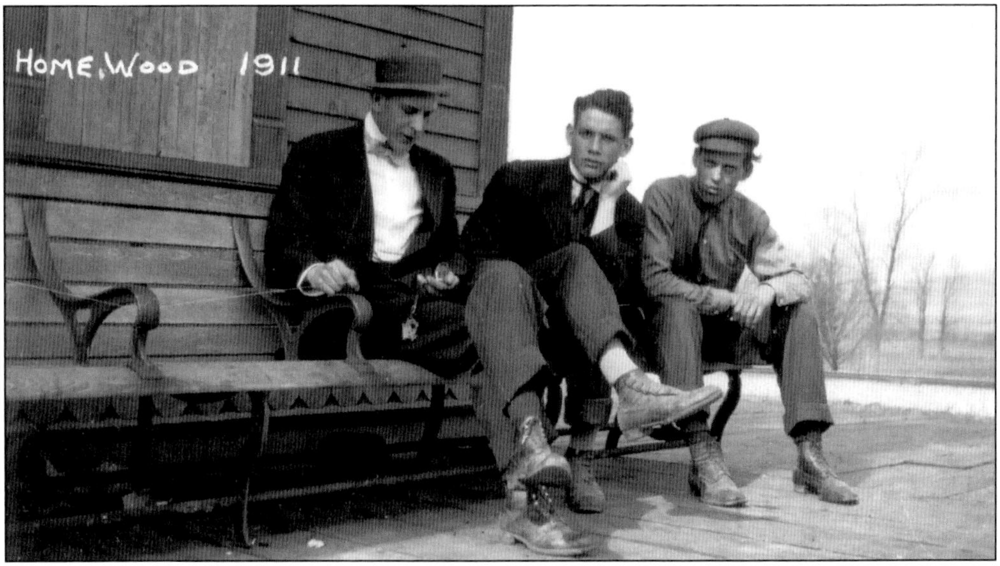

The Milwaukee Road Railroad served southwestern Wauwatosa with a stop at the Homewood station near what today is 115th Street and the Underwood Creek. Homewood was the name for this "unincorporated settlement," and 117th Street south of Bluemound Road was named Homewood Avenue. A development company that owned property in the area was also called Homewood. The train station, pictured here in 1911 with a shuttered window, was removed in approximately 1930. (WHS Photo 559.)

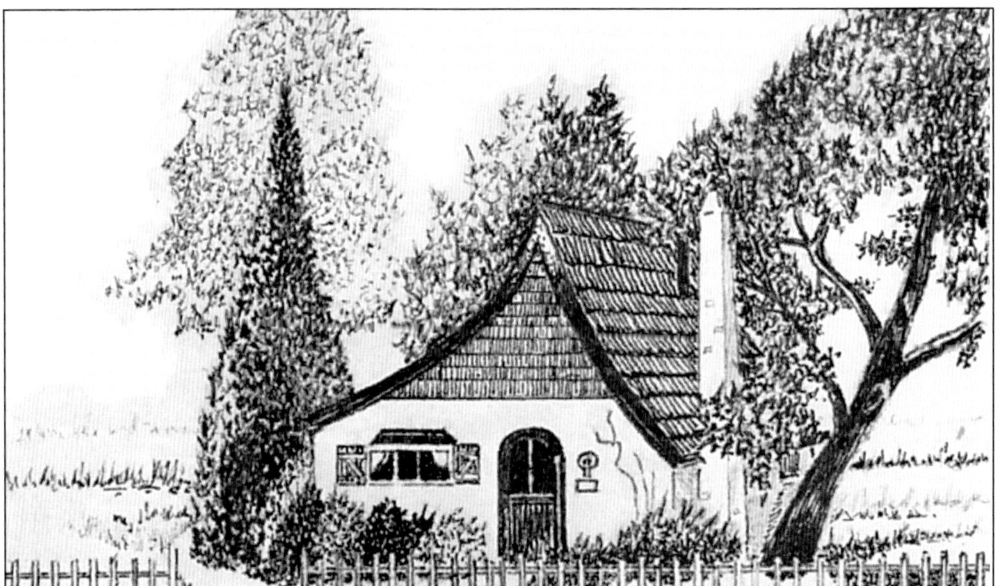

Open land surrounded the tiny "Mother Goose House," so named by Glenn Realty when they built it in 1928 at 8734 West North Avenue as a sales office for surrounding subdivisions. It closed in 1930 after the stock market crash. Neighbors bought it and in 1931 opened the Mother Goose Restaurant & Soda Grill, which operated until 1962. The building was moved in 1963 to Duplainville, an area between Brookfield and Pewaukee. (Tosart, WHS Mss. 127.)

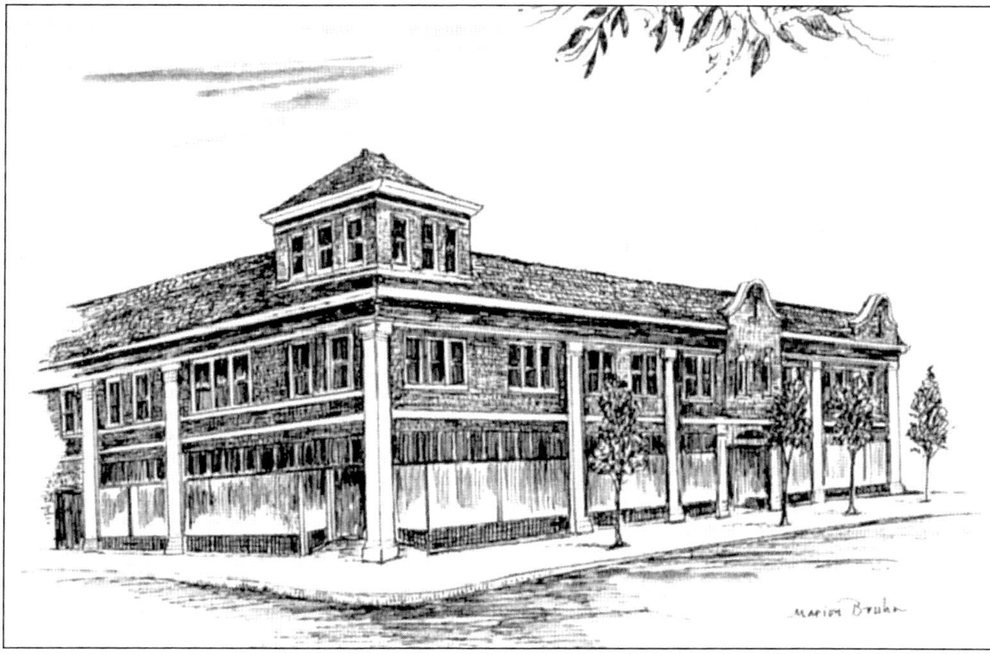

When it opened in 1928 at 7212–7226 West North Avenue, the two-story Spanish Colonial Arcade Building was "destined to be the playground of Wauwatosa." It included stores, offices, apartments, and a basement with 12 bowling lanes, 10 billiard tables, and a soda grille that became a tavern when Prohibition was repealed. When the building underwent a $1.4 million renovation in 1995, the bowling lanes were replaced by underground parking. (Tosart, WHS Mss. 127.)

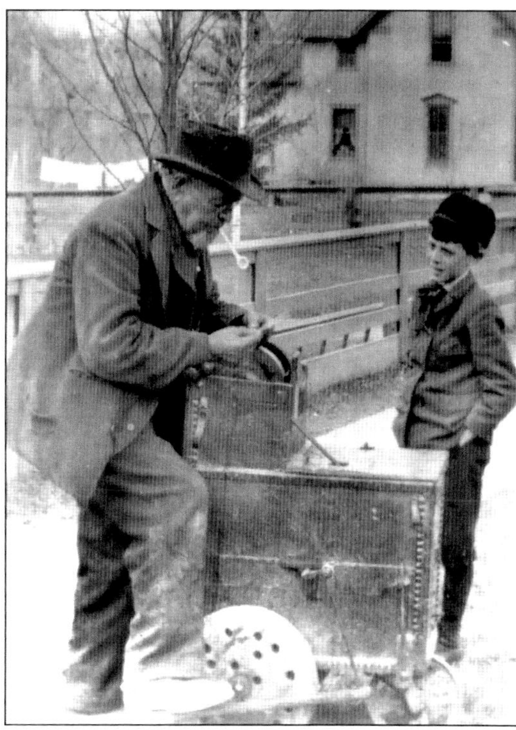

One of many vendors who regularly plied their trades on the streets of Wauwatosa in the late 1800s and early 1900s was the scissors grinder. These men took their business to the customers by pushing a cart up and down residential streets. The cart featured a foot pedal that turned a stone wheel used to sharpen knives and scissors. They made their rounds every month or two, ringing a bell to alert the neighborhood. (WHS Photo 718.)

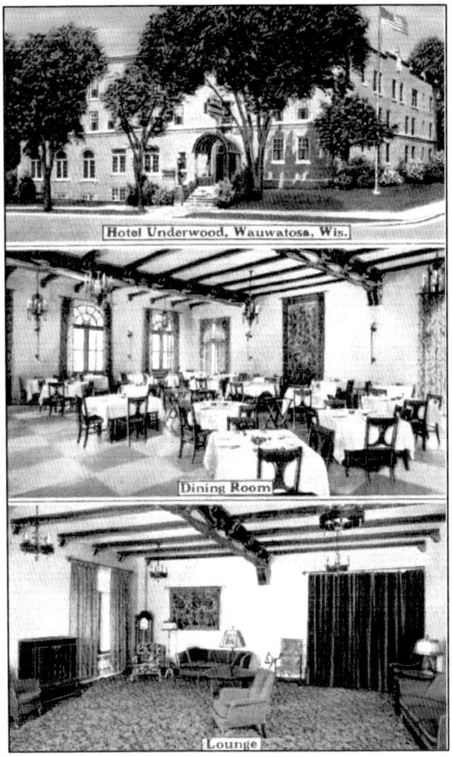

The Underwood Hotel opened in 1930 at 7416 Harwood Avenue with a dinner dance for the city's elite. It was built on the site of the home of early settler George D. Ringrose and named for Wauwatosa pioneer William O. Underwood through a Kiwanis Club contest, which drew more than 1,000 entries and awarded a $50 gold prize. A third floor was added in 1937. It was converted to apartments in 1953. (Courtesy of Judith A. Simonsen.)

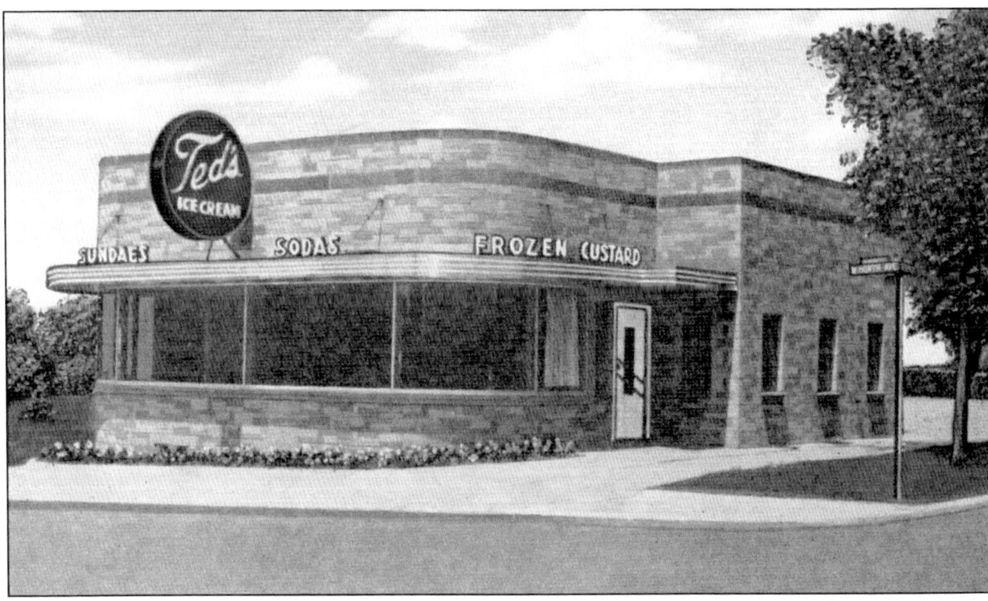

Ted Gottwein opened Ted's Home Made Ice Cream in 1941, serving eight flavors of frozen custard from 11 a.m. to midnight. Originally at 6129 West North Avenue, it moved to 6204 West North Avenue in 1948. Drive-ins hurt the night business, so Ted shifted to daytime hours in 1954 and introduced breakfast and lunch menus. Still family owned and operated, the restaurant offers the same eight flavors of custard in a largely intact 1940s décor that has been featured in television commercials. (WHS Postcard 691.)

Three

For the Common Good

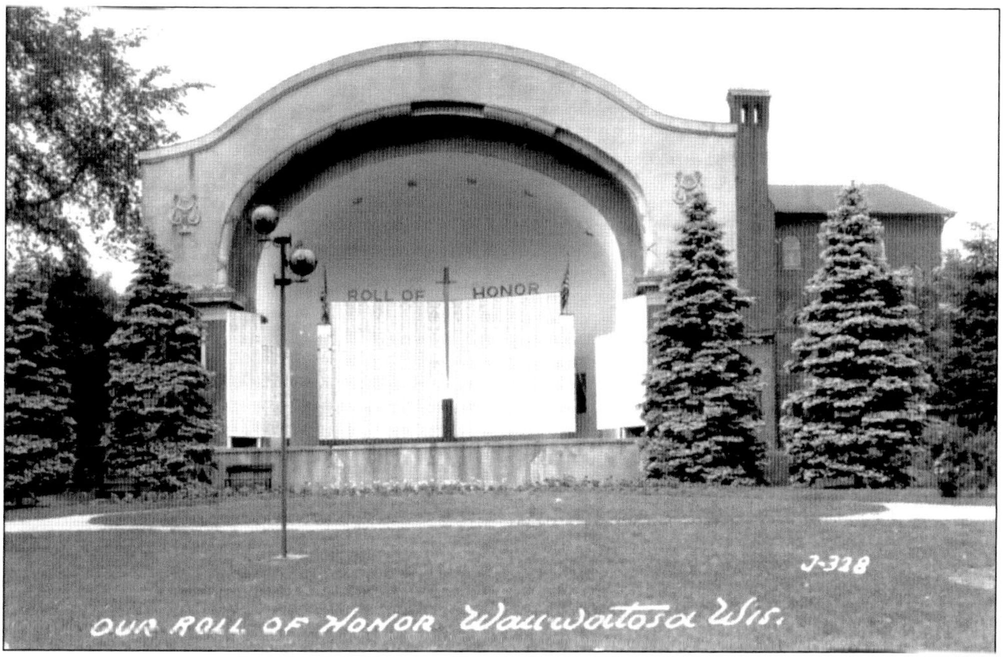

Wauwatosa's first post office opened in 1847, and by 1903 free postal delivery served most of the city. After Wauwatosa became a village in 1892, and particularly after it attained city status in 1897, many municipal services emerged. Governance at first was by an elected mayor and common council of eight aldermen. Today we have a mayor, common council of sixteen, and a city administrator. Ordinances were passed on a wide range of public issues, from regulations for dancehalls to the sale of foodstuffs. As the city grew in the 1920s, a street department and zoning board were created to oversee new roads and housing. A health department was started. The city band shell (above) erected in Root Common in 1927, displayed the community Roll of Honor during World War II. Following the war, the community began planning a civic center as a tribute and a more fitting memorial to its war heroes. The Wauwatosa Memorial Civic Center was dedicated in 1957. (WHS Postcard 631.)

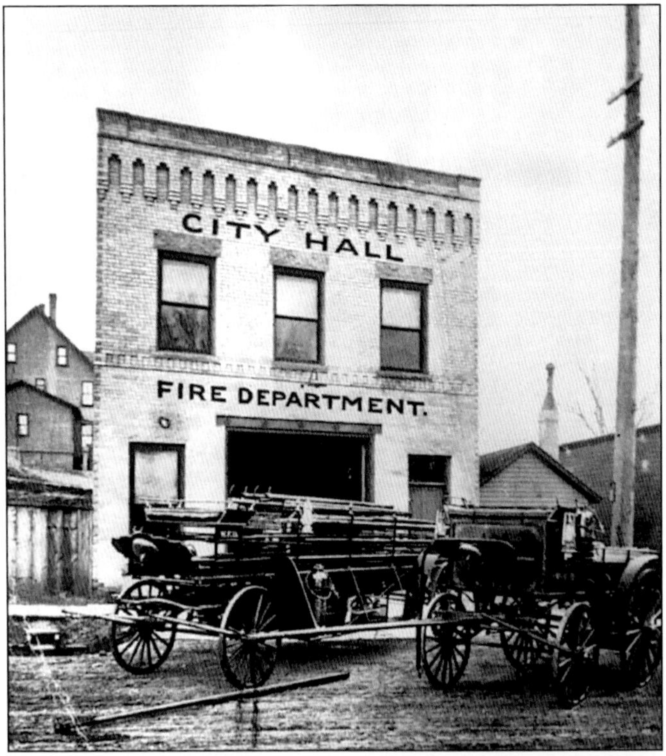

There is no mistaking the use of this building at 1430 Underwood Avenue (*c.* 1900). Completed in 1899, it housed the city hall on the second floor and the fire department below. The department's first horse-drawn ladder wagon and horse cart stand in front. On May 27, 1897, Wauwatosa became a fourth class city with Emerson D. Hoyt as its first mayor, enabling the community to authorize firefighting and other needed services. The building continues in use today as a commercial site. (Courtesy of Milwaukee County Historical Society.)

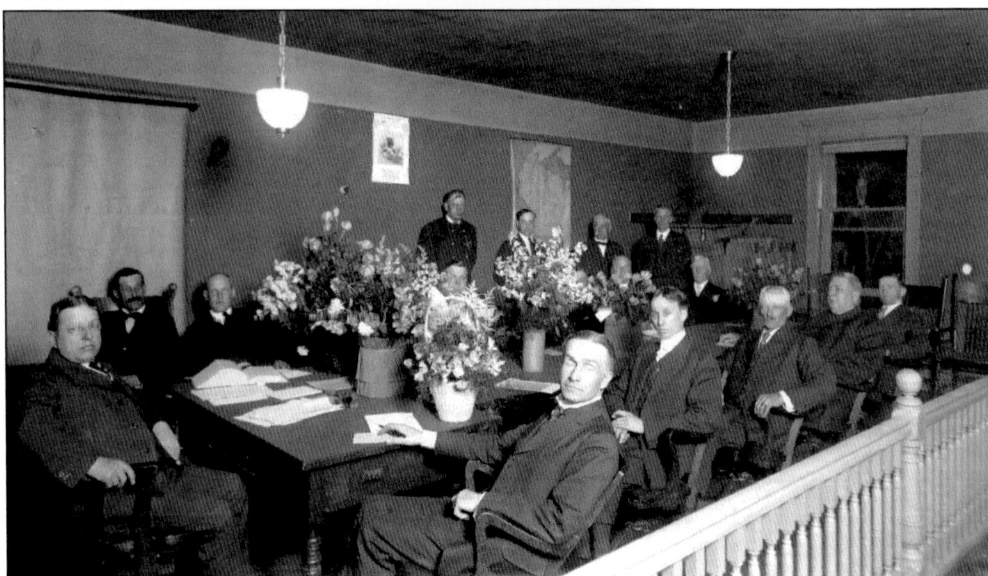

This photograph is identified only as pre-World War I, with Wauwatosa resident Dennis J. Hayes, a justice of the peace. Such justices were part-time elected Milwaukee County officials who resolved minor criminal complaints in the police courts in return for a portion of the proceeds from fines and fees. By 1910, the county ended the criminal jurisdiction of the justices of the peace, leaving them with authority for only a few misdemeanor cases and ordinance violations. None of the other individuals in the photo are identified and the occasion is unknown. (WHS Photo 719.)

With the devastating fire of 1895 a recent memory, Wauwatosa began building its own artesian well and water distribution system in 1897. The Blanchard Street Water Works (*right*), completed in April 1898, were essential to the health and safety of the growing city. Previously, firefighters were forced to rely on hand-pumping water from the river. Mr. Charles Lapham, Wauwatosa's first city engineer, designed and supervised the project. The Blanchard Street waterworks, with a flow of 450,000 gallons a day, was the first well dug. By 1903, seven and a half miles of water mains were laid, and 70 street hydrants were installed, along with some residential connections. Two 100-horsepower boilers (*below*) provided steam for the two pumps manufactured by Smith-Vaile of Dayton, Ohio. Eventually, the facility converted to electricity. By 1935, five more wells had been built, furnishing 6.2 million gallons of water per minute. Since 1959, Wauwatosa's water has come from Lake Michigan, purchased from the City of Milwaukee. (WHS Photo 721 and WHS Photo LGP 352.)

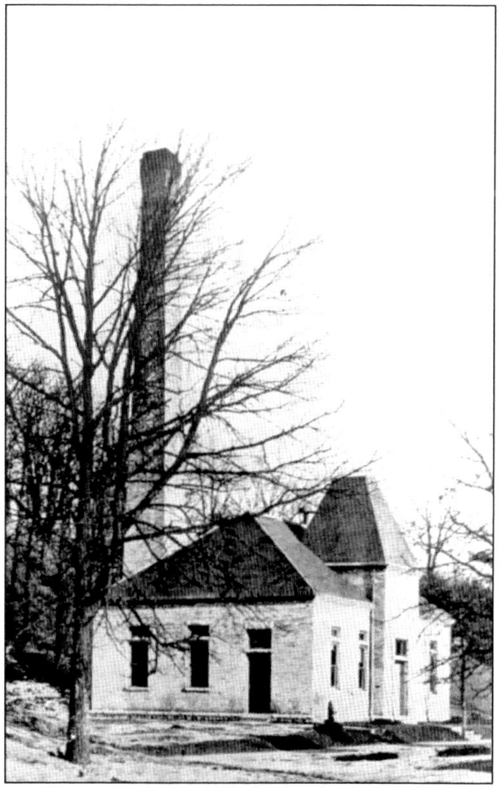

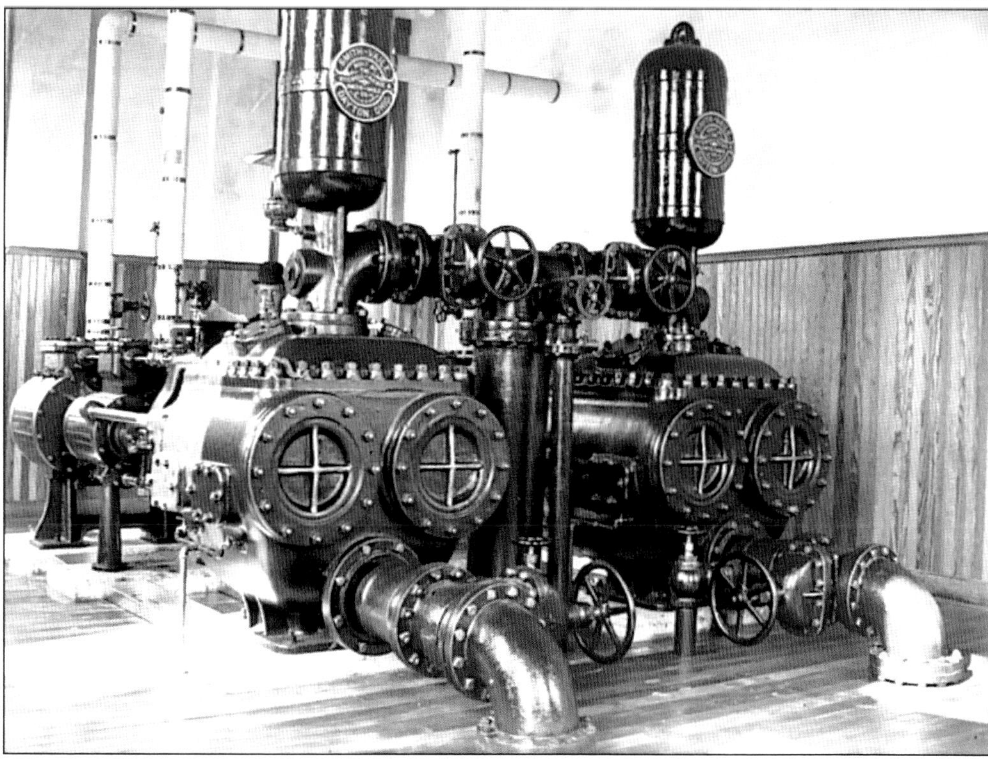

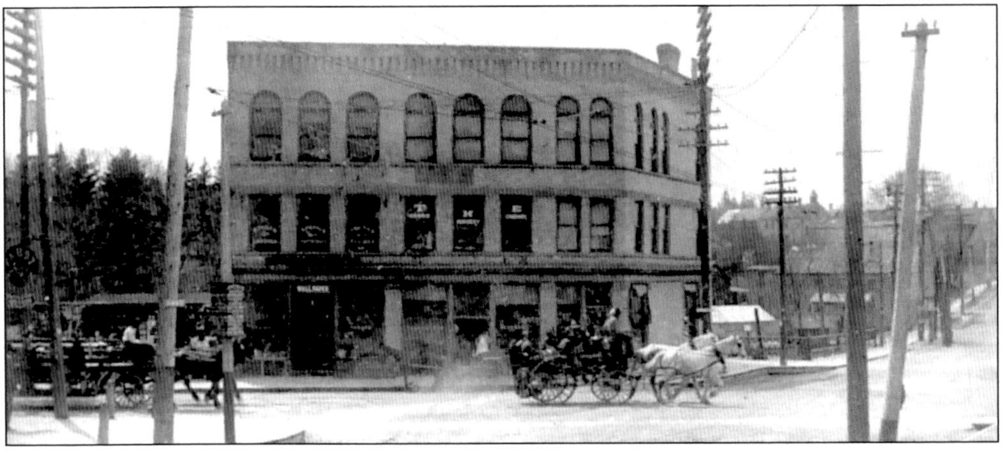

The hook-and-ladder wagon and the steam engine pumper were essential components of the city's fire-fighting arsenal. They are seen (*above*) on State Street about to cross Harwood Avenue in front of the Hemsing Block building, constructed in 1910 and still in use today. The fire department, officially established on December 19, 1899, replaced volunteers with a staff of paid, part–time firemen who earned $20 a year. They worked under the command of the first chief, J.D. Warren. Subsequent chiefs included Charles C. Jacobus, J.A. Schwaiger, John Hamme, James C. Lefeber I, Otto Garvens, Ralph Sporleder, and James C. Lefeber II, who served from 1919 to 1938. The community purchased the pumper, equipped with 1,000 feet of hose, but the firemen built the hook-and-ladder unit themselves; it was in use for 25 years. The 1909 collage shows the 22 community firefighters, with Chief J.C. Lefeber I in the center frame. (WHS Photo 434 and 718.)

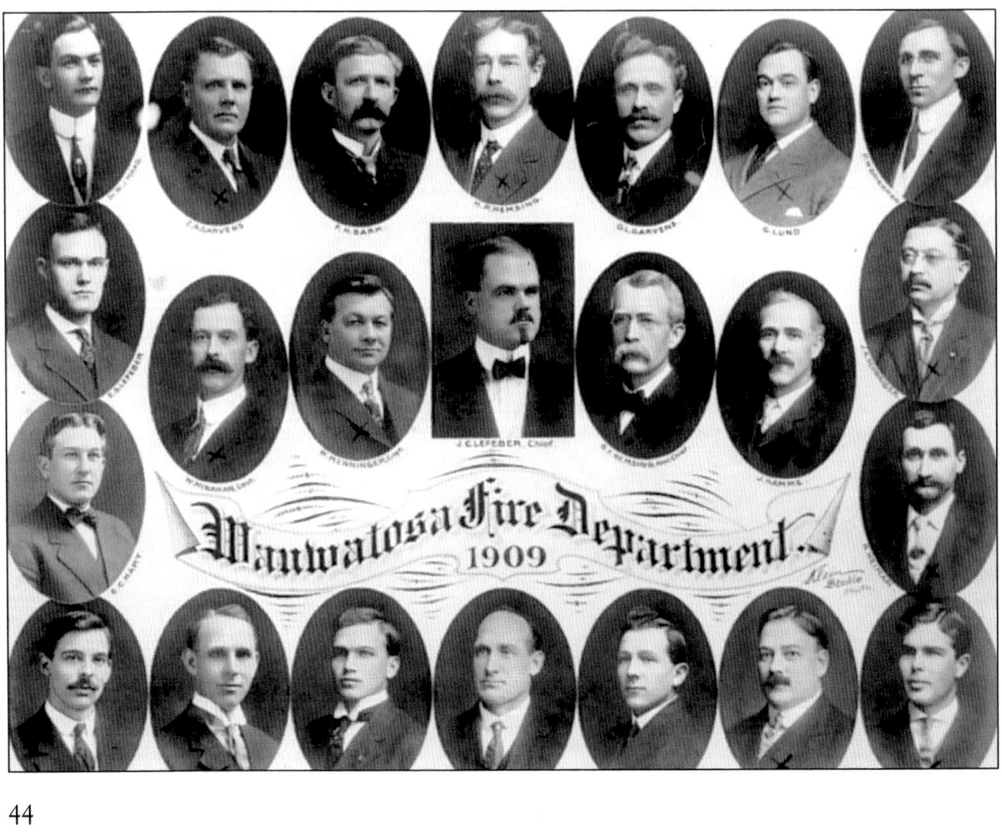

A smoky fire in March 1946 gutted the interior of Keenan's Drug Store on the southeast corner of Harwood Avenue and State Street. The fire department saved the building (see page 44, the Hemsing Block). The fire attracted great crowds and caused police to detour traffic. Auxiliary help arrived when Milwaukee sent two engines and a truck to aid the city firefighters. The fire originated in a basement pile of boxes and paper. (WHS Photo 553.)

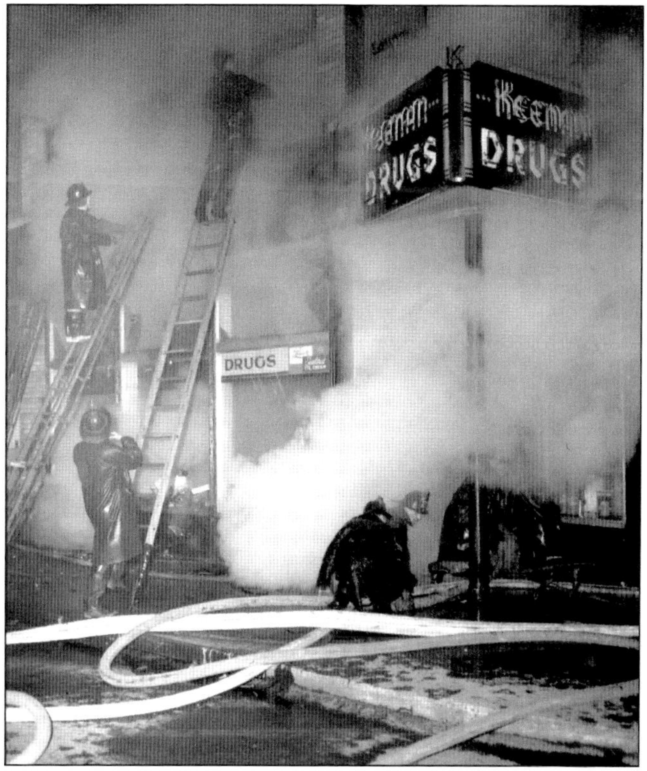

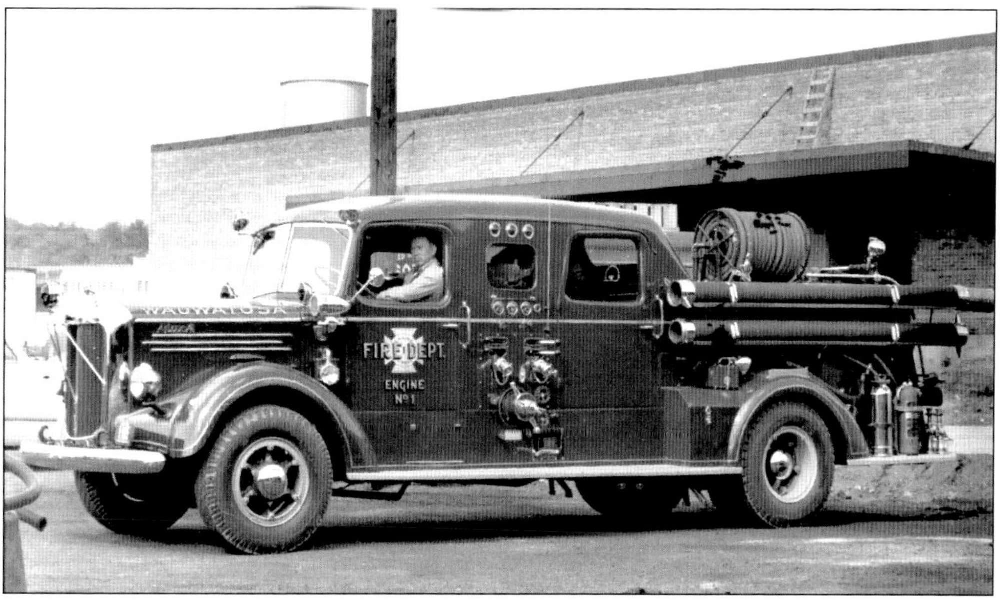

A 1947 Mack pumper truck, capable of pumping 1,250 gallons of water per minute, became part of the fire department fleet under Chief Fred Hartel. After working in cramped quarters for some time, the department had moved in 1942 to 1463 Underwood Avenue. They combined a former laundry and a new structure attached to the back of the police station to provide badly needed facilities, including dormitory space for 26 men. Douglas Dunlop became fire chief in 1949. (WHS Photo 545.)

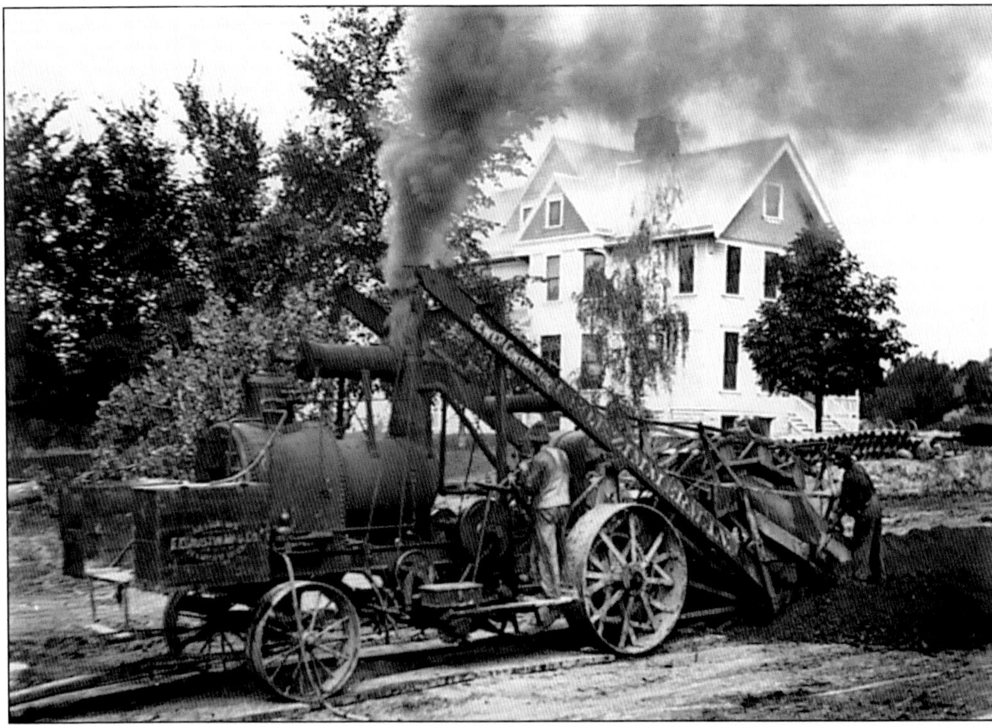

In 1901, the city began constructing a septic tank and filter disposal system to handle sewerage. Street sewers were laid in the ground with heavy equipment. This digging machine, manufactured in Harvey, Illinois, and operated by sewer contractor George E. Zimmerman, works on a city street in August 1901. By 1903, the system included a septic tank, automatic gatehouse, filter beds, and over five miles of sewers, and had operated successfully for a year. (WHS Photo LGP 72.)

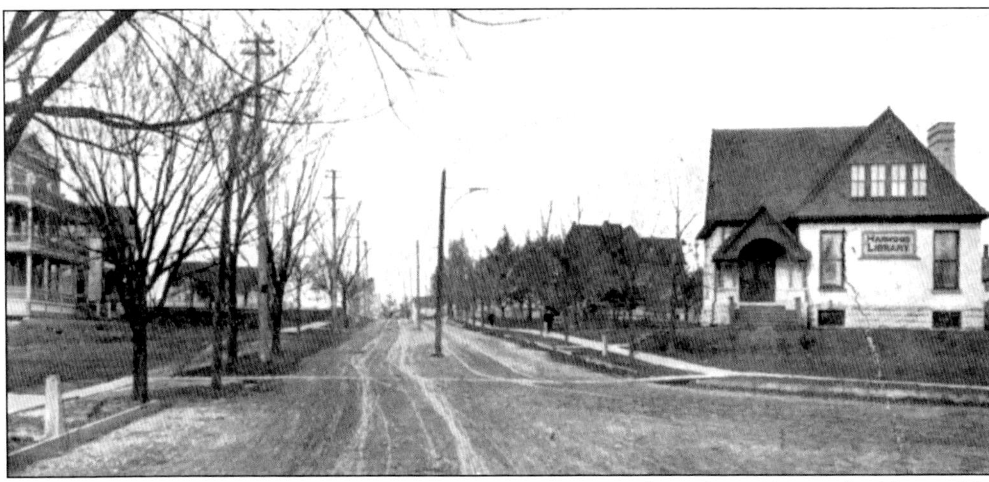

The Harwood Library and Lecture Association incorporated in the 1880s to build a public circulating library. A bequest by Oliver Harwood provided initial monies. The Harwood Library, right, was built in 1896 on land donated by James and Charles Stickney and Harry Hunter on the triangle at Milwaukee and Harwood Avenues. The building was razed in 1957. The Irvington Hotel, at left, constructed in 1895, operated until 1928. It survives today as apartments. Note the streetcar poles with conducting wire in the center of the street. (WHS Photo 27.)

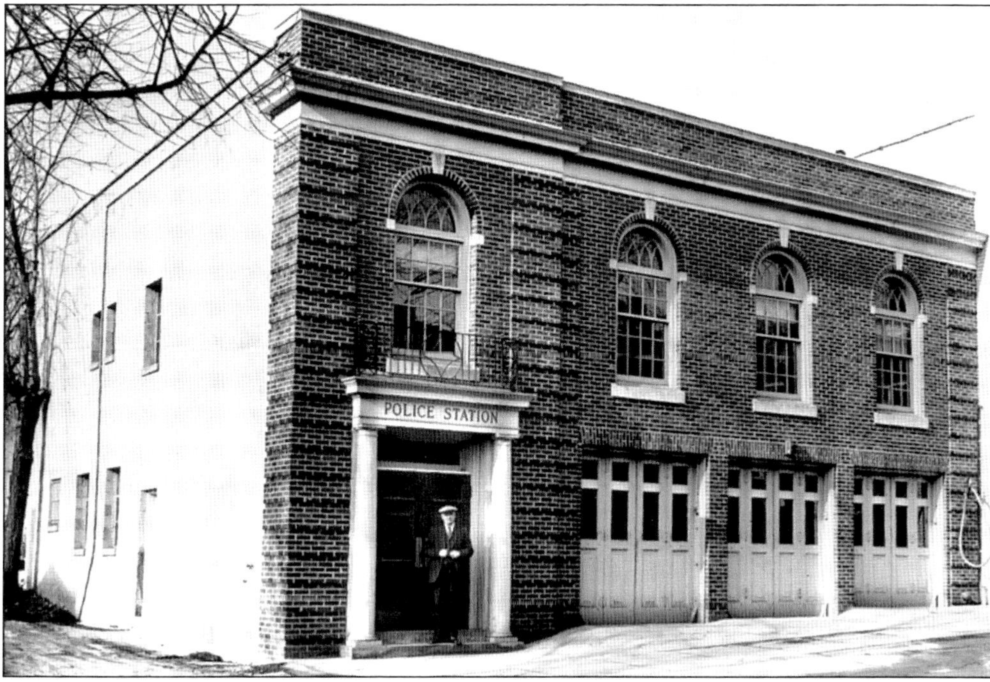

A town marshal enforced the law in Wauwatosa until the first chief of police, Julius Marquardt, took office in 1897. In 1916, the first full-time police force was authorized. The city's first police station, at 1430 Underwood Avenue, shared the building with the city hall and the fire department. The police force consisted of the chief, George W. Baltes, and two other officers. The department grew and needed its own facility, and in 1930 it moved into this new $22,000 building at 1501 Underwood Avenue (*above*). The Wauwatosa Fire Department now uses the building. The newest police headquarters is located at 1700 North 116th Street. Wauwatosa's 1940 police force is assembled in the photograph below, a testimony to the city's willingness to provide a secure environment. (Courtesy of *The Milwaukee Journal* ©2003 Journal Sentinel Inc., reproduced with permission, and WHS Photo 720.)

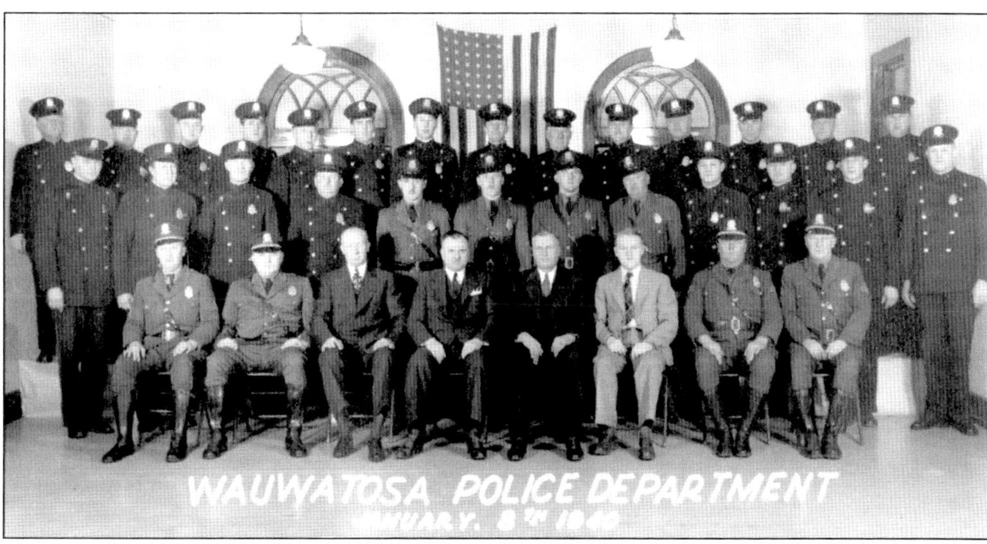

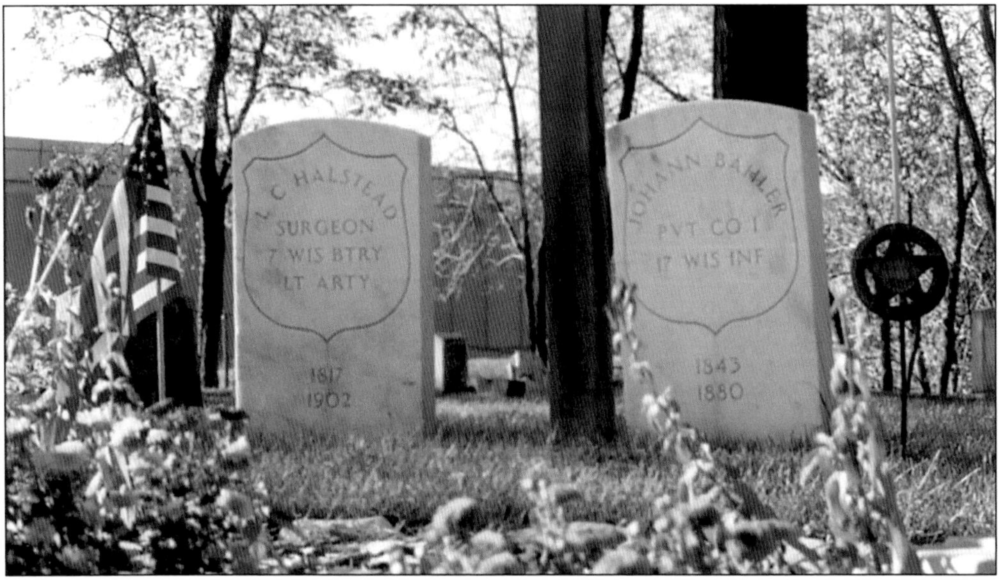

Although Oak Hill Cemetery was officially established in 1853, area farmers used the land for burials before that date—Julia Knapp's stone reads 1848. The cemetery, at 11400 West Capitol Drive, contains the graves of three Civil War soldiers, Levi C. Halstead (Halsted), an early Wauwatosa doctor, physician to the 7th Wisconsin Light Artillery; Johann Bahler, a farmer who joined the largely Irish 17th Wisconsin Infantry as a private; and David H. Bexter, another farmer, drafted into the 34th Wisconsin Infantry, eventually becoming a lieutenant. (Photo by James Ruzicka, WHS Photo 722.)

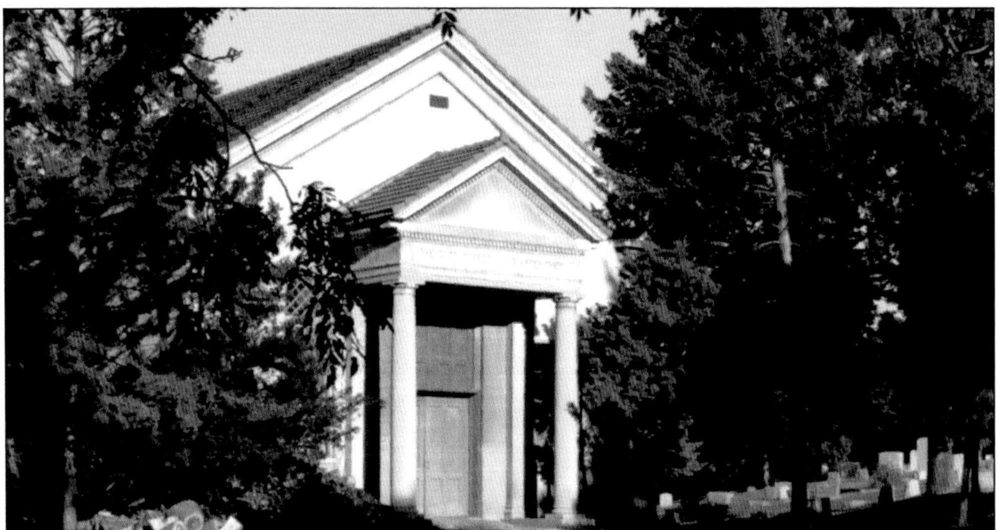

When Charles Hart's wife, Sarah, died in 1841, he established the settlement's first burial ground near the Village on Wauwatosa Avenue. In the 1860s, as the community began to grow, the cemetery and most of the graves were relocated about a mile north to the present Wauwatosa Cemetery. Enoch Underwood donated the land. In 1915 Frederick D. Underwood moved the old Baptist Church to the cemetery for use as a memorial chapel. Grave markers are seen at the right of the building. (Photo by Jerry Smaglik, WHS Photo 588.)

Four

HEALTH AND HUMAN SERVICES

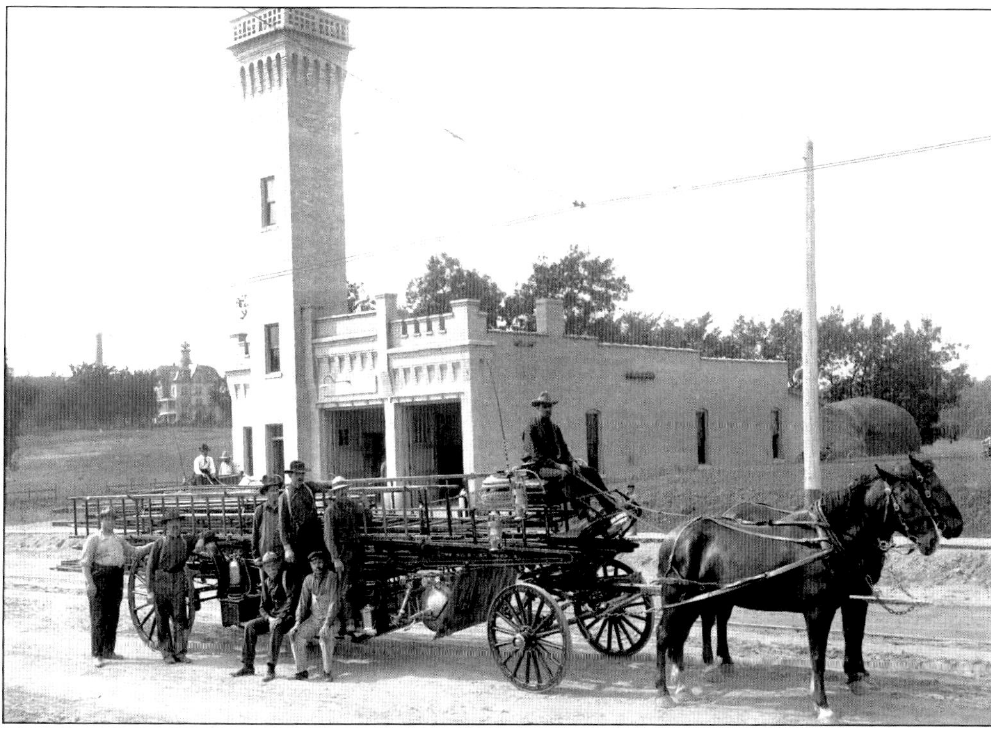

The Milwaukee County Institutions began operations in 1852 when county supervisor Hendrik Gregg offered his 160-acre farm in the Town of Wauwatosa for a county poor farm. Through the years other buildings and services were added as the county acquired more land for a total of nearly 1,200 acres, bounded roughly by Eighty-fifth and 108th Streets between Wisconsin Avenue and the Menomonee River. The complex had its own fire department (above, c. 1910). At left is the Asylum for the Insane. In addition to the county development, other early institutions in Wauwatosa served children, adults, the mentally ill, the aged, and those with special needs, such as the unwed mothers who found haven in the Martha Washington Home. (WHS Photo 555.)

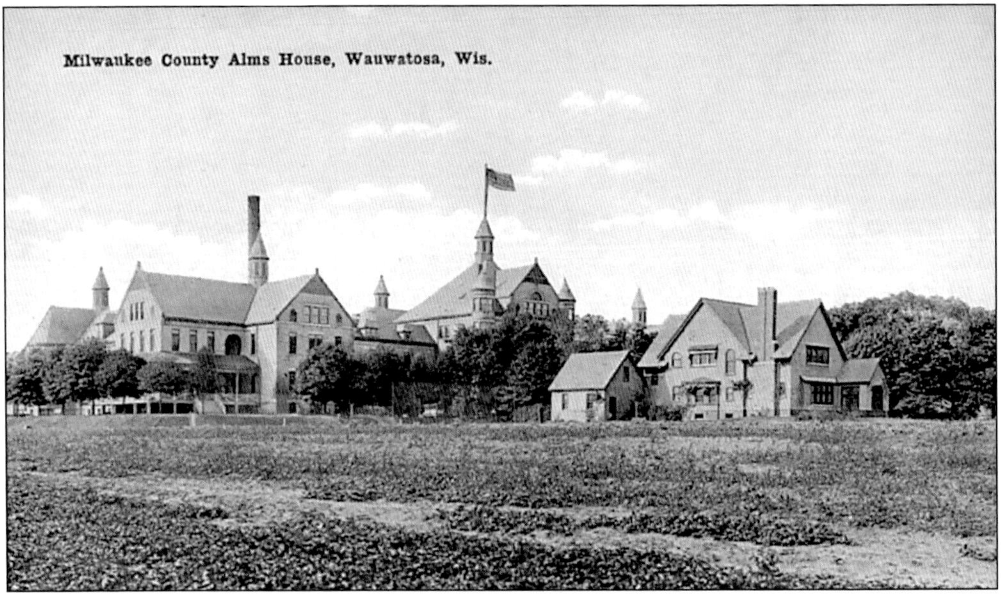

The first almshouse, or poor farm, housed 24 people in the Gregg farmhouse. It soon attracted an array of the needy, including the elderly, children, the sick, and the insane. The mixture of residents created problems that the county tried to meet in the next decades. The most urgent need was caring for the sick poor, and in 1860 a separate 31-bed county hospital opened. This postcard shows the new almshouse, built in 1890 with an addition in 1907. It was renamed the Milwaukee County Infirmary in 1917. The county farm was a thriving enterprise with gardens, barns, pastures, and grain fields. Horses, pigs, and cattle were tended by hired help and county inmates; outdoor work was seen as therapy. These resources helped sustain the residents at the various facilities. Farm workers would have used the horse-drawn wagon (*below*). (WHS Postcard 685 and Photo LGP 903.)

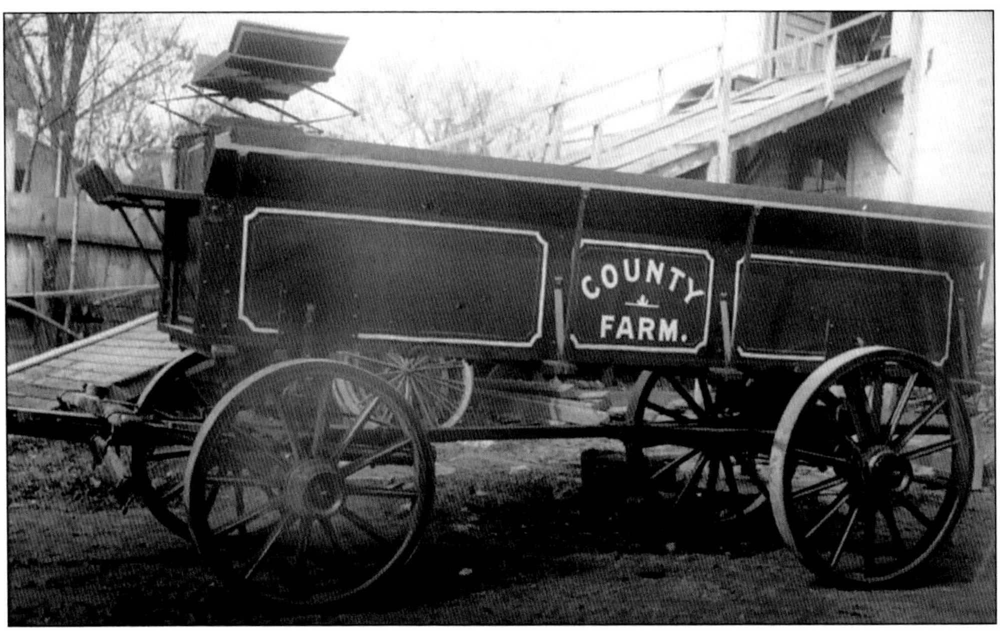

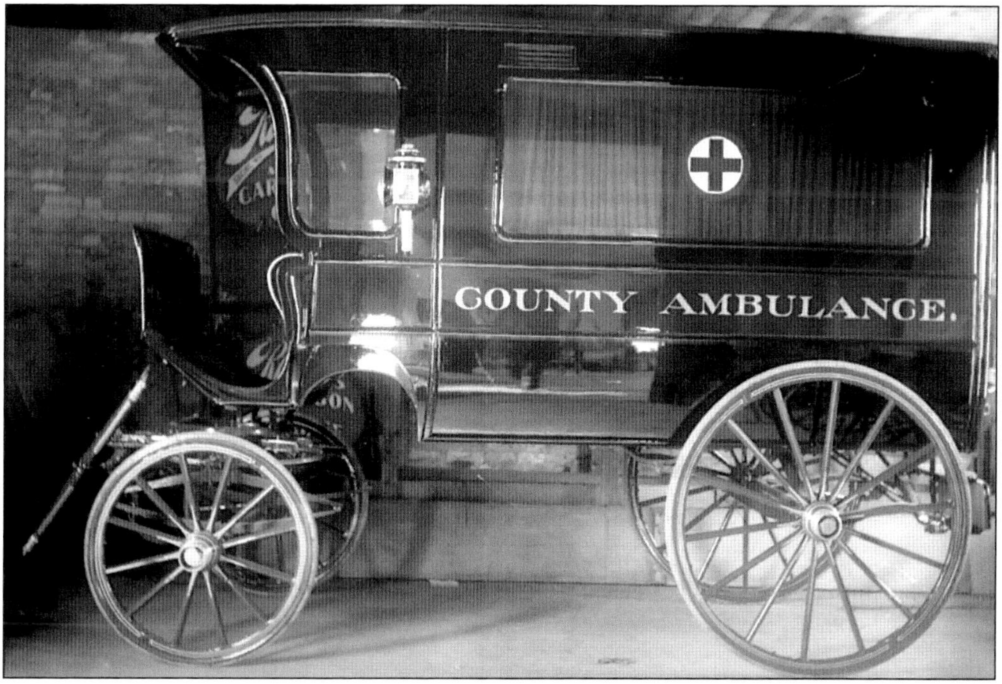

The first county hospital opened in 1860. Above is a nineteenth century horse-drawn ambulance that served patients. Wauwatosan Dr. Fisk H. Day regularly treated patients at the institutions as a county physician. An advocate for humane treatment of the sick and insane, Day frequently raised the ire of the county board with his criticism of practices and building conditions. In 1876, he became the first medically trained administrator at the hospital. The 1860 hospital burned down in 1880 and was rebuilt that year. That new building, with additions, is seen at the upper left in the photo below. In the wake of scientific discoveries of the 1870s relating bacteria to disease, the 1880 hospital began to adopt new sanitary practices and treatments, as well as surgery, and added an integrated medical education component. In 1930 an up-to-date, 650-bed Milwaukee County General Hospital opened (*below*). It was razed in the 1990s. (WHS Photo LGP 904 and Courtesy of James Cerletty.)

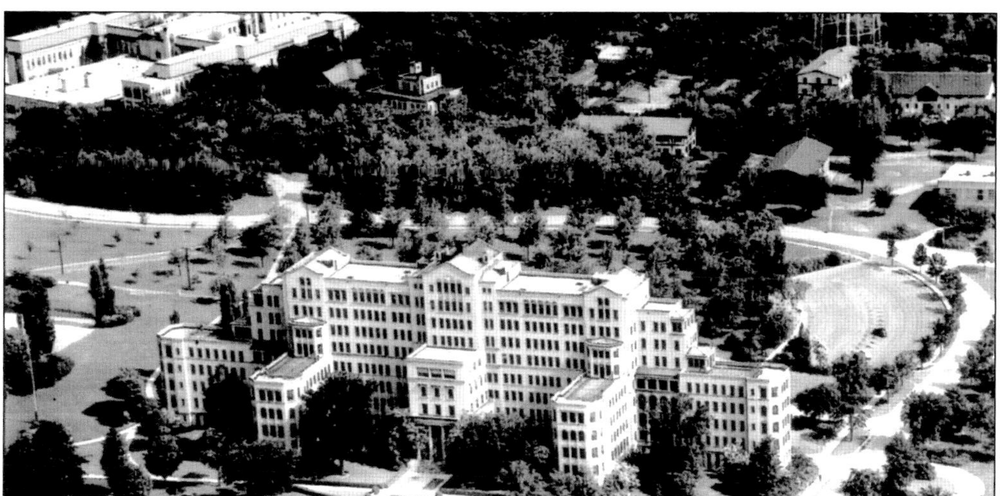

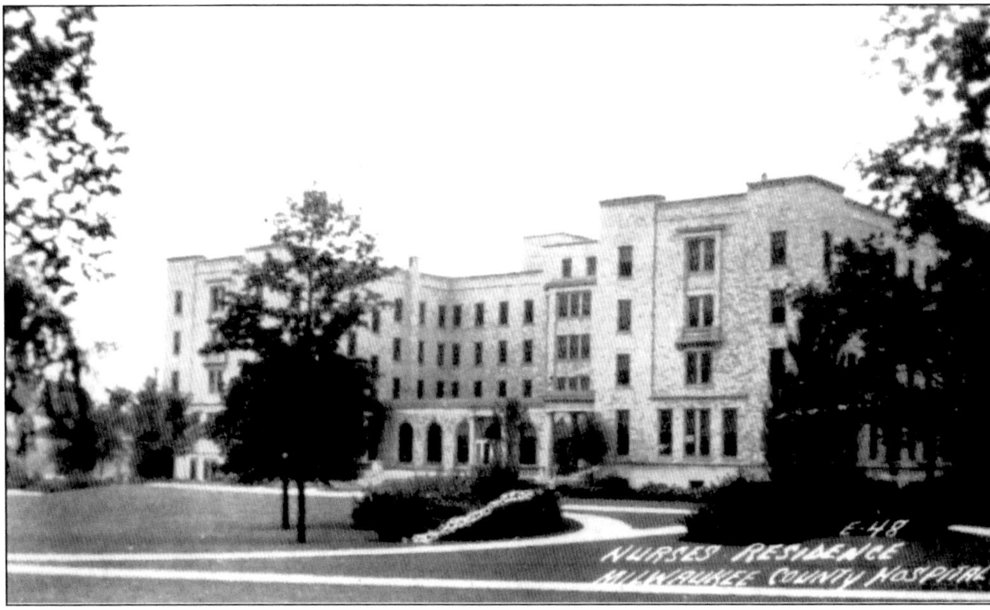

Patient care improved at the county hospital when its superintendent, Dr. M.E. Connell, and his wife, Dr. Anna Gregory Connell, started a nursing class in 1887. The next year the county board approved a two-year diploma training program and 13 young women enrolled as students. This nurses' residence hall was completed in 1933, located west of the hospital. Designated a Milwaukee County Landmark in 1989, it was subsequently razed. (WHS Postcard 678.)

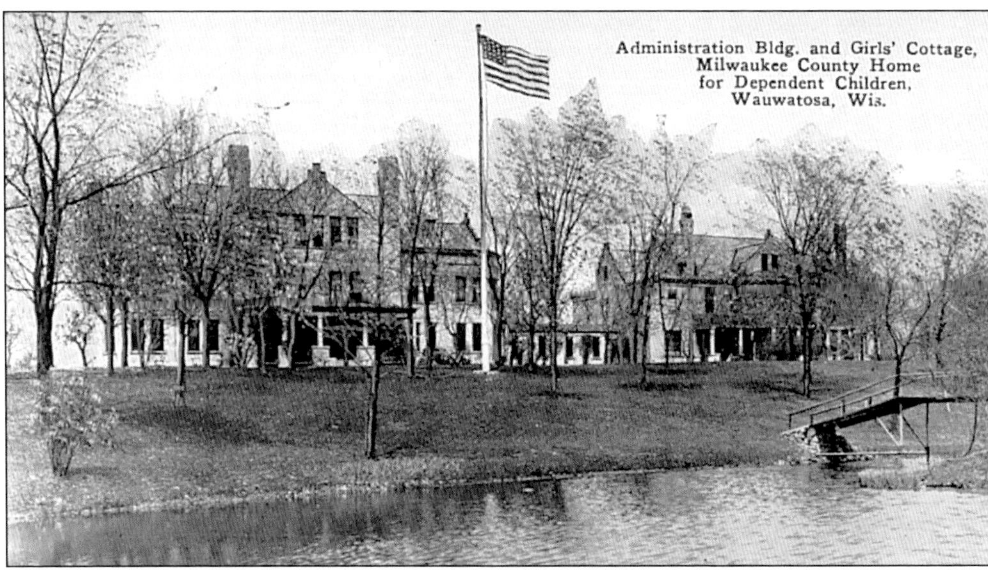

A state law of 1875 prohibited housing minor children in county poor houses. In 1882 the county opened a temporary children's home to handle transients. Public pressure from home-care advocates and increasing numbers of dependent minors compelled the county to act, and the Home for Dependent Children opened in 1898. It became part of a complex, shown in this postcard, which eventually included a facility for infants and hospital care. Many children became long-term residents, and educational and recreational programs were instituted. (WHS Postcard 619.)

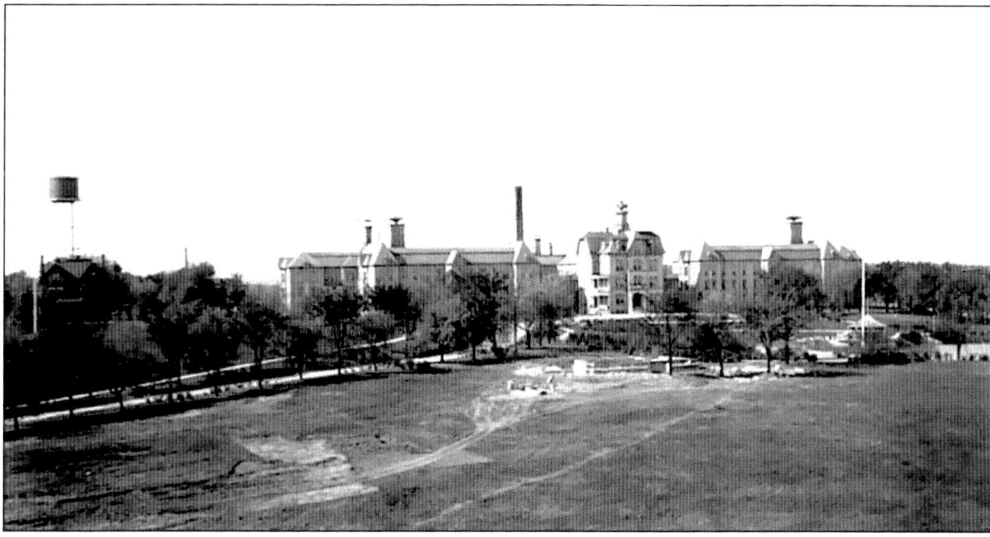

Treatment of mental illness was slower to advance than care for medical and surgical illness. The state opened two asylums in 1860 and 1873, but they quickly became overcrowded. This 1904 image (*above*) shows the asylum complex Milwaukee County built, and below is a close-up of its beautiful park-like grounds. Previously many mentally ill Milwaukeeans had been placed in a separate "insane section" of the county almshouse, which was woefully inadequate. Dr. Day, local reformers, and the State Board of Charities and Reform pushed for change. Ultimately a state-legislated county-state program led to the Milwaukee County Insane Asylum, which opened in 1880 with 275 beds. In 1889 a separate Asylum for the Chronically Insane opened for permanent care, and the older building became the Milwaukee County Hospital for the Acute Insane, for "curable" patients. Medical advances in the twentieth century have offered dramatic new treatments to help the mentally ill. (WHS Photo LGP 905 and 428.)

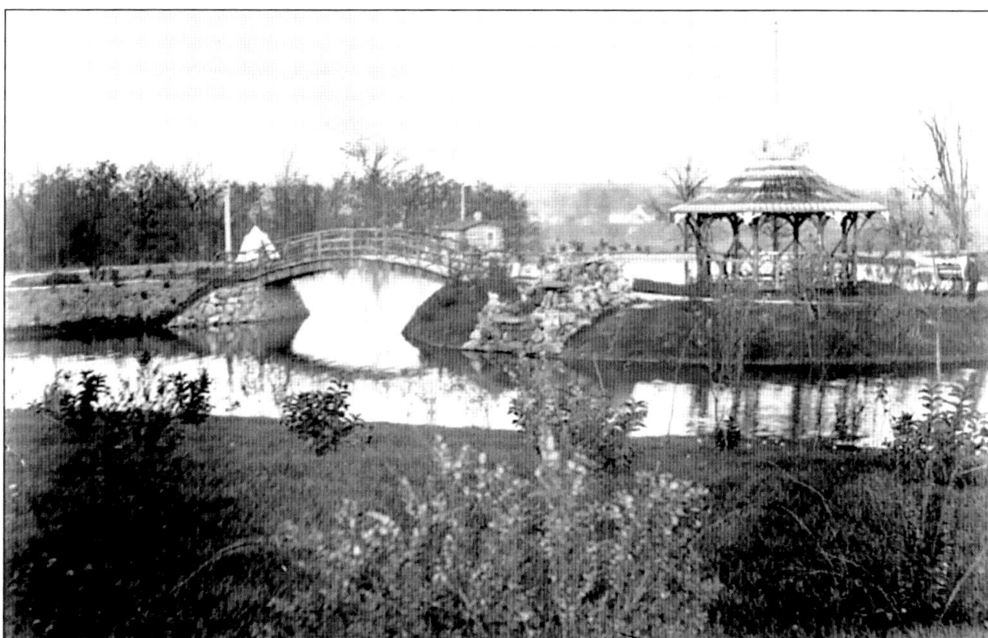

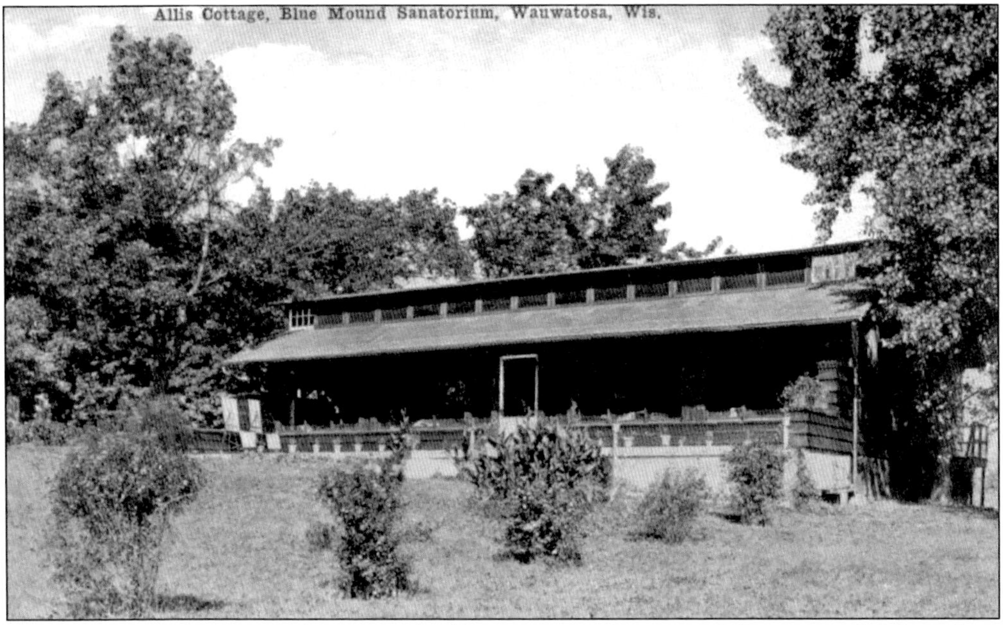

Tuberculosis (TB) was one of the most deadly contagious diseases and the National Tuberculosis Prevention Movement educated the public in the early twentieth century. Milwaukee physicians were alarmed at the increase in cases. In 1907, the Blue Mound Sanatorium, one of the first specialized facilities here, was built in the Town of Wauwatosa—their Allis Cottage is shown. In 1921, the county purchased this sanatorium to treat children, renaming it the Blue Mound Preventorium, an adjunct of Muirdale Sanatorium. (Courtesy of Len Borkowski.)

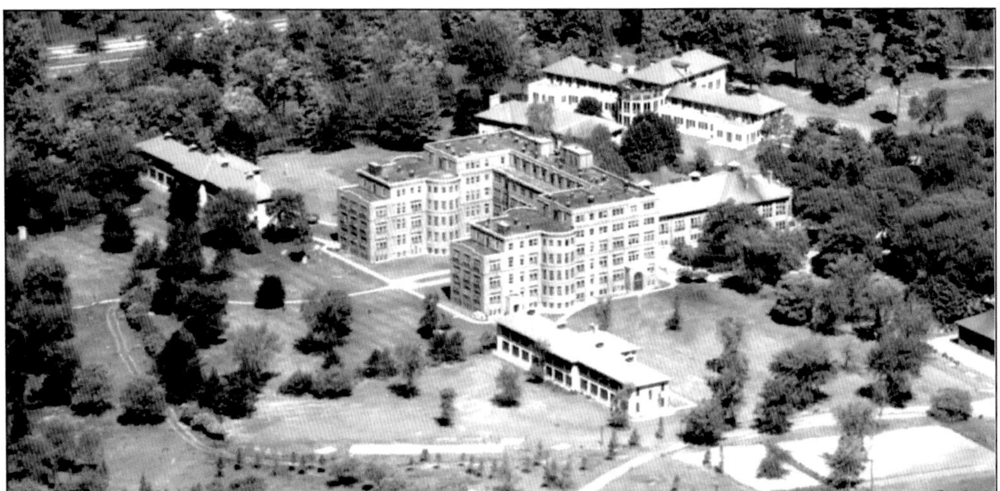

Milwaukee County met TB head-on, obtaining approval for the 1913 construction of the Muirdale Sanatorium on the county grounds on the southeast corner of present Mayfair and Watertown Plank Roads. Named for Wisconsin naturalist John Muir, the facility was unique. It had cottage-like arrangements to keep patients together, and treatment insisting on the therapeutic value of cold, dry air. Medical progress after World War II essentially conquered this dreaded disease, and the complex closed in 1978. (Photo by Greenberger Air Pix, Courtesy of James Cerletty.)

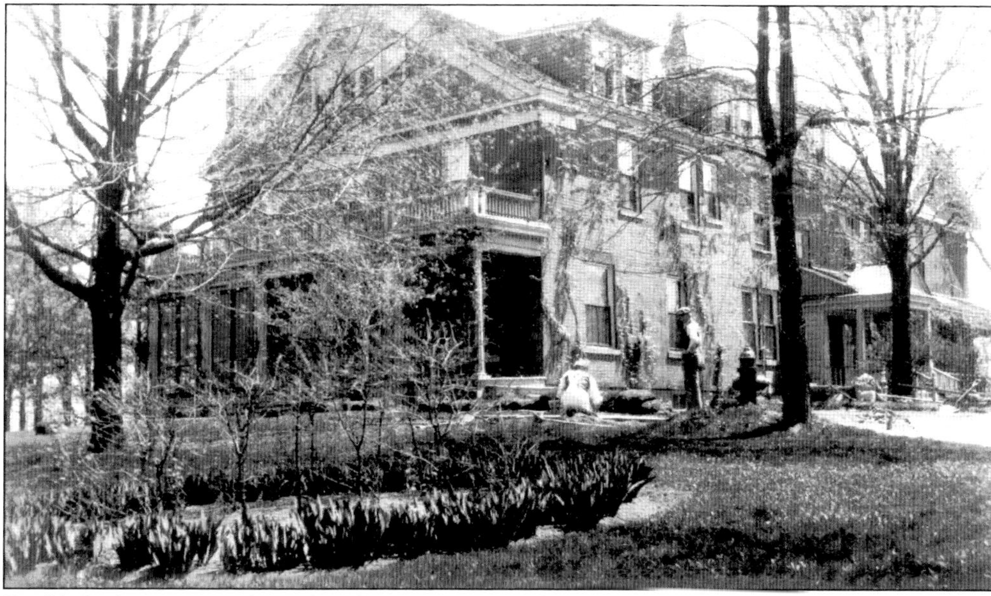

Established in 1884 as the Milwaukee Sanitarium, this psychiatric facility had only five medical directors in its first 73 years. The second, Dr. Richard Dewey, directed the hospital the longest, 24 years, and became closely associated with it. He instituted a cottage system with a homelike atmosphere. One of these cottages is shown in this postcard. This private institution paralleled the county services but attracted clients from a wider geographic area. In 1964, the name changed to Milwaukee Psychiatric Hospital. (WHS Postcard 669.)

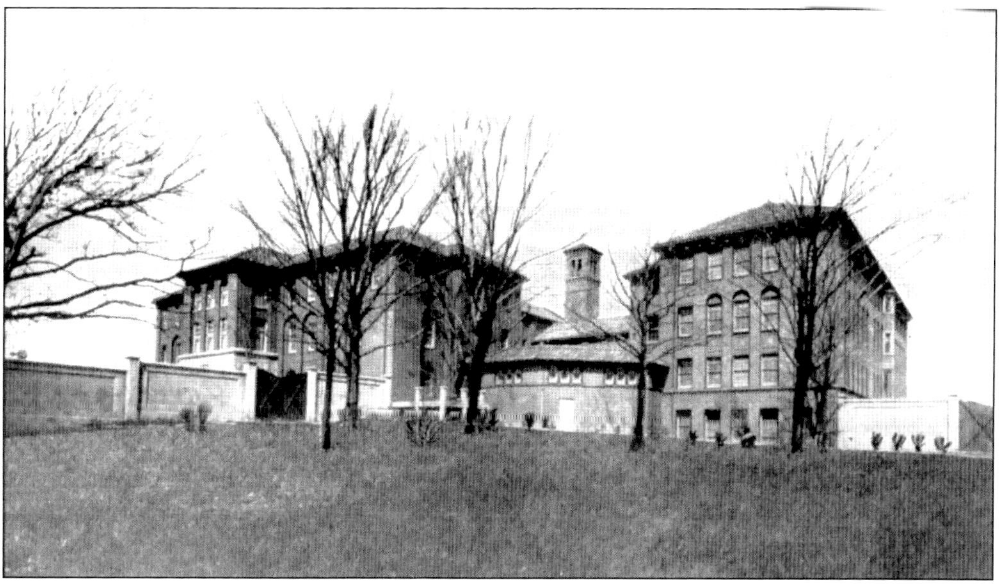

The Sisters of the Good Shepherd opened the House of the Good Shepherd in the late nineteenth century and established a permanent site at 8830 West Blue Mound Road. This Catholic facility served as a home for delinquent girls and women. The postcard view is from approximately 1924. Four-year-old Wisconsin Lutheran College purchased the complex in 1977. The perimeter walls were removed, but the original buildings are now an integral part of the college's expanded campus. (WHS Postcard 656.)

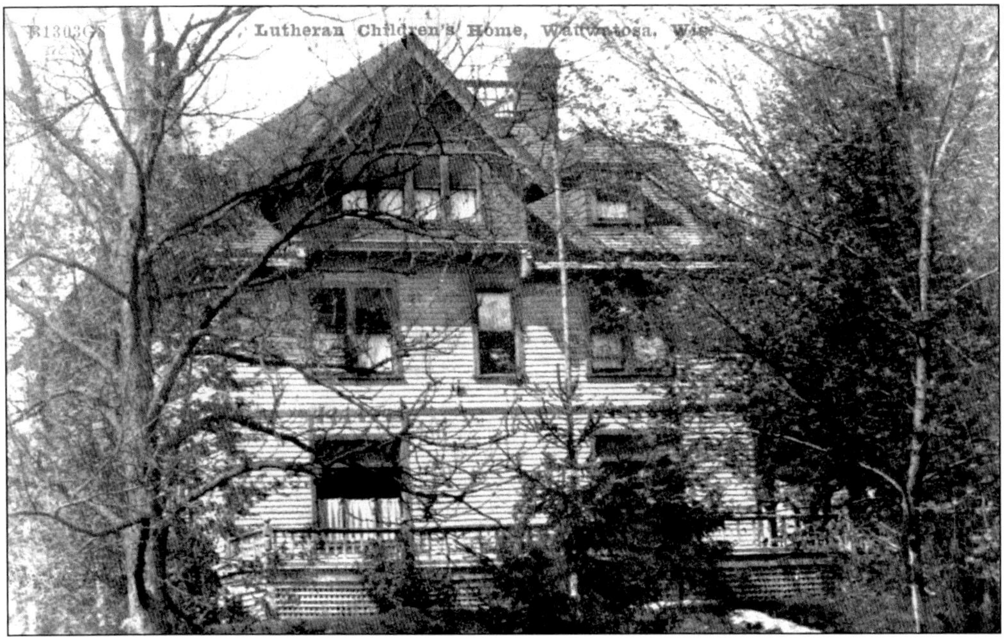

The Lutheran Children's Home (*above*, c. 1910), incorporated in 1896 by the Lutheran Kinderfreund Society, served dependent and neglected children from throughout the State of Wisconsin. Initially on West Milwaukee Avenue, it was located for most of its operation at 8138 Harwood Avenue. It closed in 1966. The Lutheran Altenheim Society of Wisconsin purchased a farmhouse and land on the northeast corner of North and Wauwatosa Avenues in 1906, and established a Home for Aged Lutherans that accommodated 15 people. In 1908, 15 more beds were added, and in response to an urgent need, a building (*below*) was erected three years later with a capacity of 90 residents. The facility continues today as the Lutheran Home, in a new building on the original land. The Wisconsin and Missouri Synods supported both of these endeavors. (Courtesy of Len Borkowski and WHS Postcard 642.)

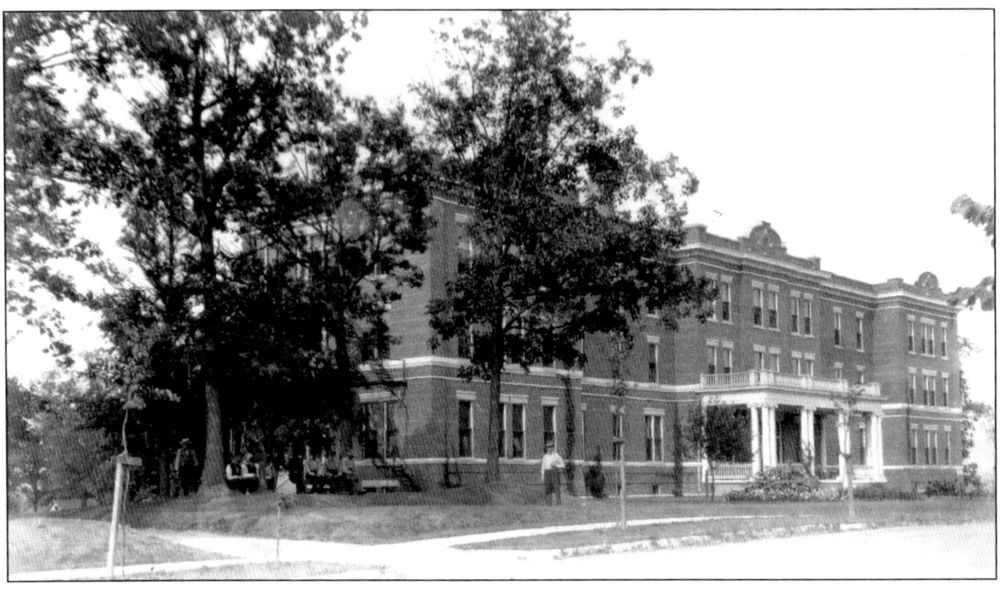

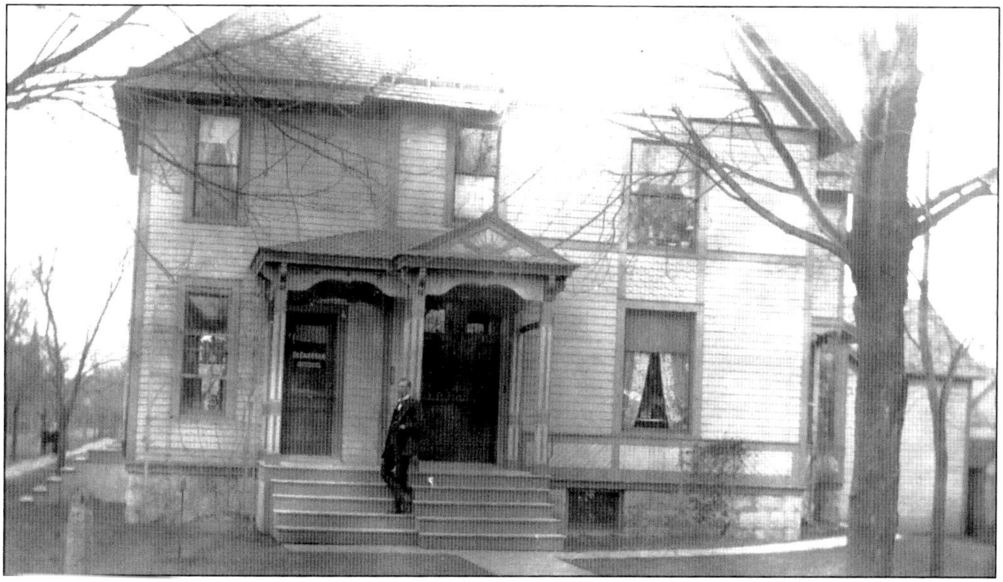

Wisconsin-born Dr. James W. Cairncross graduated in 1875 from Bellevue Medical College in New York, and set up practice in Mukwonago. In 1888, he moved to Wauwatosa. Dr. Cairncross stands on the steps of his home/office on Milwaukee Avenue near the corner of Church Street. The right-hand door is the family entrance, while the left door lettering reads "Dr. Cairncross Office." Dr. Andrew Clark, Wauwatosa's first physician, was succeeded by Dr. Levi C. Halstead (Halsted) in 1848. (WHS Mss. 133.)

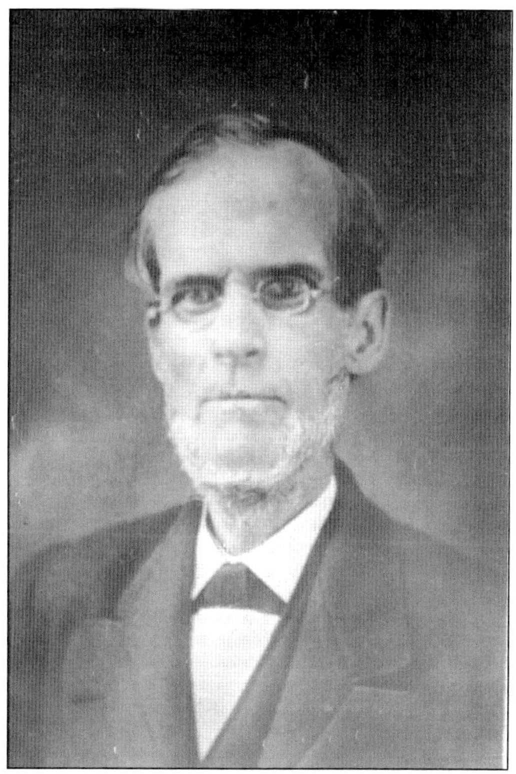

In 1844, Dr. Robert J. Faries became the first resident dentist in Milwaukee. The Faries family enjoyed country living and in 1856 built Wauwatosa's first brick house, an Italianate villa with a three-story tower. It stood on the site of the present Carmelite Sisters Provincial Motherhouse at 1230 Kavanaugh Place. In 1857, Faries left his Milwaukee partner and moved his office to his Wauwatosa home, becoming Wauwatosa's first dentist and practicing here for nearly 20 years. (Courtesy of Milwaukee County Historical Society.)

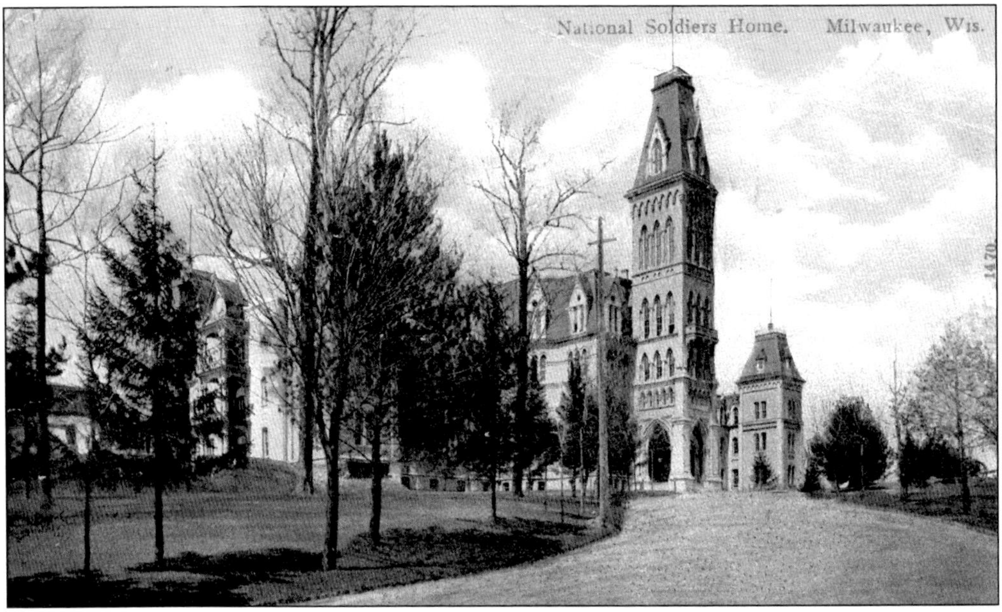

Following the Civil War, the federal government planned National Homes for Disabled Volunteer Soldiers. Milwaukee women recognized the need and in 1865 held a fair, which raised more than $100,000. They then successfully requested that one of the homes be located here. The site chosen lay in the southeast corner of the Town of Wauwatosa. In 1867, the first domiciliary building (*above*) opened, designed by renowned Milwaukee architect E. Townsend Mix. The magnificent tower of his Gothic Revival structure overlooks a cluster of buildings erected through the years, including a theater and the home's own post office, Wood, Wisconsin. This landmark building still has a commanding site at the present Veterans Administration Center and is commonly known as Soldier's Home. A postcard (*below*, c. 1913) depicts a military burial at what is now Wood National Cemetery. (Courtesy of Judith A. Simonsen.)

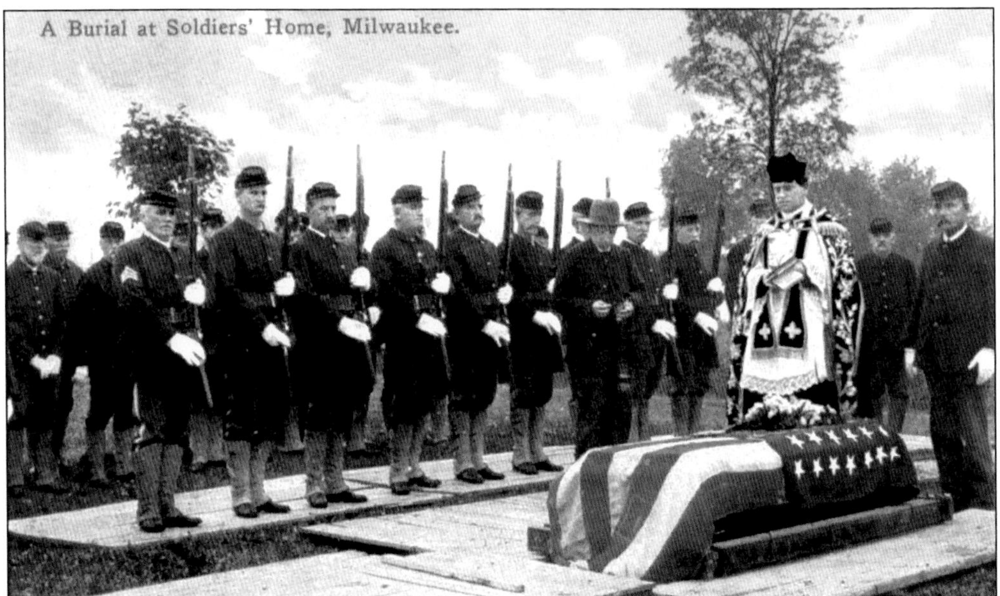

Five

Educating the People

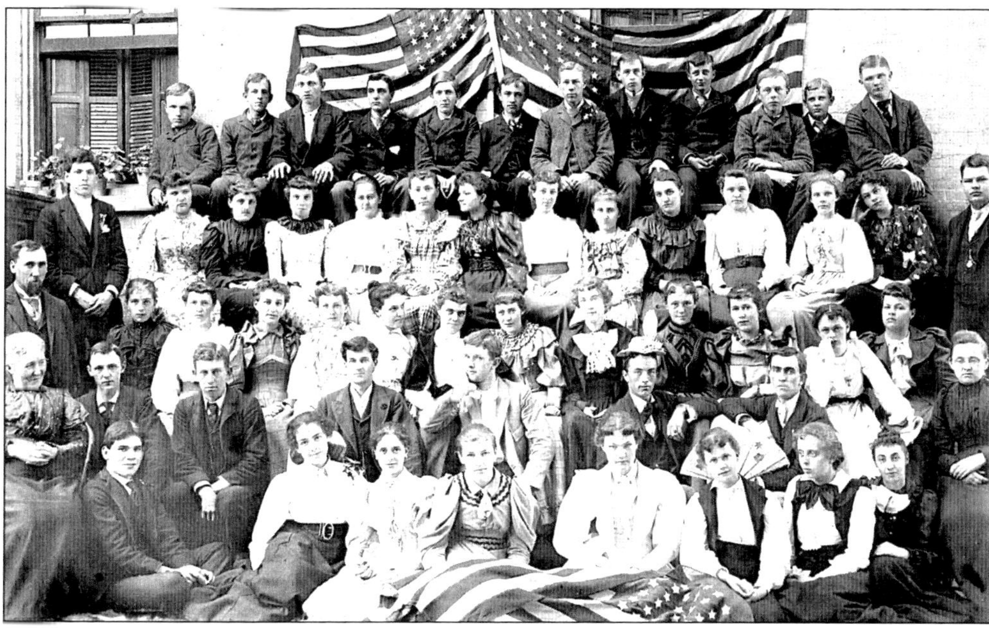

Leading citizens formed private schools to meet the need for education in the early years. The Underwood family established the first known school in Wauwatosa at the Mark Johnson farm. In 1841, town school districts were created and one-room schools followed. Scores of youngsters received their formal education in these multi-grade facilities. Until 1861, the Town of Wauwatosa had its own superintendent, later sharing that person with the Town of Granville and the Town of Milwaukee, outside of the city. A private institution of note was the Wauwatosa Academy founded by A.H. Dengel, a graduate of Amherst College; a catalogue of instructors and students survives from 1856. This Wauwatosa High School class picture of 1890 includes the principal, Professor A.W. Smith, pictured at left in the middle row. He gave impetus to a progressive expansion of the school curriculum, forming the basis of later educational development. Over the years, Wauwatosa has offered students a sound program of education. (WHS Photo 732.)

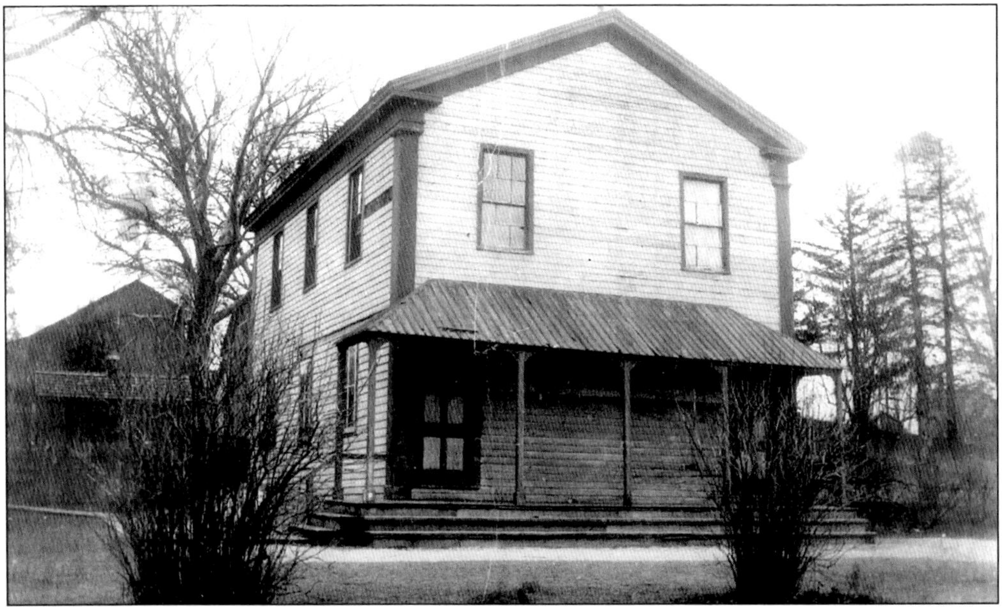

The first public school opened in 1838 in the home of Gideon Wales, just west of the Village. The first teacher, Elizabeth Boyden, had seven pupils. When the school (above) was built in 1841, it had only one floor. It was located just north of Root Common, about where St. Bernard's Church is today. The school was also used on alternating Sundays by Methodists, Baptists, and Congregationalists to hold their church services. The building later served as the Wauwatosa Town Hall. (WHS Photo 158.)

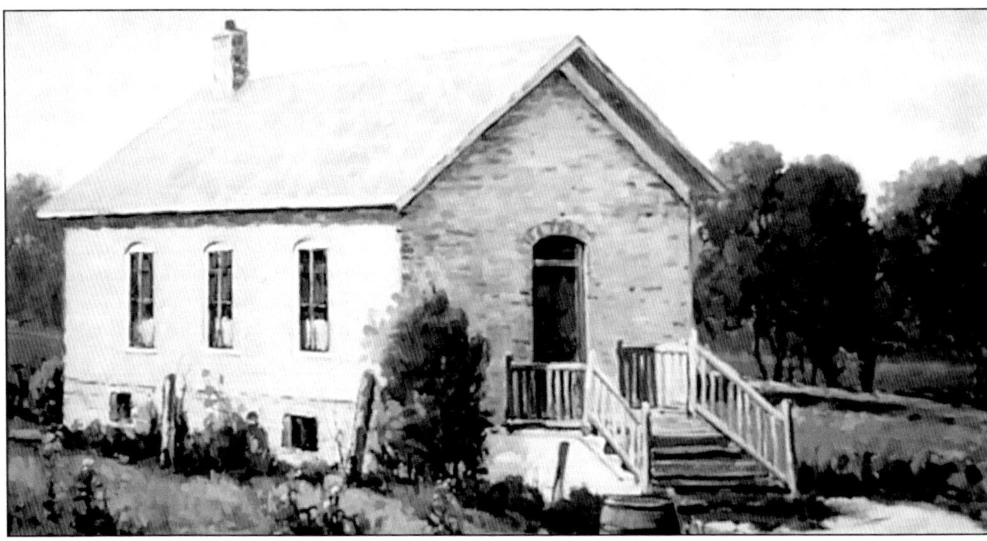

In 1841, a one-room school, 16 feet by 20 feet, was built of logs on the northwest corner of Mayfair Road and North Avenue, referred to as the Gilbert neighborhood. An 1846 frame structure served until this cream brick building was erected in 1877. It was called the Fisher School, after the Yankee farmer William I. Fisher, a founder of the school and nearby landowner. This 1937 painting by H.J. Stoltenburg, noted Milwaukee landscape artist, hangs in the Wauwatosa School District administration building, a gift from the artist. (Courtesy of Wauwatosa School District, WHS Photo 726.)

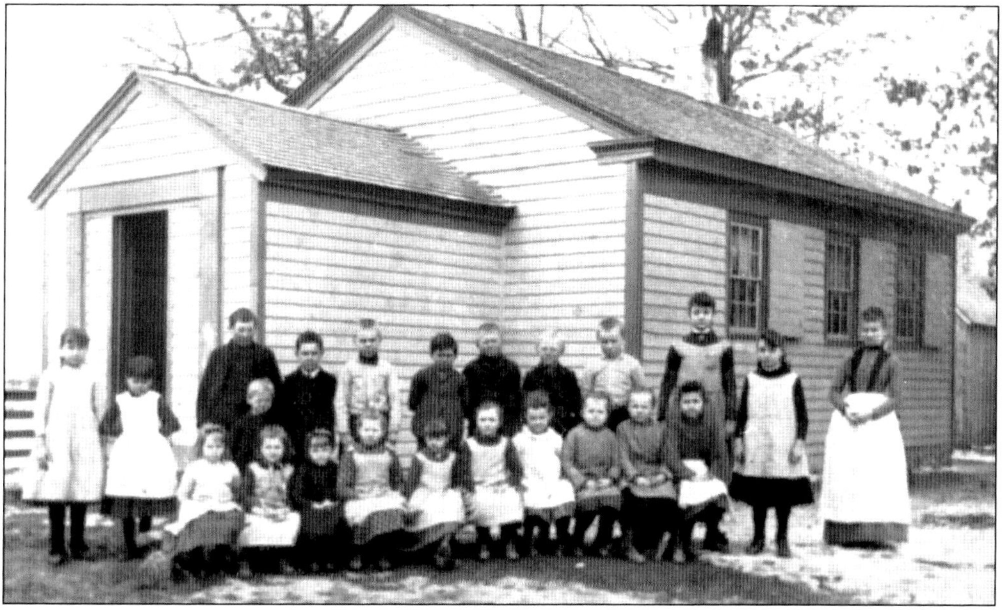

District #10 school, later called Underwood School honoring pioneer William O. Underwood, was first a log building on the southwest corner of Mayfair and Watertown Plank Roads. In the mid-1870s, the school moved to the northwest corner of Potter and Mayfair Roads and was used until 1917. Pupils stand in front of the clapboard-covered structure with their teacher (c. 1890). The present Underwood School is in the same general location, at 111th Street and West Potter Road. (WHS Photo 733.)

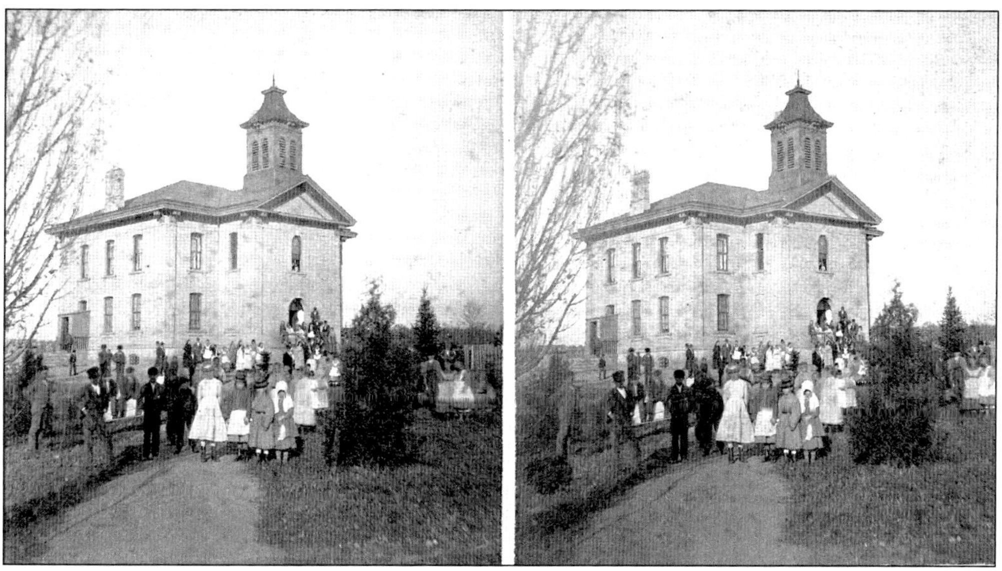

Wauwatosa's first high school was built in 1871on the north side of Milwaukee Avenue, near Wauwatosa Avenue. Its design is similar to Italianate schoolhouses built in Milwaukee at that time. A combined educational facility, it housed the high school on the upper floor and a grade school on the lower. Wauwatosa was very progressive in education when one considers that Milwaukee had built its first public high school only a few years earlier. This rare stereoscopic view was taken between 1871 and 1875. (WHS Photo 734.)

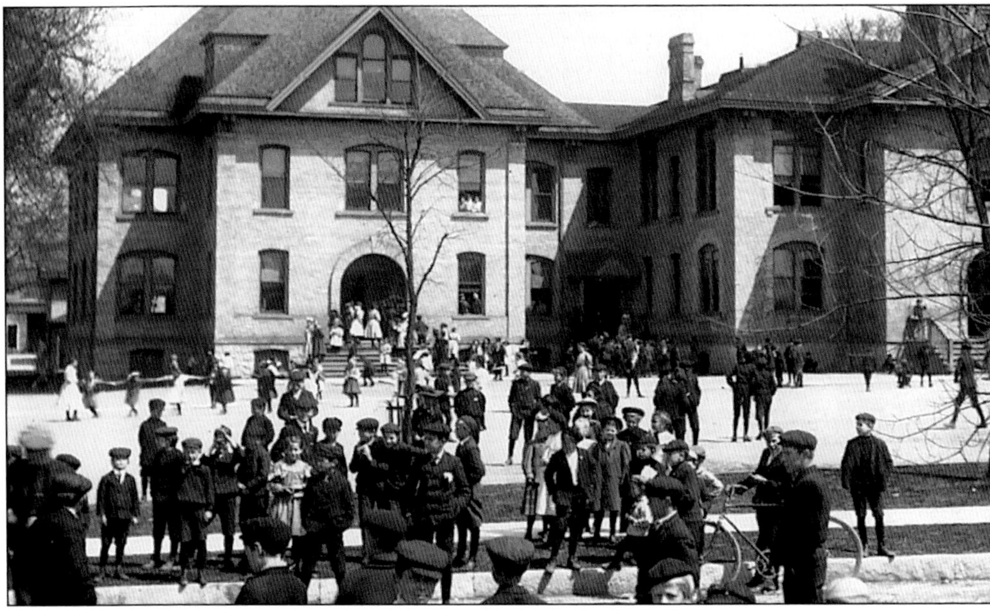

The 1871 high school and grade school soon became cramped. In 1876, a building, in a similar style, was erected next door to the west, with a connecting passage, extending the building to the corner of Wauwatosa Avenue. Children (*above*, c. 1900) enjoy recess. The newer structure housed the high school and the older one the elementary grades, beginning with kindergarten. Note that remodeling at some point changed the windows on either side of the front entrance and on the side of the old school. This complex served student needs until the turn of the century. In 1906, a two-story, red brick high school opened across the street on the northwest corner of Milwaukee and Wauwatosa Avenues, adequate until the 1930s. The site (*above*) remains in educational use and today Wauwatosa East High School stands on its expanded grounds. The 1911 first-grade classroom (*below*) was taught by Miss Chamberlin, standing center in the back row with her serious looking pupils. (WHS Photo 728 and 730.)

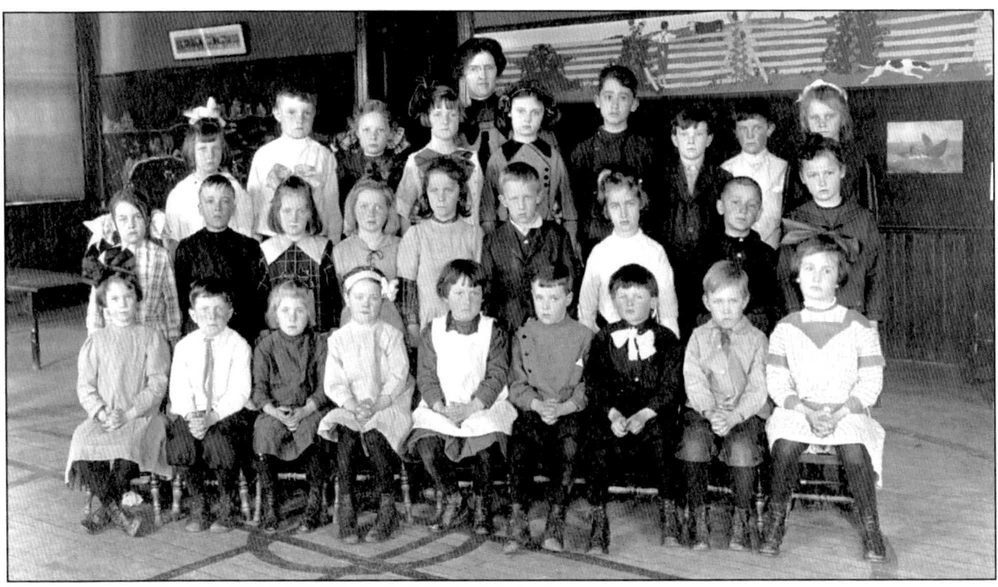

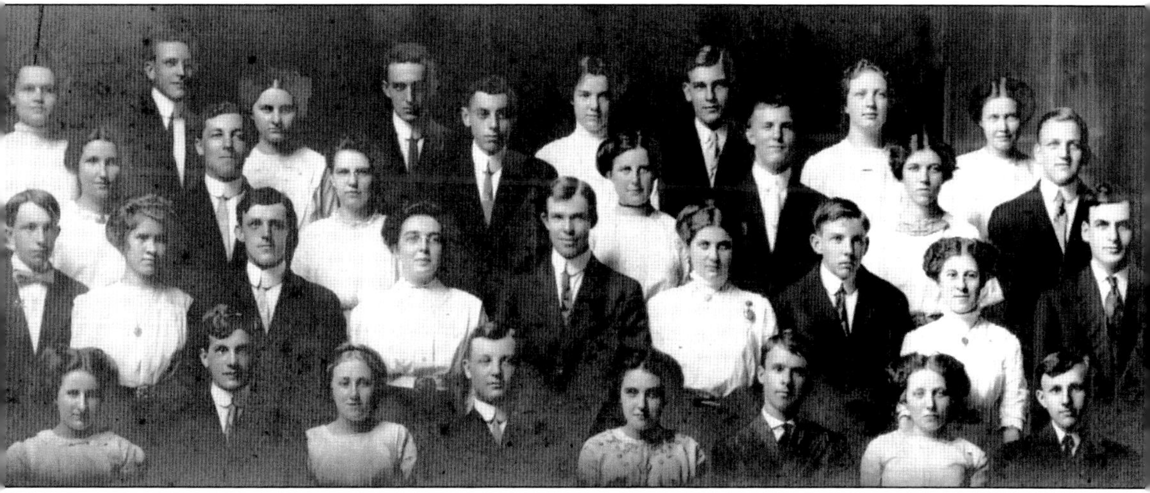

Until well into the twentieth century, most people in this country did not graduate from high school. This photo of the 1911 Wauwatosa High School graduating class (*above*) shows a group of fortunate young men and women prepared to face the rigors of the adult world. Their class motto was "Finish what you begin." Commencement exercises at the First Congregational Church had a 15¢ admission. In the second row, far right, is Howard Wells, the only identified student. Sports were part of education. The Wauwatosa High School football team of 1901 is seen below. The players did not have the protective gear worn today, nor were the teams as large as is common now. From left to right are the following: (front row) Elmer Pilgrim, O. ?; (second row) Alister Currie, Jim Lefeber, Otto Zillmer, John Craft, Percy Meyers, Lester Pavy; (back row) Art ? (sitting), Ed Pares, Everett Hart (kneeling), Don Fisher, Walter Wood. (WHS Mss. 129 and Photo 729.)

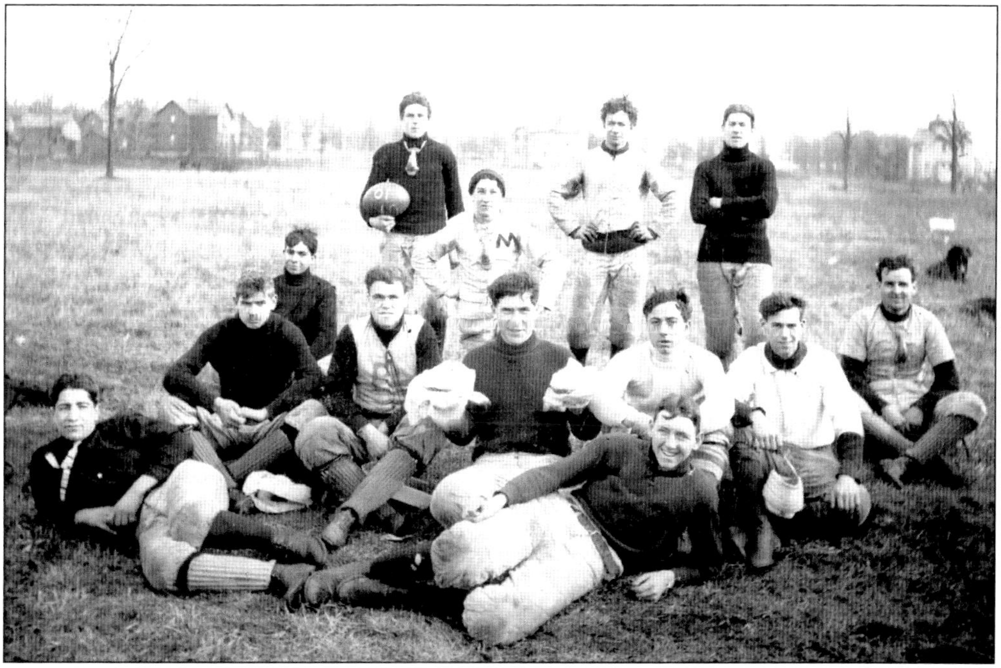

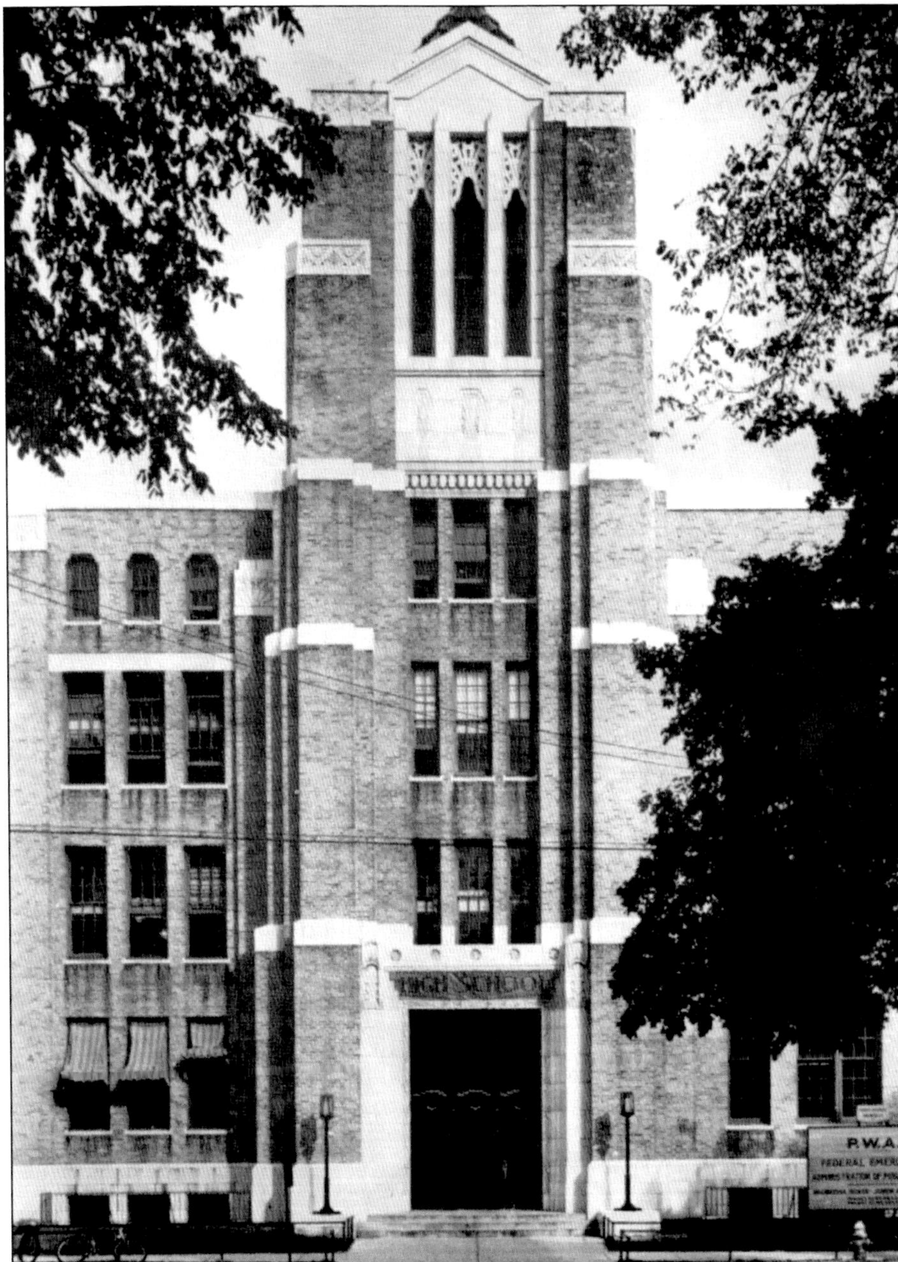

A new Wauwatosa High School was built in 1931 along the east side of Wauwatosa Avenue, north of Milwaukee Avenue. In the Art-Deco style, it had a stunning tower. Extensive additions in the late 1930s, to expand the size and utility of the school, extended the building to and around the corner of Milwaukee Avenue, onto the site of the first high school, and included a tunnel to connect to the old high school across Wauwatosa Avenue. During major remodeling in the 1970s, the tower was removed. This image of the main entrance is from the 1942 *Cardinal Pennant* yearbook. The book contained photos of Wauwatosa graduates who were serving in the military. When the city gained a second high school, Wauwatosa East kept this name for its yearbook and Wauwatosa West took the name *Olympian* for its book. (WHS Yearbook Collection.)

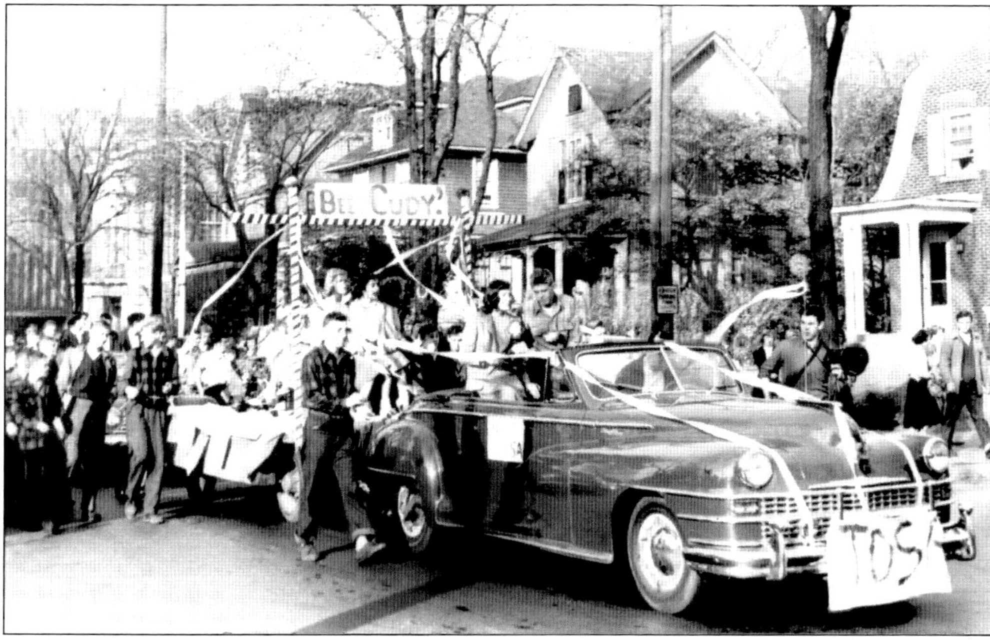

Parades with student-decorated floats have long been part of high school homecoming celebrations. In this picture of Wauwatosa High School's 1948 homecoming, students are showing off their enthusiasm for the upcoming game with Cudahy High School. With the sign "Beet Cudy," the group proceeded south on Wauwatosa Avenue. The high school is in the background at the left. Unfortunately, the Wauwatosa football team lost the game 19-34. (WHS Mss.134.)

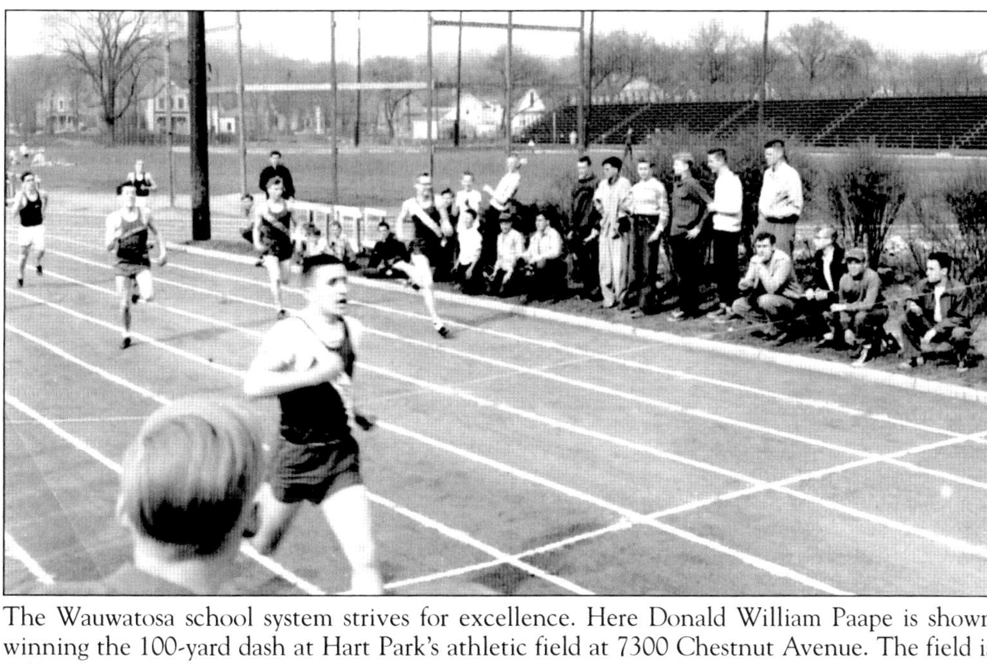

The Wauwatosa school system strives for excellence. Here Donald William Paape is shown winning the 100-yard dash at Hart Park's athletic field at 7300 Chestnut Avenue. The field is still used today for Wauwatosa East's track and football events. An all-round Tosa High School athlete (track, football, and diving) and scholar, Paape was captain of the 1949 football team and went on to study at the University of Wisconsin in Madison. (WHS Mss.134.)

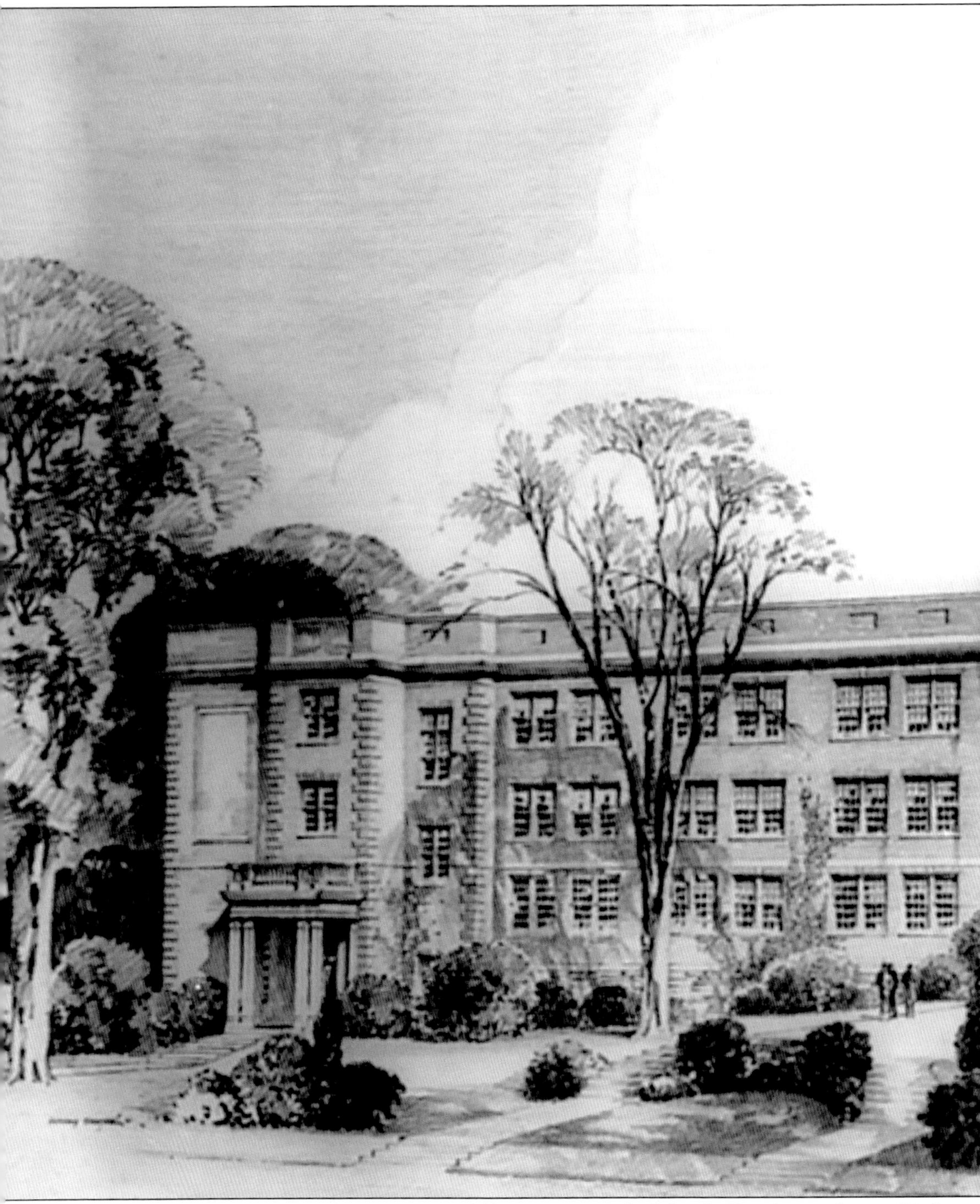

To ease overcrowded conditions at Longfellow Junior High School, Hawthorne Junior High was constructed in 1931 at 7700 Portland Avenue. It opened in 1932 with 225 students, all living south of the railroad tracks in the Village. The impressive red brick Georgian Revival style building, designed by the firm of Herbst & Kuenzli Architects, had a tower that became a landmark in the neighborhood. Students at Longfellow and Hawthorne combined in writing

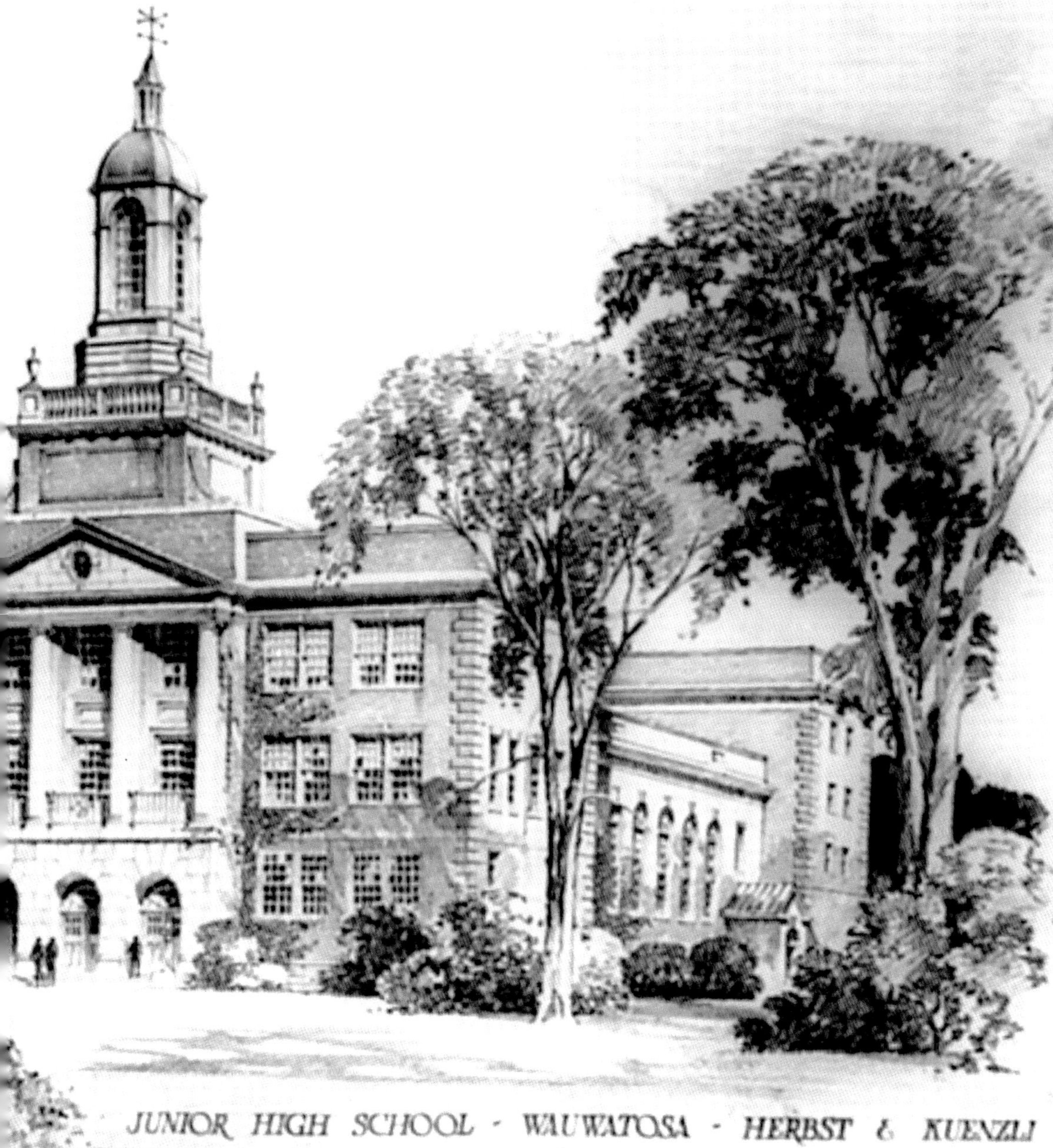

a school paper called the *Junior Journal*, in October 1932, to encourage cooperation between the two schools rather than rivalry. In 1981, the school board voted to close Hawthorne as a school and make the building available for other uses. Today it is a private residential building. (WHS Print Collection.)

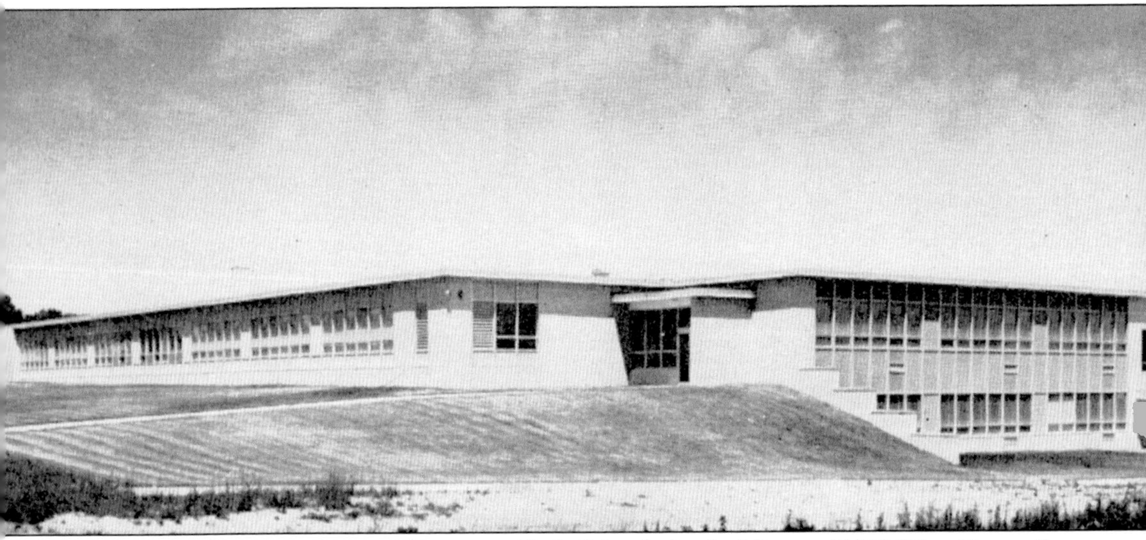

Because of overcrowding at Wauwatosa High School, this building at 11100 West Center Street served as Wauwatosa West High School from its opening in 1961 until 1970. When West opened, Wauwatosa High School became Wauwatosa East High School. A few years later, Longfellow Junior High School needed relief. A new West high school was constructed in 1969 next door to the existing school. A fire (arson) caused almost two million dollars damage and delayed its opening. This 1961 school building became Whitman Junior High. (WHS Mss. 73.)

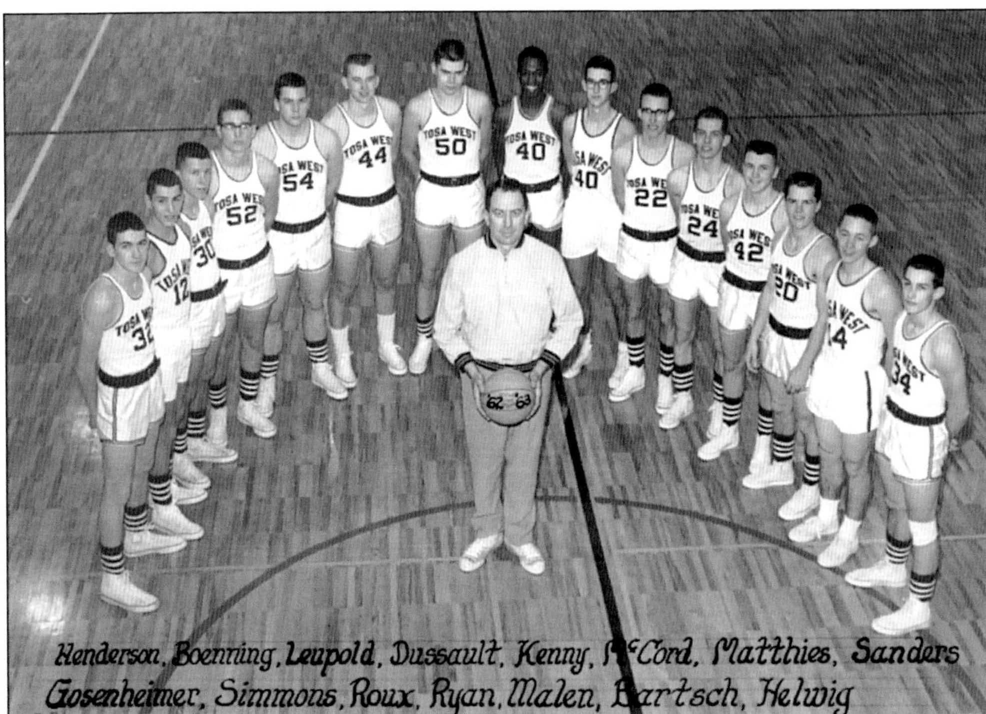

Sports were an important part of school life, and in the 1962–1963 school year there were many choices open to both boys and girls. This is the Wauwatosa West High School boys' basketball team coached by Warren Cartier, center of photo. (Courtesy of Warren Cartier.)

During the 1920s, the city population tripled. Many residents now lived north of North Avenue and east of Wauwatosa Avenue. Ground was broken for Roosevelt School in 1929. Construction cost $136,813 and the school opened in March 1930. Initially it had eight classrooms on the first and second floors; later five more classrooms were added on the third floor. As enrollment continued to rise, additions were constructed in the 1940s and 1950s; in 1993 four new classrooms and a gymnasium were added. These pictures from 1935 capture a kindergarten study of the native-American peoples who first lived in the area that became Wauwatosa. The costumes and papooses were made of burlap, probably sewn by the parents. Marilyn Miller is second from left in the top two pictures. The children learned about the music and dance, represented in the lower picture. (Courtesy of Marilyn Miller Farmer.)

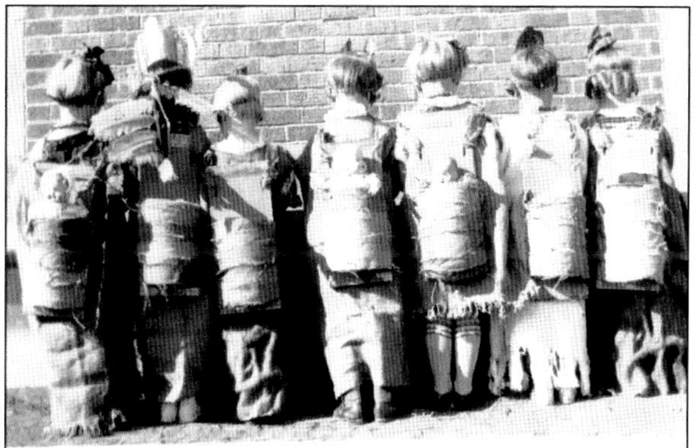

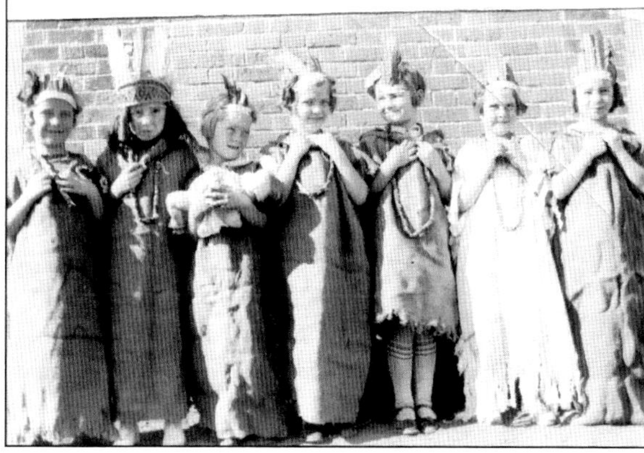

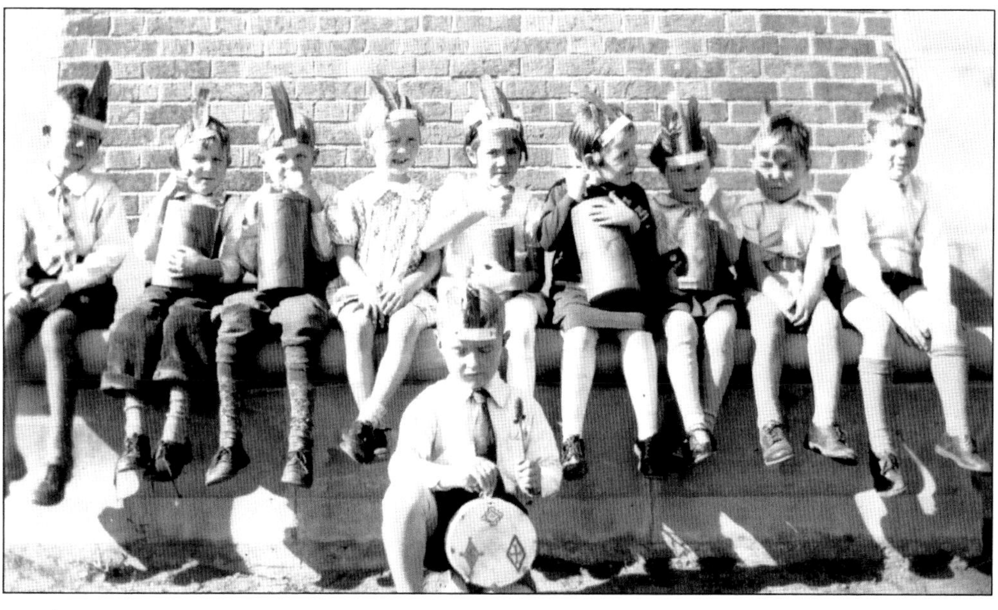

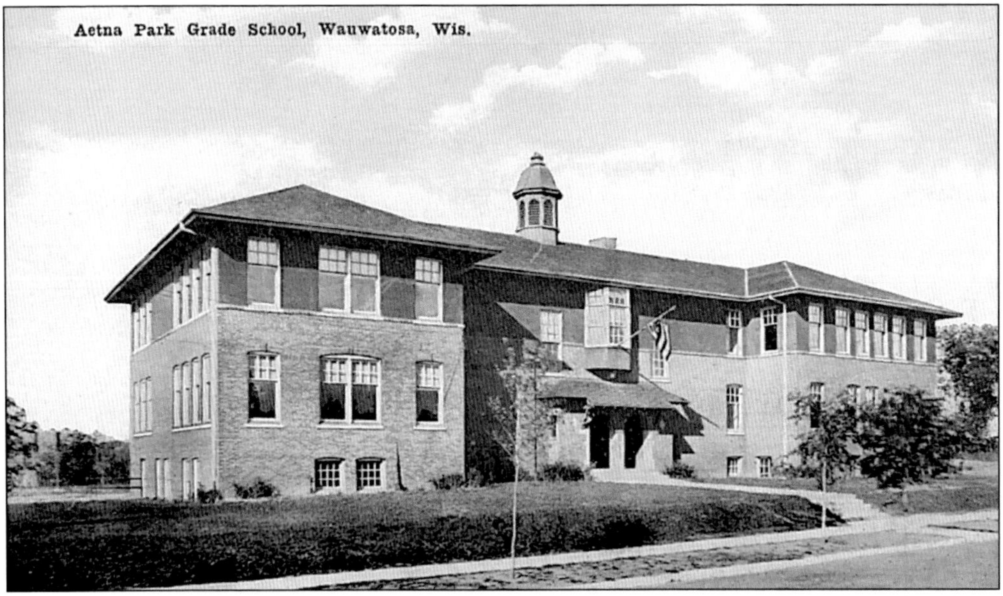

Aetna Park School at Aetna Court and Seventieth Street, completed in 1924, served students south of the Village railroad tracks. It was renamed Jefferson School in the early 1930s. In 1957, a replacement for Jefferson School was built, and children helped move supplies to the new school in May 1959. On June 8, two boys broke into the old school, setting mops aflame to light their way. A four-alarm fire resulted that destroyed the building. (WHS Postcard 800.)

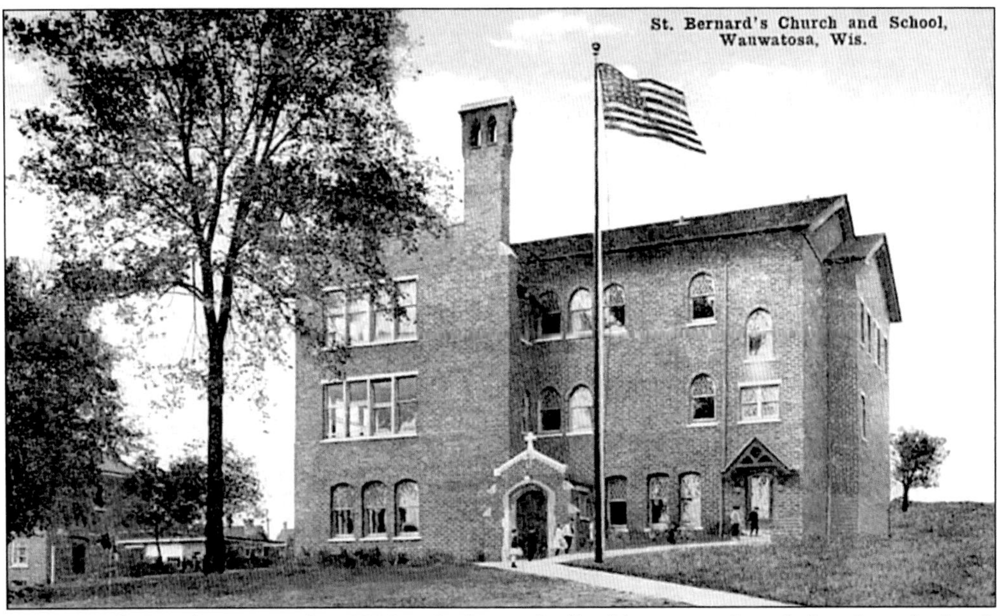

St. Bernard's Parish organized in 1911 with the goal of building a combined church and school. Land purchases in 1911 and 1915 gave them the site, still in use today. The school opened in 1919 with two rooms for four classes taught by Dominican sisters who resided at the St. Thomas Aquinas Convent and made the daily trip to teach by streetcar. A convent was completed at St. Bernard's in 1922. By 1935, there were five parochial schools in Wauwatosa—three Lutheran and two Catholic. (WHS Postcard 672.)

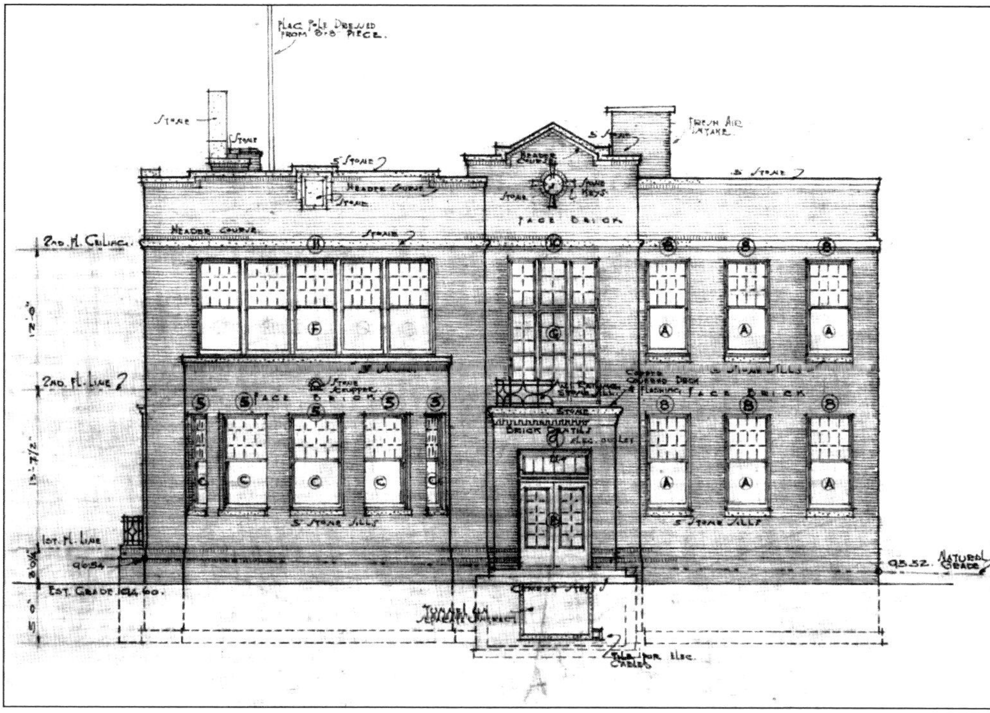

The presence of children in the Milwaukee County Almshouse in the 1850s presented a difficult problem. To effect a degree of separation from adult residents and provide an education for the youngsters, a school was erected in 1858. Ultimately, children's facilities were built, and the Plank Road School opened in 1925. Milwaukee architect Robert A. Messmer designed the school in the Colonial Revival style. It was razed in 2001. (WHS Blueprint Collection.)

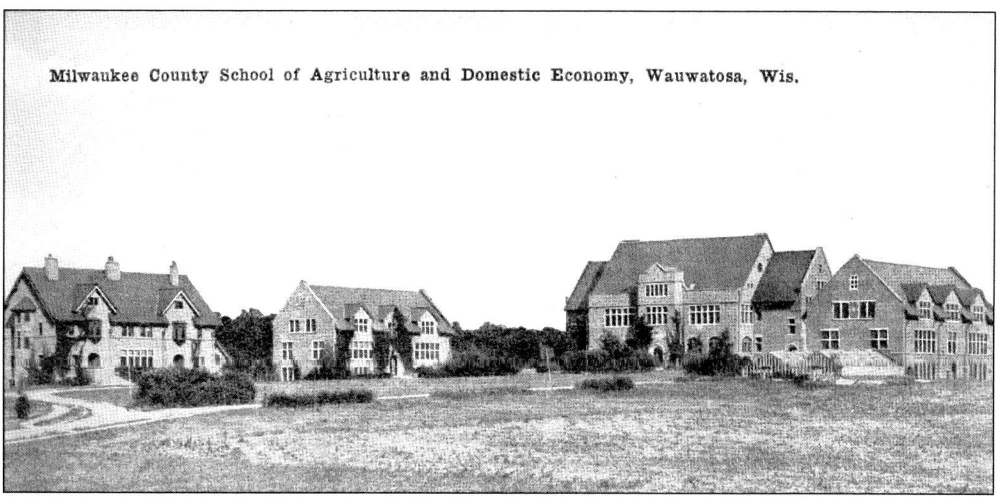

The School of Agriculture and Domestic Economy for high-school age boys and girls opened on the Milwaukee County Institution Grounds in October 1912. The school provided training in farming and home economics. The students produced prize-winning exhibits at the Wisconsin State Fair. Eminent Milwaukee architect Alexander C. Eschweiler designed the five Neo-Gothic Revival buildings. Despite its success, the school was judged too costly because of declining enrollment and was closed in 1928. Four of the buildings remain today. (WHS Postcard 684.)

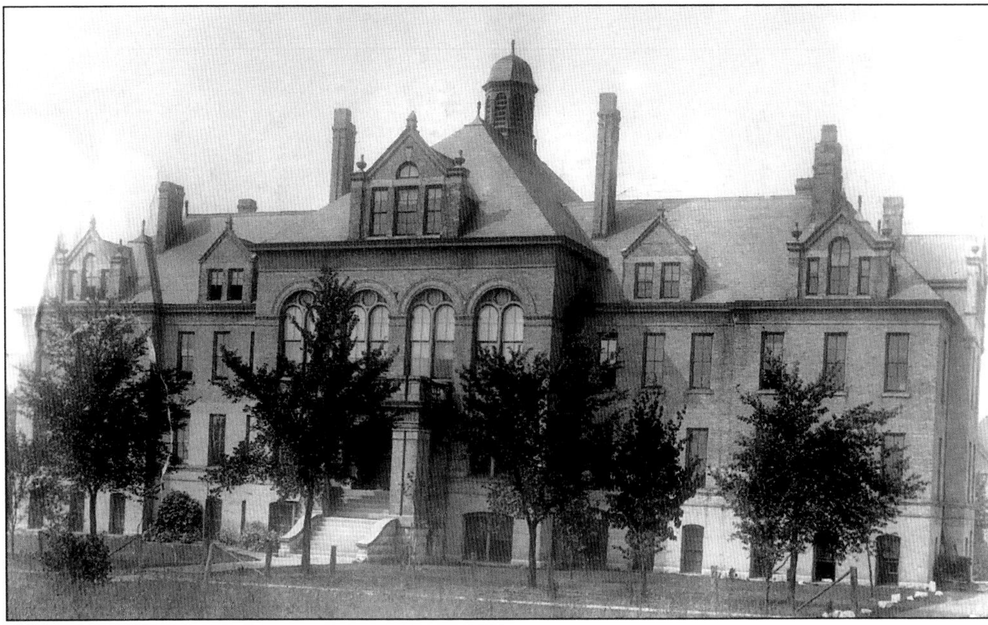

The Wisconsin Synod of the Evangelical Lutheran Church dedicated its new Theological Seminary on September 17, 1893. It stood on the southwest corner of North Sixtieth and West Lloyd Streets, previously part of the Pabst farm. Frederick Pabst, head of the Pabst Brewery, donated the land for educational purposes. The building was a combined classroom-dormitory, and, in addition to it, three homes were erected for faculty. Total construction costs were $38,600. Classes began the day after the dedication. (WHS Photo 235.)

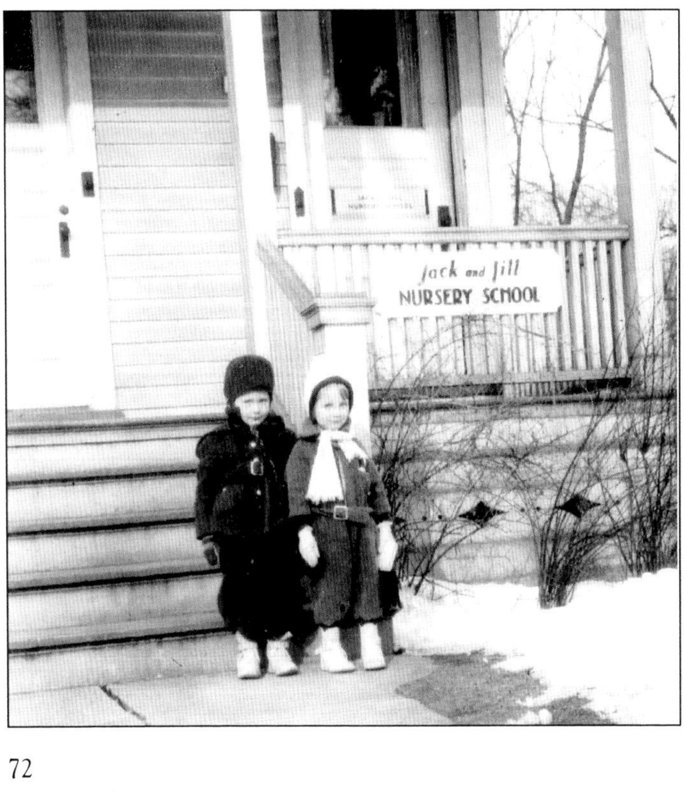

In the early 1930s Alice B. and Helen M. Smith set up a nursery school at 1755 North Seventy-fifth Street and named it the Jack and Jill Nursery School. The two little girls are Peggy Winding Haesler, left, and Barbara Davidson Baumann, right. The operation apparently had a short existence, as there were no listings in the Wauwatosa City Directory after 1941. The house was razed for the Wauwatosa East High School athletic field. (Courtesy Barbara Davidson Baumann.)

Six

Our Faith Grows Deep

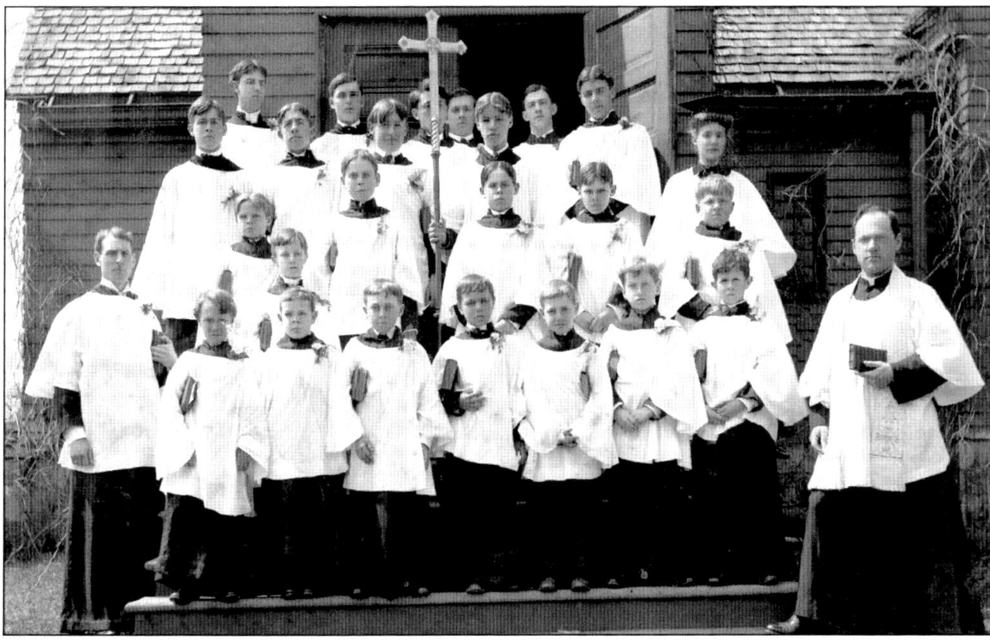

Presbyterians, Congregationalists, Episcopalians, Baptists, Methodists, Catholics, and Lutherans established themselves in the Town of Wauwatosa between 1837 and 1882. Initially, itinerant preachers led meetings of the faithful. A Presbyterian minister preached the first sermon here in 1838 in Jonathan Warren's house. Folks gathered in cabins, farmhouses, taverns, and schoolhouses to worship. The first Sunday schools in 1840 included those organized by the Methodists, Baptists, and Congregationalists. Gradually church buildings were erected. The Baptists built in 1852 and the Congregationalists in 1853—both rang new church bells for the first time in 1855. The community's faith played an important role in the fabric of Wauwatosa life. By the 1990s, Wauwatosa had more than 40 churches. Along with sermons, music played a significant role in most churches. The 1905–1906 boys' choir from Trinity Episcopal Church stands with Edward Bair front row, left, director; Miss Franklin (possibly the organist) third row, right; and the Reverend Mr. James Kieb front row, right. (WHS Photo 735.)

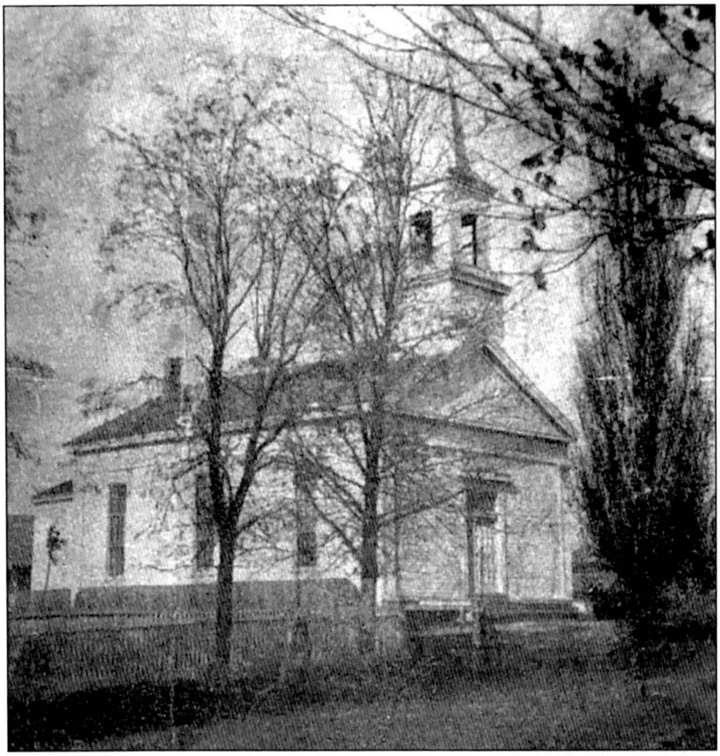

Eleven people gathered in the log dwelling of Richard Gilbert Sr. to organize the First Congregational Church of Wauwatosa in 1842. The congregation purchased land in 1853 on Church Street, from Charles Hart for $50 and built this meeting house for $3,347.80. A parsonage was erected across the street in 1884. Remodeling of the church in 1888 included adding a basement. The last services were held in this structure in July 1919. (Courtesy of Milwaukee County Historical Society.)

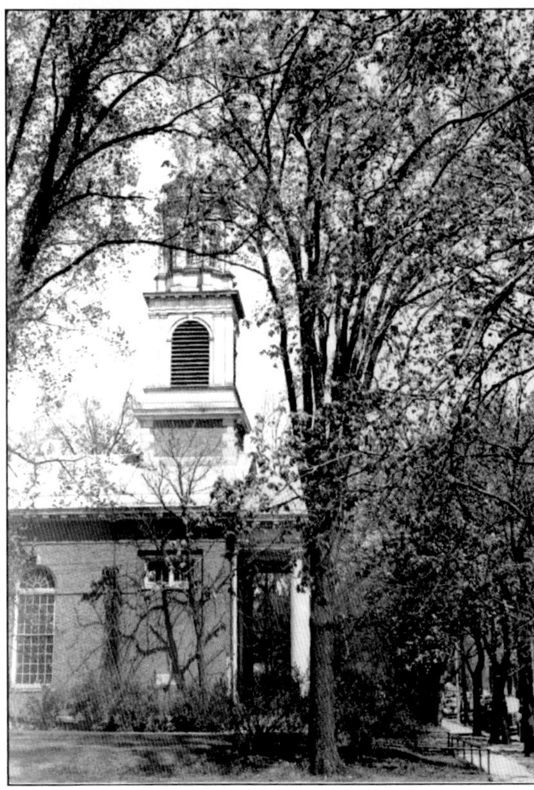

Between 1919 and 1921, a new Congregational meeting house was constructed of red brick. It incorporated the old building, which was turned 90 degrees and moved to the rear of the new structure for use as a social and multi-purpose hall. The new entry has a massive portico and a 124-foot Christopher Wren spire, a replica of one in Williamstown, Massachusetts. The steeple contains four bells, including the original from 1855. Parishioners have gathered on this spot for over 150 years. (WHS Photo 589.)

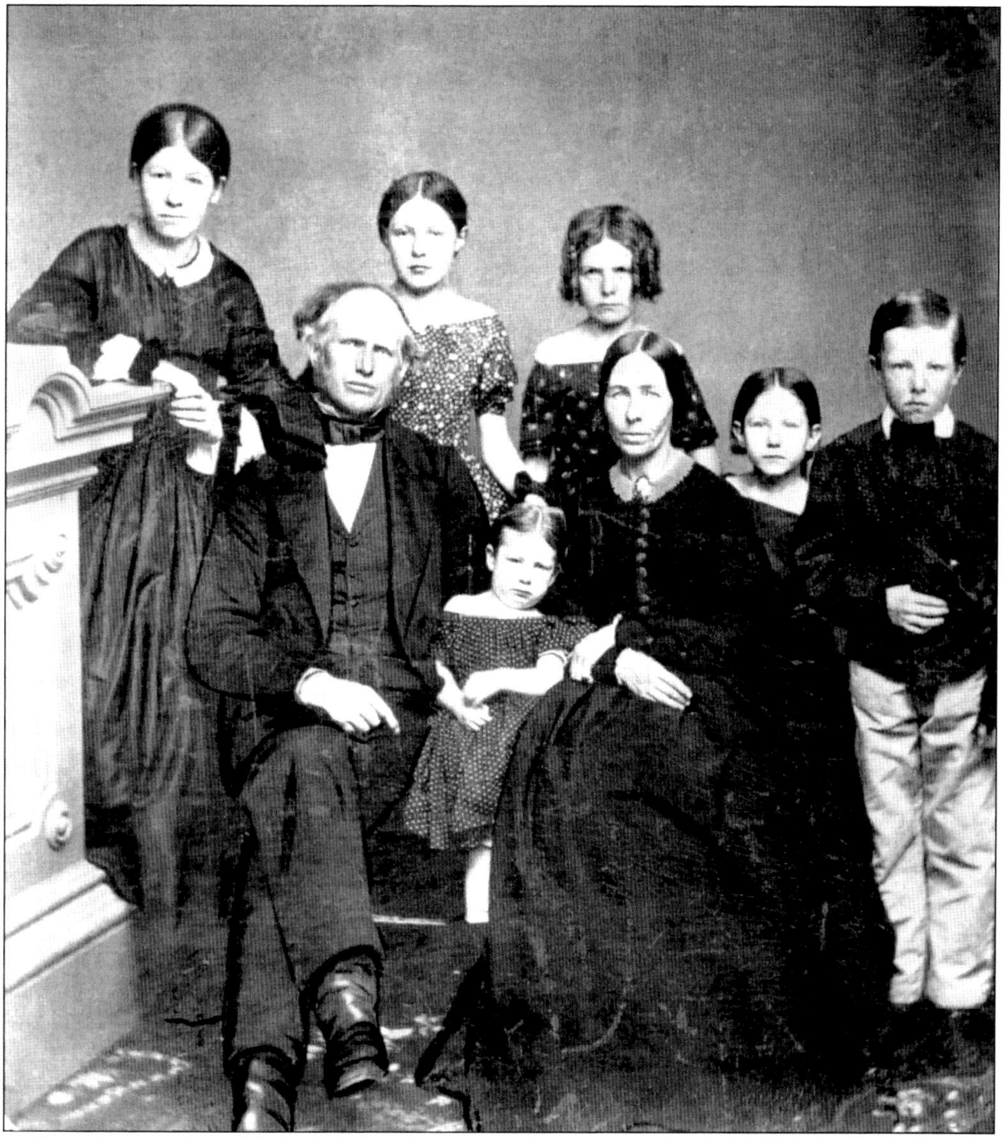

Luther Clapp graduated from Williams College in 1841 and from Andover Theological Seminary in 1845. He came from Massachusetts to be ordained a minister in Wauwatosa that year. At 25 years of age he had accepted a call to serve the First Congregational Church three years after its organization—three pastors had preceded him. The Reverend Mr. Clapp ministered to his flock for nearly 30 years, overseeing the construction of the first meeting house in 1853. Called "Father Clapp," he was highly regarded by his parishioners. He established the first select school, comparable to a high school, in his home. Luther and his wife, Harriet, had six children, seen in this 1862 family grouping. From left to right: (front row) Reverend Mr. Clapp, Grace, Mrs. Harriet P. Clapp, and Wardlaw; (back row) Harriet, Emma, Mary, and Sarah. Note the clothing and hairstyles of Mrs. Clapp and her daughters. (WHS Photo 736.)

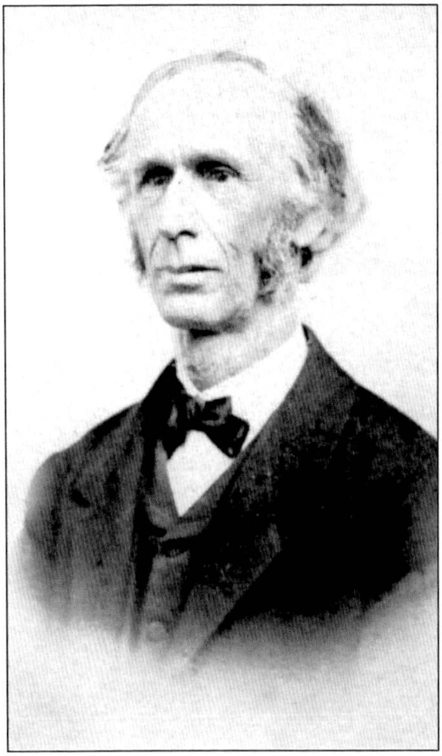

The Baptist church organized in 1845. Elder W.R. Manning served as pastor until the 1849 ordination of Elder Enoch D. Underwood (left), who ministered to the congregation for 38 years. A Greek Revival church with a bell tower was built in 1852 on the southwest corner of North and Wauwatosa Avenues, at a cost of $2,800. Underwood and his congregation were abolitionists and active in the Underground Railroad, which assisted slaves to reach freedom in Canada. (WHS Mss. 112.)

The First Baptist Church moved to a new Victorian Gothic building (below), dated 1887, on the corner of Seventy-fifth Street and Hillcrest Drive. The Reverend Mr. E.O. Smith stands at right. A rededication service in 1907 changed the name to Enoch D. Underwood Memorial Baptist Church. In 1954 the congregation dedicated a new building on Hillcrest at Wauwatosa Avenue. The Latvian Evangelical Lutheran Holy Trinity Church of Milwaukee purchased the old church and held their first service there in February 1961. (WHS Photo 736.)

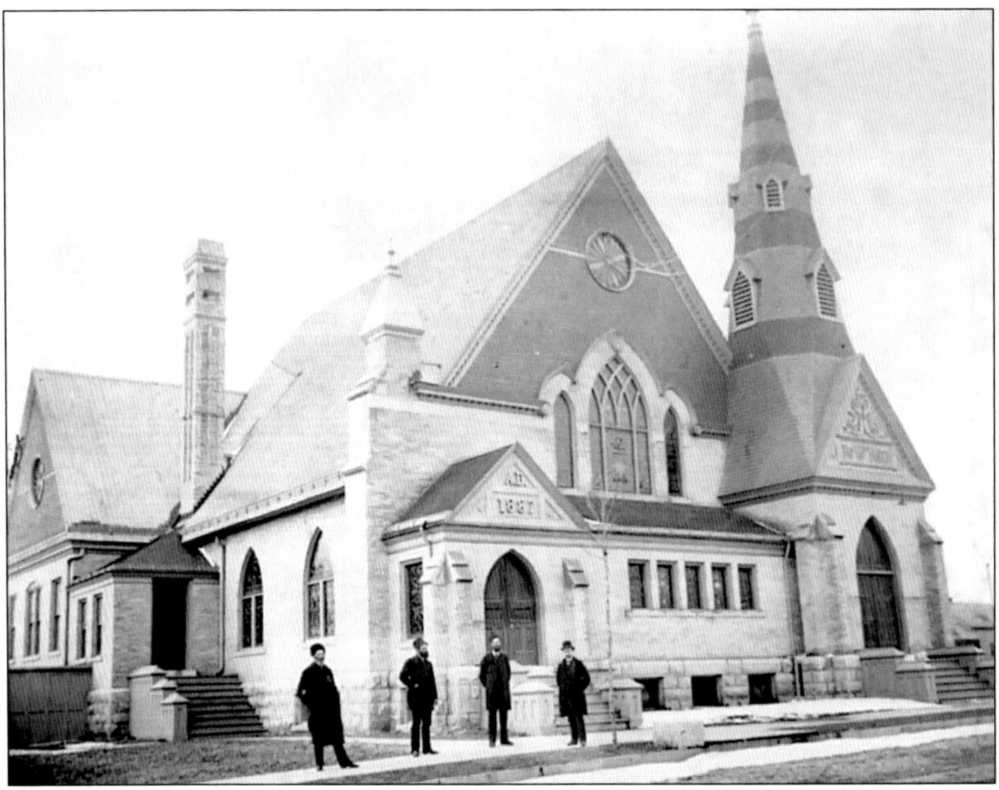

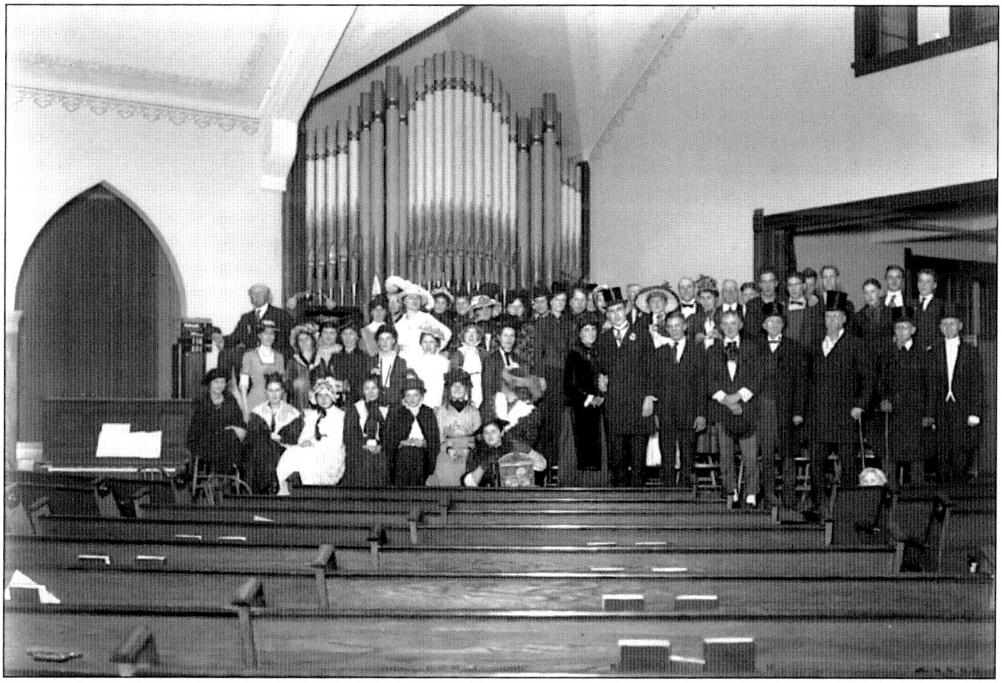

At the 100th anniversary of the Baptist church, members dressed in period costumes and re-enacted services of an earlier era. The ornate stenciling on the walls and ceiling reflects the Victorian design of the 1887 structure. The pipe organ was purchased in 1907 from a $2,500 gift made to the church by Frederick D. Underwood, at which time he requested the church name be changed to honor his father, Enoch. (WHS Photo LGP 906.)

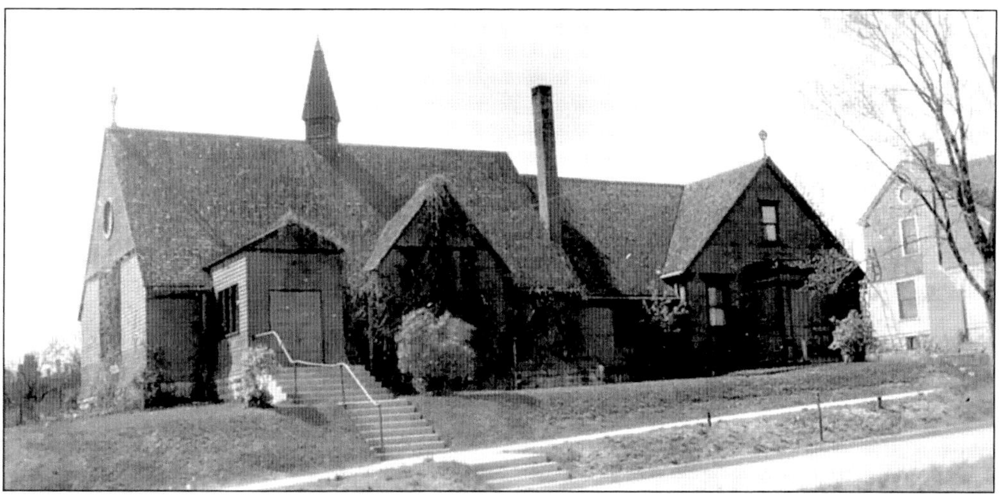

Bishop Jackson Kemper recorded in his diary that the first Episcopal church services in Wauwatosa were held March 11, 1844. Meetings followed in private homes until the St. John's Mission was formed and the group purchased the school building (see top photo page 60) for worship. In 1889, a lot on the northwest corner of Church Street and Milwaukee Avenue was purchased for $348 from J.M. Warren, and this house of worship was built. Formal organization followed, along with the name Trinity Church. (WHS Postcard 666)

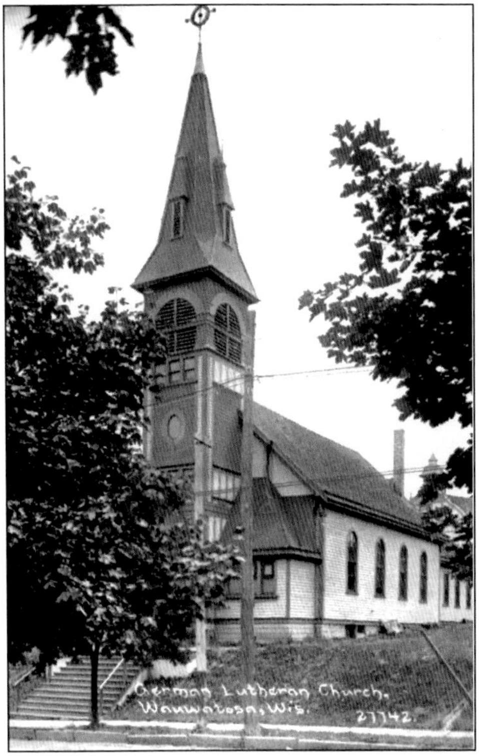

A Milwaukee Lutheran theology student, William Rader, preached the first sermon to the 24 organizing families of St. John's Evangelical Lutheran Church on January 22, 1882. This congregation, of German heritage, purchased land at the southwest corner of Harwood and Dewey Avenues and built their church that year. Following his ordination, Rader returned to serve as the first pastor for 22 years. Services were held in the German language. In 1888, the Lutherans erected the first parochial school in the city. (Courtesy of Len Borkowski.)

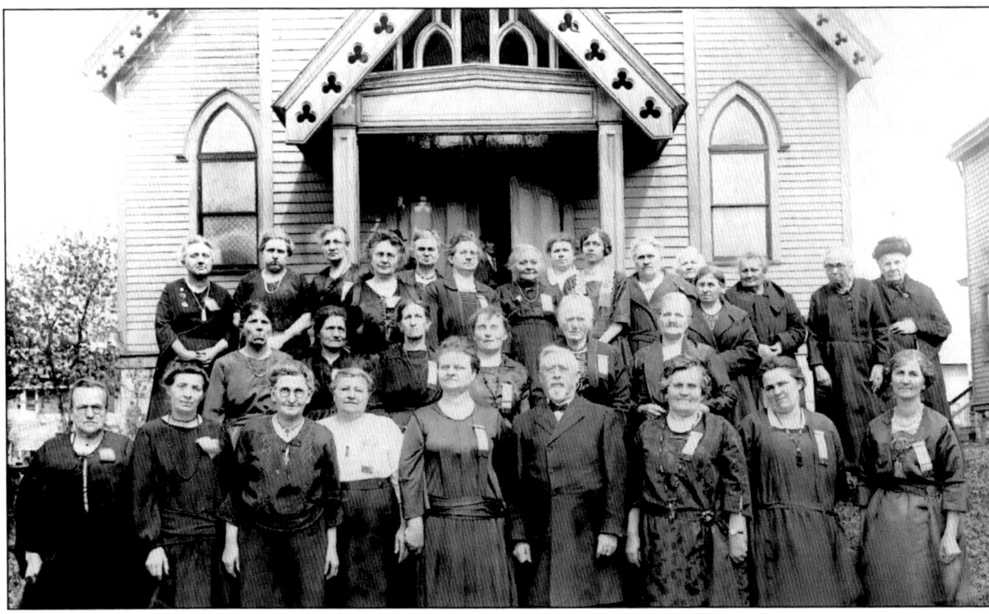

This undocumented image from the early twentieth century captures a group of people in front of the small frame Gothic church at 1510 North Seventieth Street. The date of construction is unknown. In 1903, St. Paul's Evangelical Church, also known as the German Evangelical Church, was organized at this site. It moved in the 1950s, and the Apostolic Christian Church occupied the building until the 1970s, when the present church congregation of Holy Angels Old Catholic Cathedral chose the building for their worship center. (WHS Photo 756.)

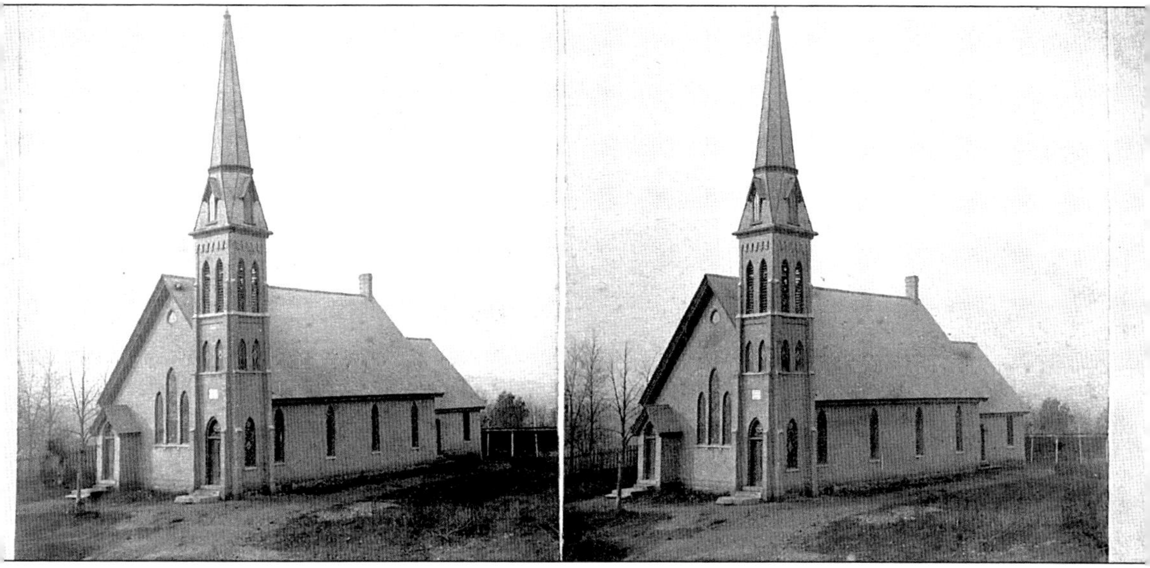

A rare stereoscopic image (*above*) shows the Methodist Church erected in 1870 on Wauwatosa Avenue just north of the Village. The first Methodist Episcopal Church incorporated on May 22, 1848. In 1869, 42 members purchased this site for $200, and then proceeded to mortgage their own properties to finance the church construction, raising a total of $5,482. At the dedication in the spring of 1870, the building was debt free. On Sunday, May 25, 1919, crowds gathered to witness the spectacular fire that destroyed the Methodist Church (*below*). The cause was determined to be a defective flue. Wauwatosa firefighters were joined by the Milwaukee County Institutions fire department, but their efforts could not save the 1870 structure—all that remained were the tower and a side wall. The congregation rebuilt. In 1969, the Methodist Church merged with the Evangelical United Brethren Church to form Wauwatosa Avenue United Methodist Church. (WHS Photo 600 and 592.)

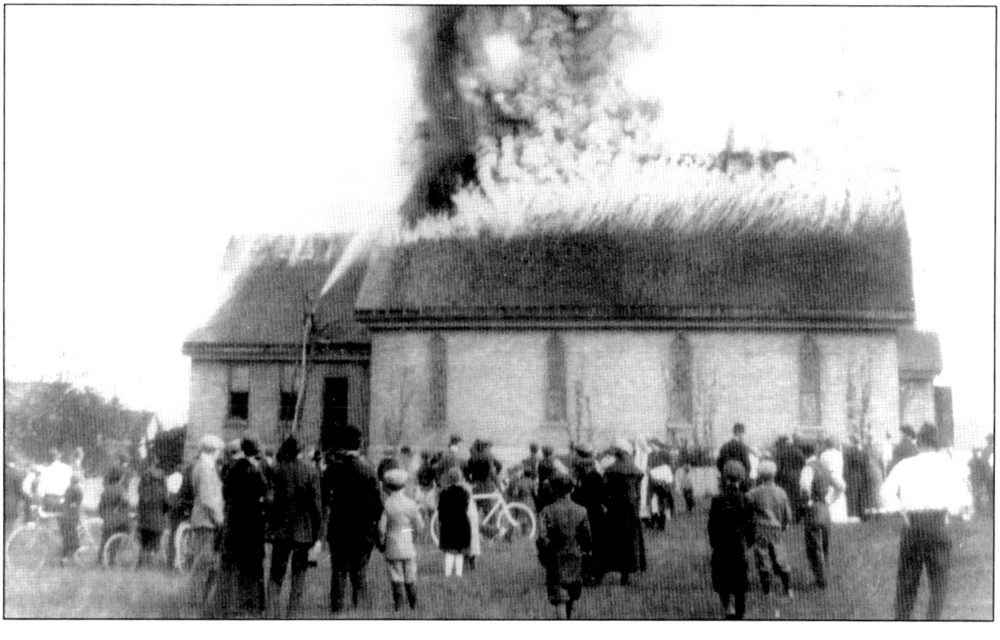

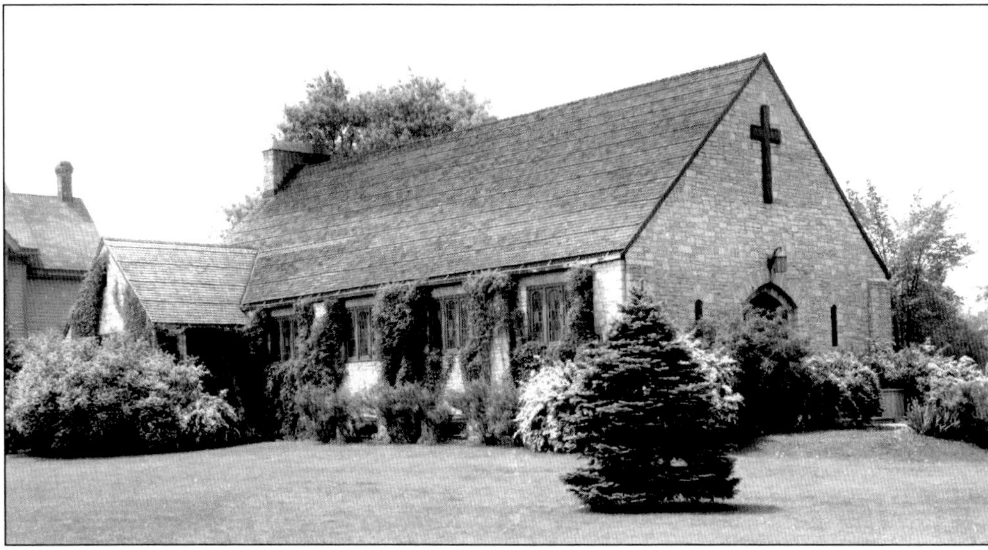

The Reverend Mr. William C. Stump organized St. Matthew's Evangelical Lutheran Church in May of 1920 to offer Lutherans worship in the English language. By January 1921, services were held in this English Gothic parish house on the southwest corner of Wauwatosa and Milwaukee Avenues. The first minister, Pastor William Niebling, served from 1921 to 1967. A new Lannon stone church building was dedicated in 1950, replacing the old structure, followed by an educational addition in 1964. (WHS Postcard 668.)

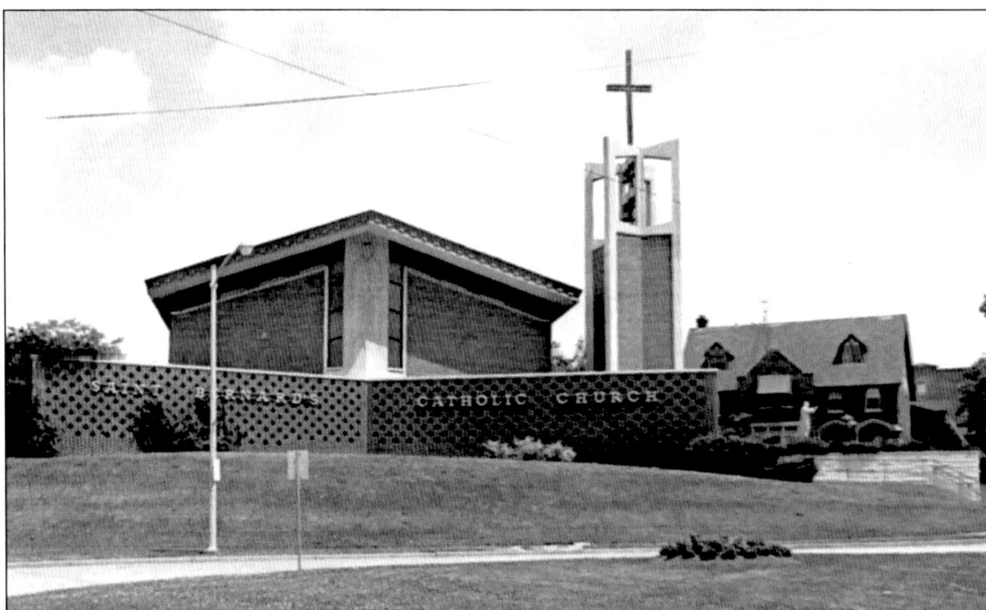

The 1880 Holy Cross Catholic Church, far to the east in the Town of Wauwatosa, served area Catholics. In 1911, a parish organized in Wauwatosa and Msgr. Bernard Traudt held the first Mass; the parish name honored him. The old Riddle home, north of Root Common, was purchased and used from 1912 to 1918, until the first church and school were completed. A new St. Bernard's Church, at the same location, was dedicated in 1963; the old convent is at the right. (Photo by Victor Cordes, WHS Photo 609.)

Seven

VOLUNTARY ORGANIZATIONS

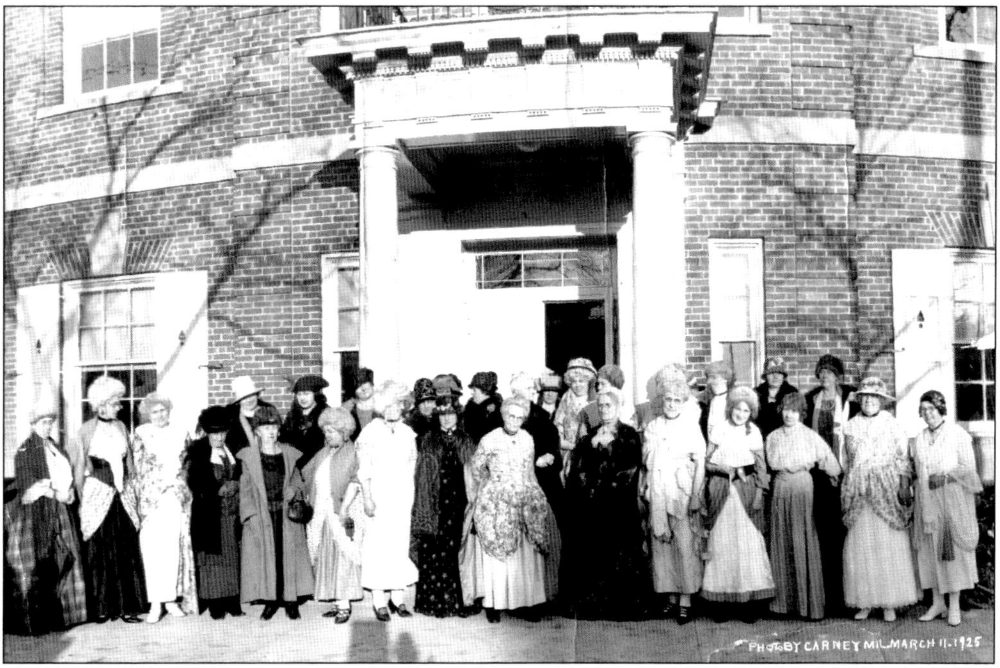

The Wauwatosa Woman's Club was founded in 1894, at a time when women nationally were forming clubs for intellectual enrichment and social activities and to foster civic involvement. On March 11, 1925, their Georgian clubhouse, on the southeast corner of Wauwatosa and Milwaukee Avenues, was dedicated on land donated by Emerson D. Hoyt. A member said, "The clubhouse stands—the visible show of an idea." Three days of celebratory events included a historical costume party and the ladies in their finery were captured on film in front of their building. The club also housed the only woman's club museum in the state. The club is still active; its building is a Wauwatosa and Milwaukee County Landmark and listed in the State and National Registers of Historic Places. Through the years, many other organizations, from the Twentieth Century Topic Club to the Wauwatosa Camera Club, have provided outlets for a wide range of citizen interests. (WHS Photo 739.)

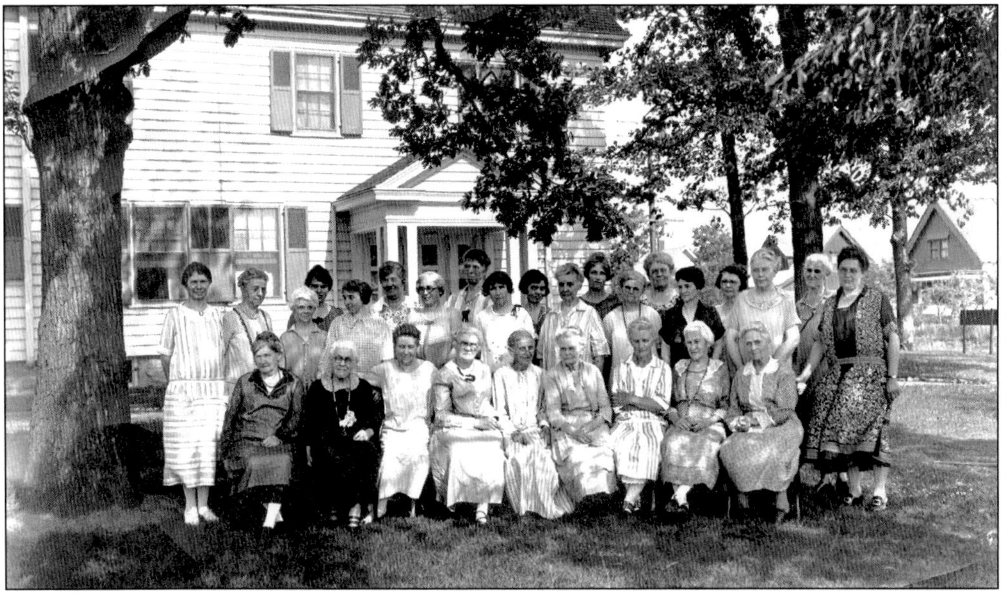

The Wauwatosa Pioneers Club was originally a 1921 fund-raising circle of the Wauwatosa Woman's Club. When the circles were discontinued, this group decided to keep their format and form a new organization. Frederick D. Underwood offered a house at 8612 West North Avenue for use as their clubhouse. The members gathered in front of their club home for this picture in the 1920s.With diminished membership, the group disbanded in 1992. (WHS Photo 737.)

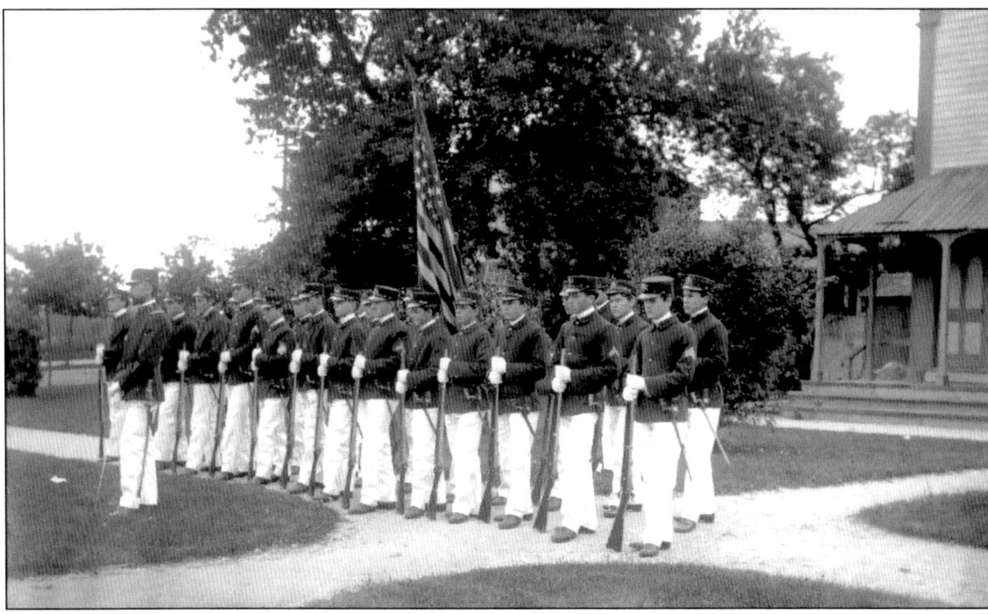

The Minute Men were a patriotic military and social group at the turn of the nineteenth century. Renamed the Wauwatosa Light Guard, they drilled and marched in Memorial Day parades and appeared at other community events. They held encampments with mock battles. The Wauwatosa Light Guard also fielded both a baseball and a football team in season and presented plays. Members stand at parade rest on Memorial Day 1905, at Root Common in front of the Town Hall. (WHS Photo LGP 907.)

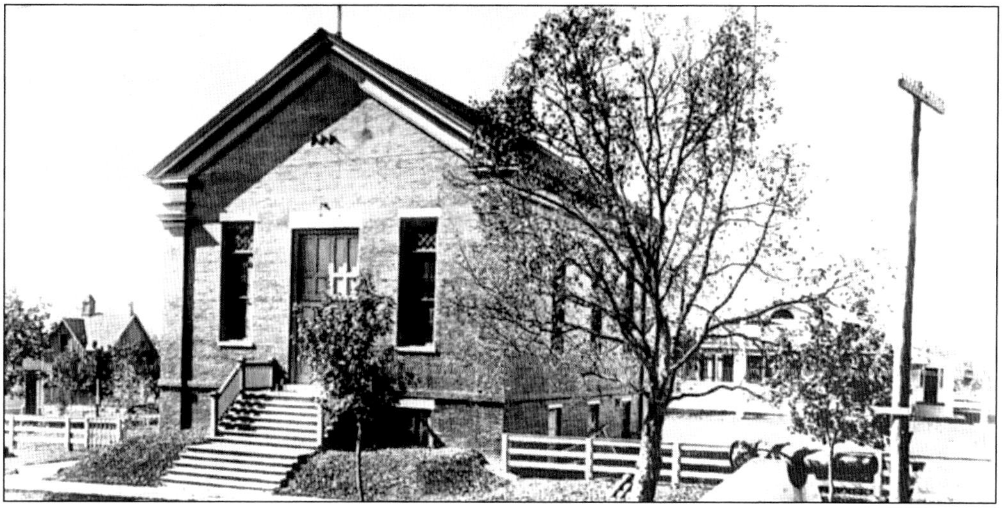

Frederick D. Underwood promoted the idea of a permanent meeting hall for the Wauwatosa Light Guard. He had purchased the original First Baptist Church for $3,000 in 1888. Underwood renovated the old building, which faced Wauwatosa Avenue, for use by the Light Guard as an armory (*above*). Note the cannon at the right and the absence of the original steeple. The stock certificate of Mr. H.D. Fuller for five shares in the Armory Hall Association, dated April 5, 1905 (*below*), supported this effort. Underwood later preserved the structure by moving it to the Wauwatosa Cemetery. The building at the right of the armory is possibly a portion of the one-story house that Underwood built for himself and later expanded with a second floor (see page 118). (WHS Photo 270 and Mss. 131.)

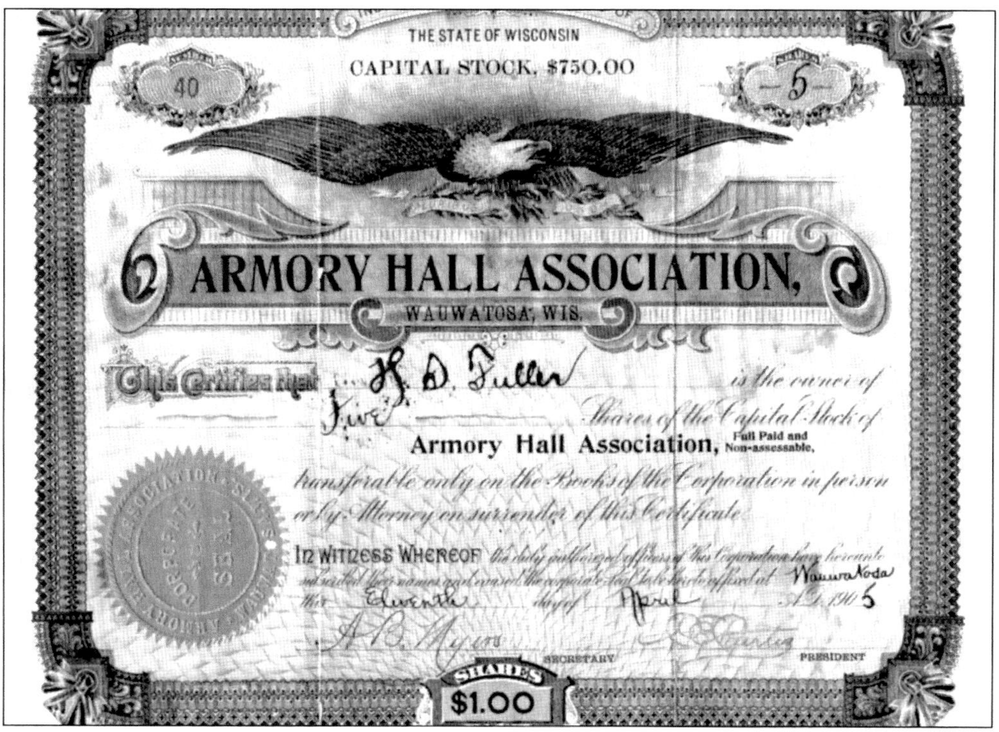

THE STATE OF WISCONSIN

CAPITAL STOCK, $750.00

40 — 5

ARMORY HALL ASSOCIATION,

WAUWATOSA, WIS.

This Certifies that H. D. Fuller is the owner of Five Shares of the Capital Stock of **Armory Hall Association,** Full Paid and Non-assessable, transferable only on the Books of the Corporation in person or by Attorney on surrender of this Certificate.

In Witness Whereof the duly authorized officers of this Corporation have hereunto subscribed their names and caused the corporate Seal to be hereto affixed at Wauwatosa this Eleventh day of April A.D. 1905

A. B. Myers, Secretary

President

SHARES $1.00

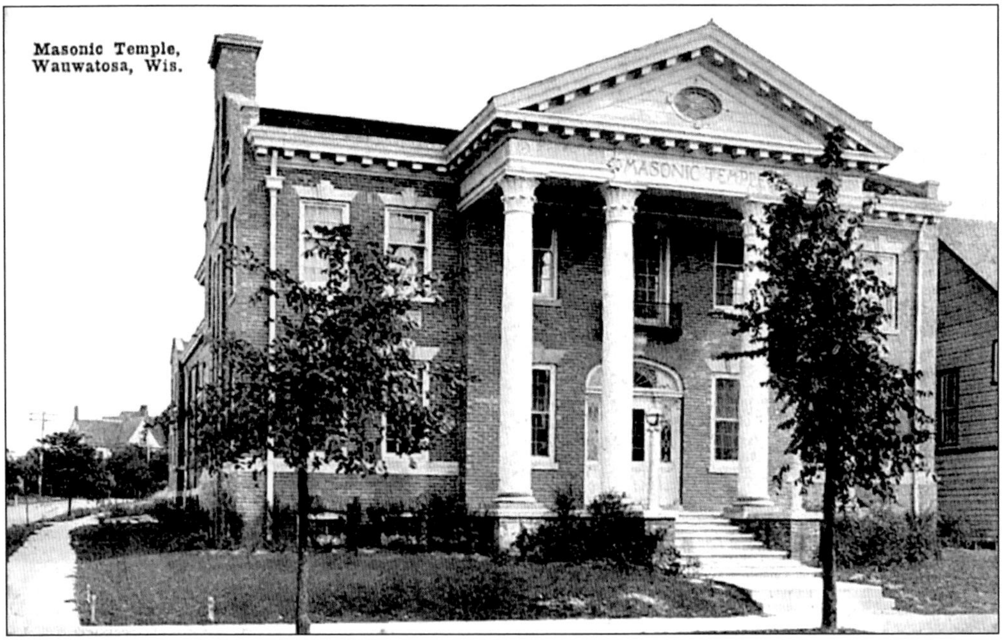

Organized in 1869, Wauwatosa Lodge No. 267 F. & A.M. Grand Lodge of Wisconsin built their own structure in 1918, at 1532 Wauwatosa Avenue. At one time their membership reached 900. The building was sold to the Irish Fest organization in 1998 and it houses their J.J. Ward Irish Music Archives. Masonic members now meet in the West Allis Lodge building and offer three $1,000 scholarships to Wauwatosa high school students. (WHS Postcard 662.)

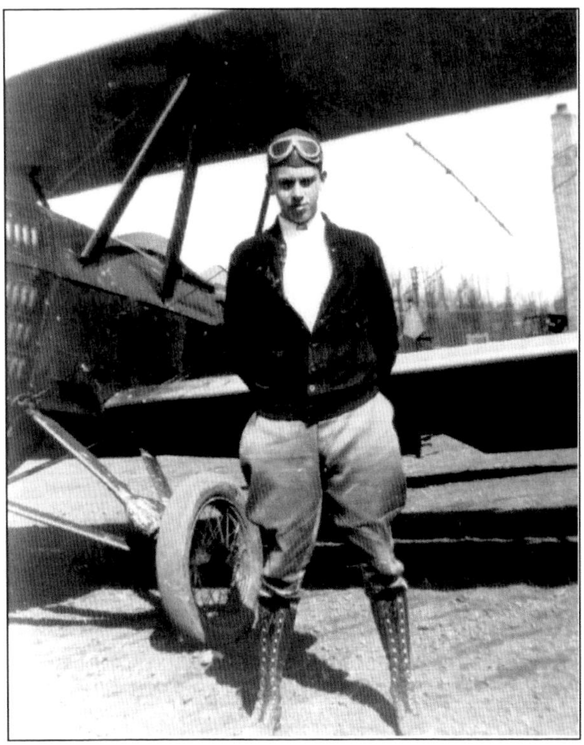

Air cadet James Seton Gray Jr. stands next to a plane at the Milwaukee County Airport in 1929. Born in 1914, he was, at age 16, the youngest licensed pilot in the United States. He became the first Double Eagle scout in Wisconsin—Eagle Scout and Quartermaster Sea Scout. After graduation from Wauwatosa High School in 1932, Gray joined the U.S. Navy. He retired a captain in 1966, the recipient of many awards and medals. (WHS Photo 738.)

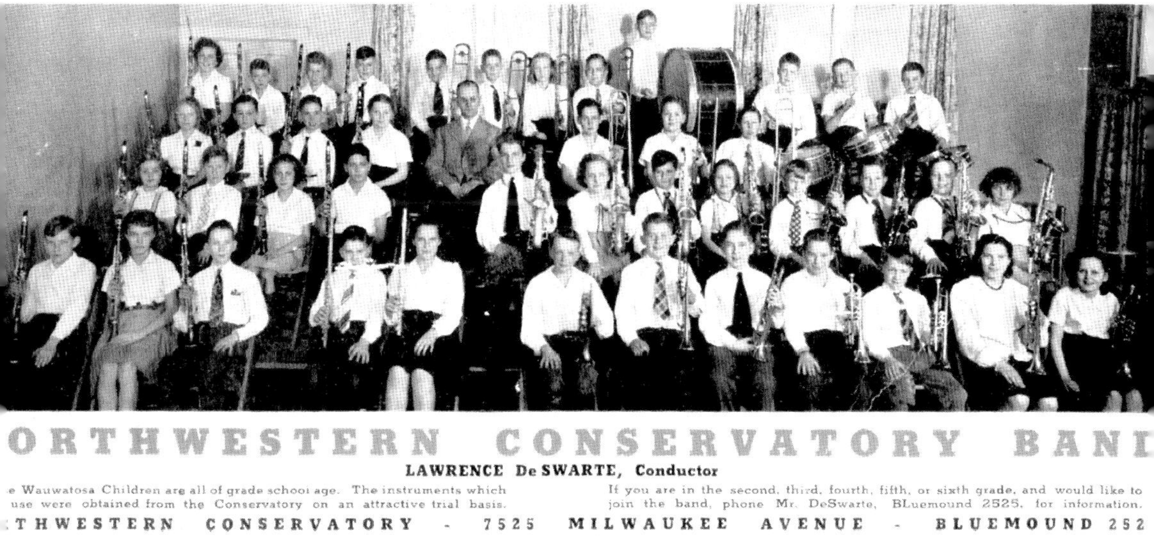

The Northwestern Conservatory Band offered Wauwatosa children in grades two through six the opportunity to perform musically. Instruments could be obtained on a trial basis and lessons were offered through the Northwestern School of Music at 7525 Milwaukee Avenue (building razed). The conservatory operated from the 1920s to the late 1940s. The school was a family affair, with Lawrence DeSwarte as president and band director, his wife, Ada, as office secretary, and their son Keith an instructor. (WHS Mss. 155.)

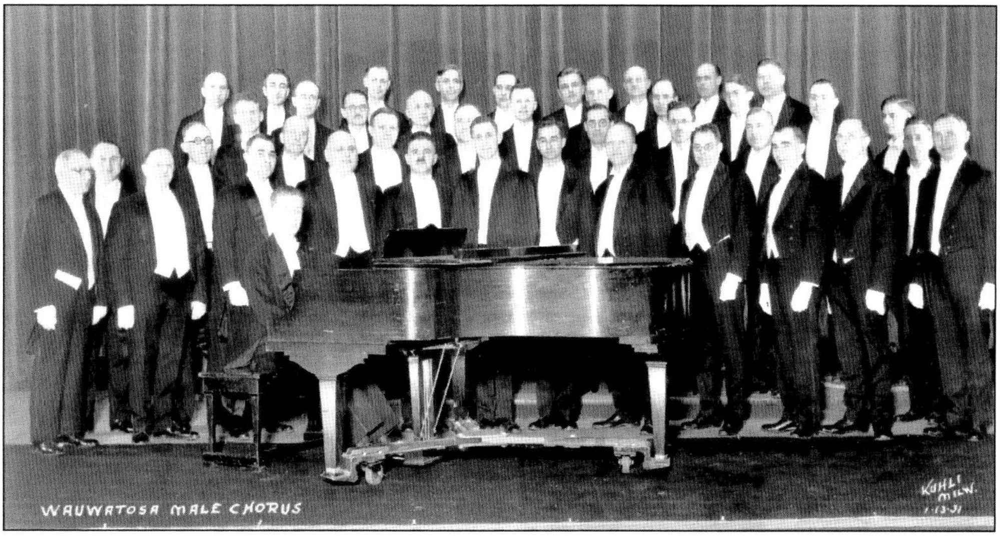

The Wauwatosa Male Chorus, organized in 1930 under the direction of Samuel A. Thorne, a professor at Milwaukee State Teachers College (now UW-Milwaukee), became a popular and highly sought after performing group. Composed of professionals and businessmen, the chorus gave concerts locally and in nearby cities, taking the stage in full dress suits, white ties, vests, and wing collars. Their repertoire included religious, classical, and popular songs. They prided themselves on committing all pieces to memory. (WHS Mss. 109.)

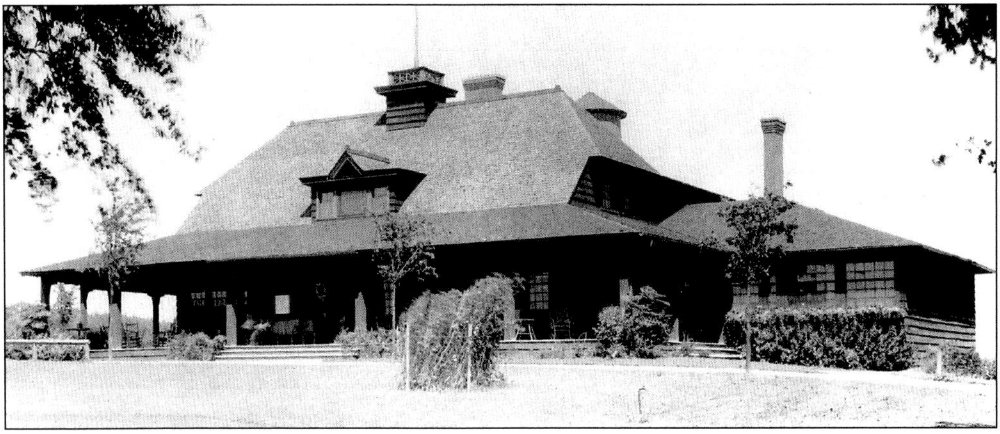

Three golfing buddies founded one of the earliest private clubs in the state, the Blue Mound Golf and Country Club, which celebrated its 100th anniversary in 2003. On land leased from Jacob Wellauer, north of Bluemound Road and west of Sixty-eighth Street, this clubhouse and links opened in May 1905. The club purchased its own land and in May 1926 it opened at its present location (see page 122). The original site became a public course before being subdivided for homes. (Courtesy of Blue Mound Golf and Country Club.)

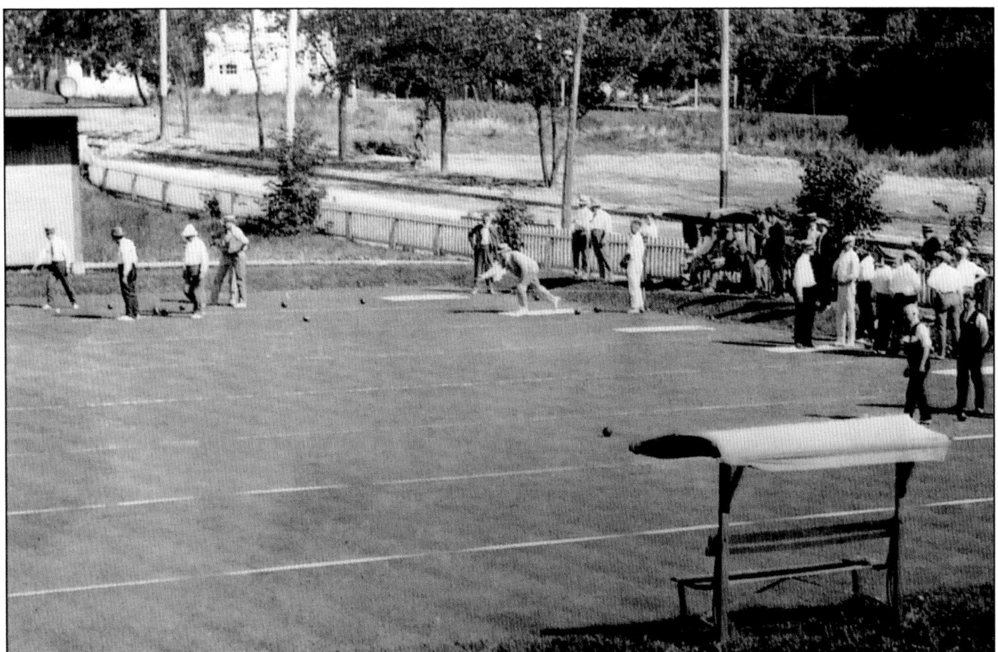

Stickney Field Club began in 1913 at approximately the 7800 block on Stickney Avenue, on property donated by Frederick D. Underwood. A family club, it had a two-story frame building with locker rooms, four clay tennis courts, horseshoe pitch, children's playground, picnic area, and a bowling green for lawn bowling, seen here in 1924. Members built a shed and ice surface for two lanes of curling, in 1920. The Wauwatosa Curling Club used the facilities until moving both the shed and their activities to Hart Park in the mid-1920s. (Courtesy *The Milwaukee Journal* © 2003 Journal Sentinel Inc., reproduced with permission.)

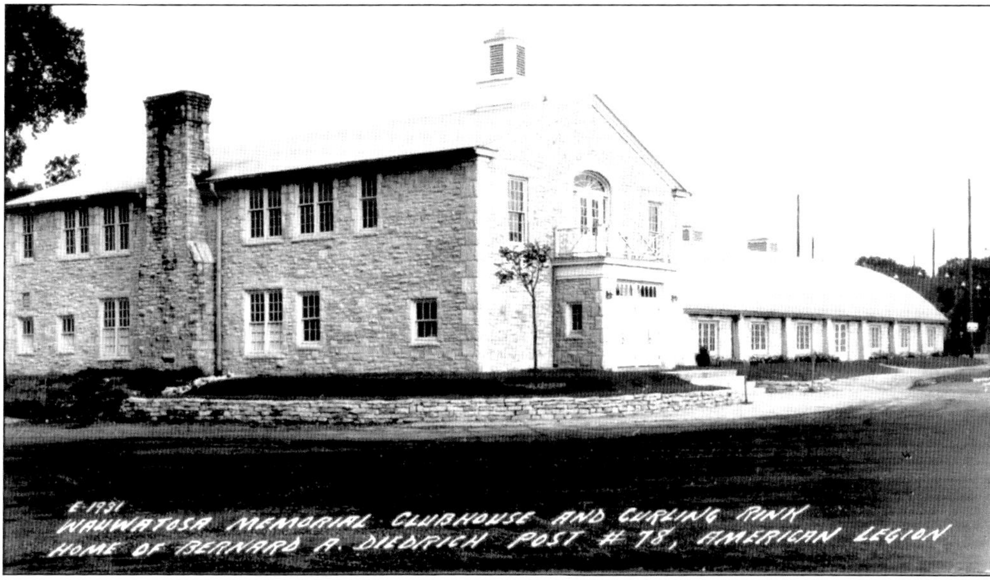

Between 1939 and 1941, a federal W.P.A. project built the Wauwatosa Recreational Building in City Park, renamed Hart Park in 1960. Designated a community memorial clubhouse, it housed Milwaukee's first indoor artificial ice rink and offered public skating to music and ice for curling. The building was renamed in 1974 for city forester Howard Muellner. The Bernard A. Diedrich Post #78 of the American Legion also used it as a clubhouse. (WHS Postcard 671.)

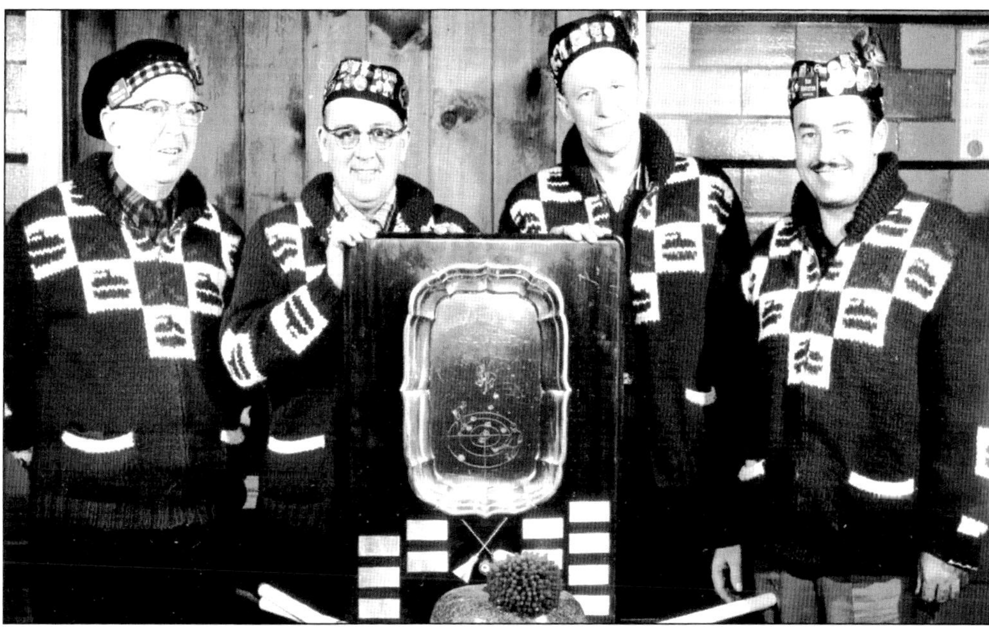

The sport of curling, believed to have been invented by the Scots in the seventeenth century, gets its name from the curved route, or curl, the stone takes as it glides over the ice. Pictured here, c. 1955, in their curling sweaters and displaying their commemorative pins on their hats are, from left, "Skip" Hubert "Doc" Roberts, "Third" Earl Easton, "Second" Carl Stuart "Stu" Haagensen, "Lead" Robert Houston—winners of the First Event in Wauwatosa Men's Invitational Bonspiel (tournament). (Photo by Erv Nell, WHS Mss. 130)

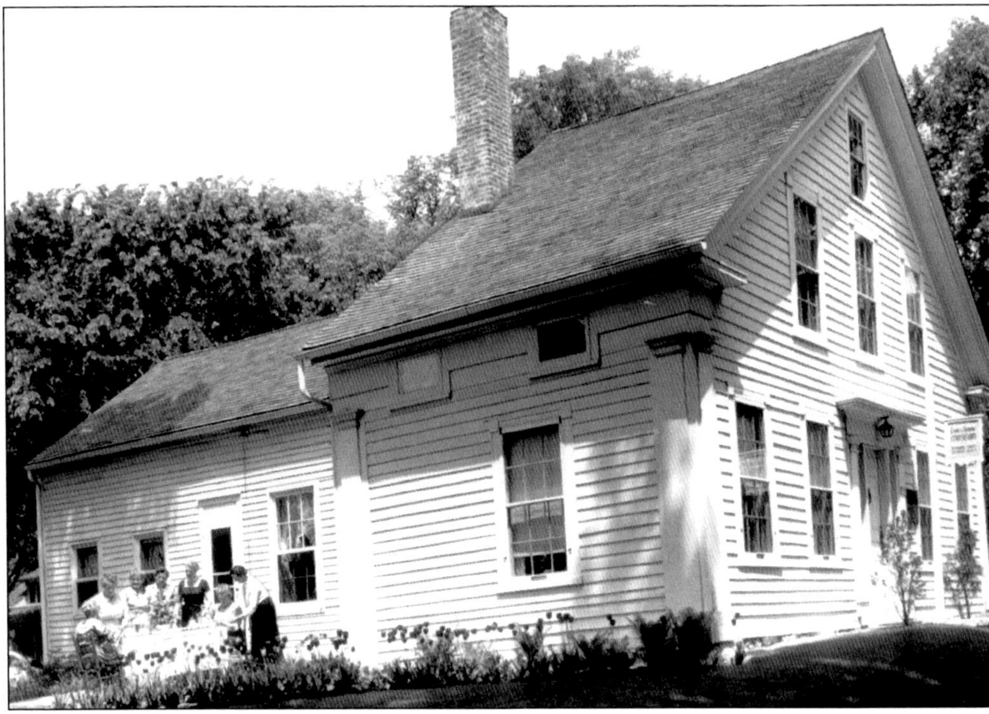

In 1956, garden club members posed outside the 1844 portion of the city's oldest home, built by Oliver Damon. His son Lowell added the front in 1846. The Alexander Rogers family donated the property to Milwaukee County Historical Society in 1941. In 1948, an area garden club landscape project expanded to include work on preserving the interior. The County Society recently has undertaken major renovation of what is now the Lowell Damon House Museum at 2107 Wauwatosa Avenue. The neighborhood association maintains the gardens. (WHS Photo 760.)

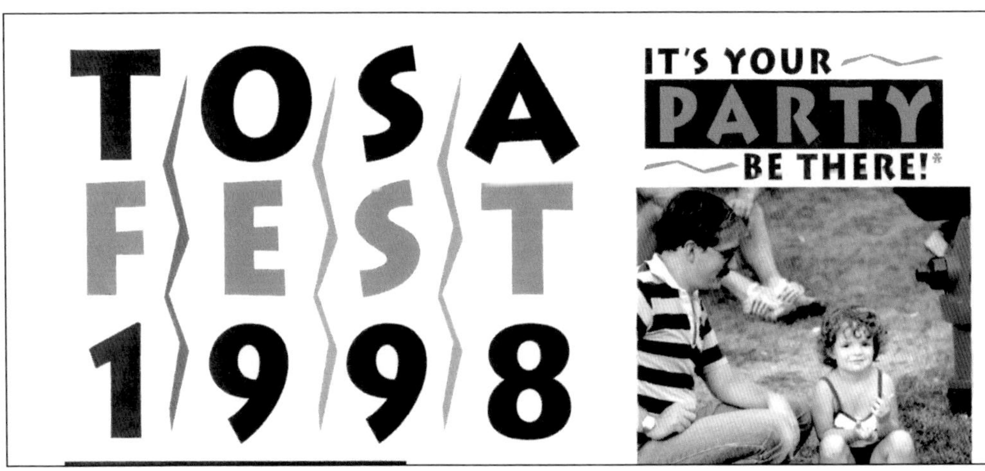

Begun in 1979, TosaFest features family fun, food, and free entertainment to celebrate Wauwatosa's historic Village and community spirit. Proceeds help multiple community projects, such as education, safety, and neighborhood improvement. Countless volunteers work virtually year round to produce this event, which entertains and benefits the entire community each fall. Inserted into this publicity brochure is a photo from the early 1980s of a past organizer, Charles Causier, and his daughter Beth. (WHS Mss. 38 and Courtesy of Kathy Causier.)

Eight

People, Pleasures, and Pastimes

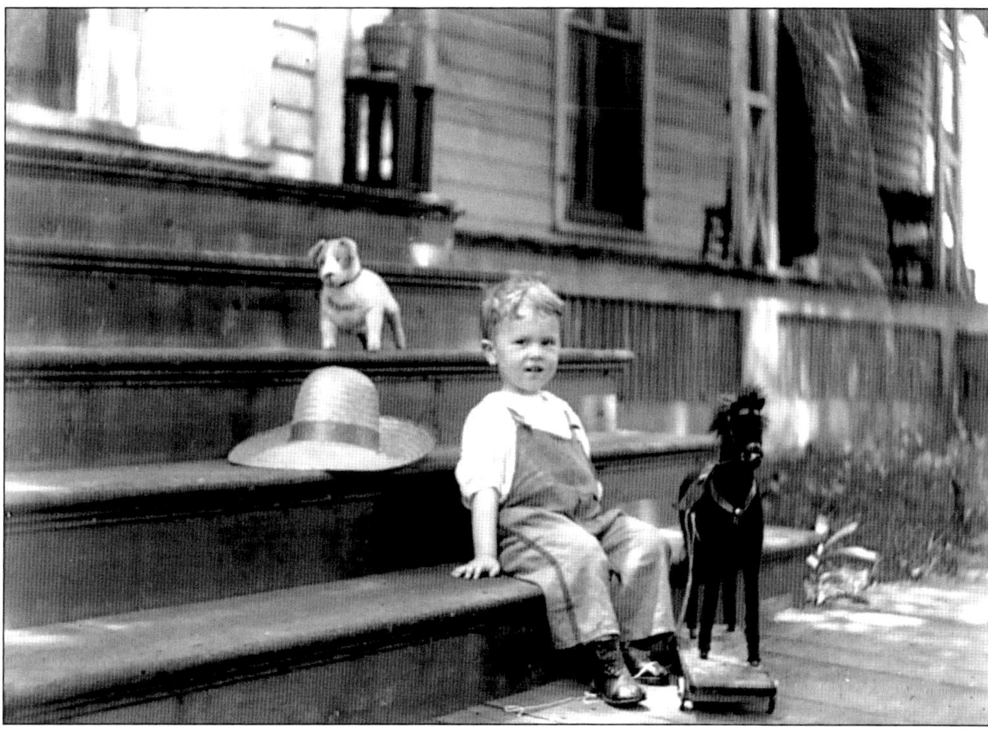

As leisure time increased in the nineteenth century, people enjoyed a variety of activities. Outdoor sports, stereoscopic viewers, music, and games such as charades and cards provided amusement. On New Year's Eve of 1889, for a 25¢ ticket, one could attend a "Candy Pull Social" at Lefeber's Hall. One could read the local newspaper or attend the first motion pictures in town at the Delight Theater on State Street in 1911. The radio of the 1920s added another diversion. Nineteen acres were purchased for City Park in 1921, and a football field, baseball diamonds, and tennis courts were developed in what is now Hart Park. On a warm summer day, young Edward Lefeber takes a break from his busy playtime activities (c. 1900). For just a moment, the camera has drawn his attention away from his pull-toy horse and stuffed dog. (WHS Photo LGP 869.)

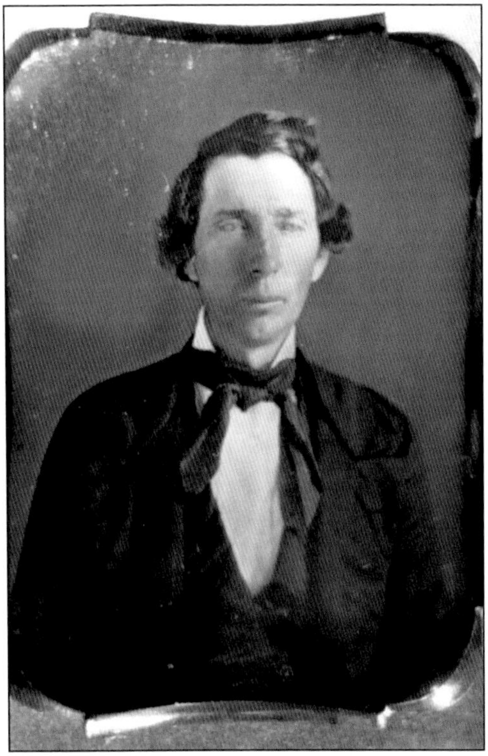 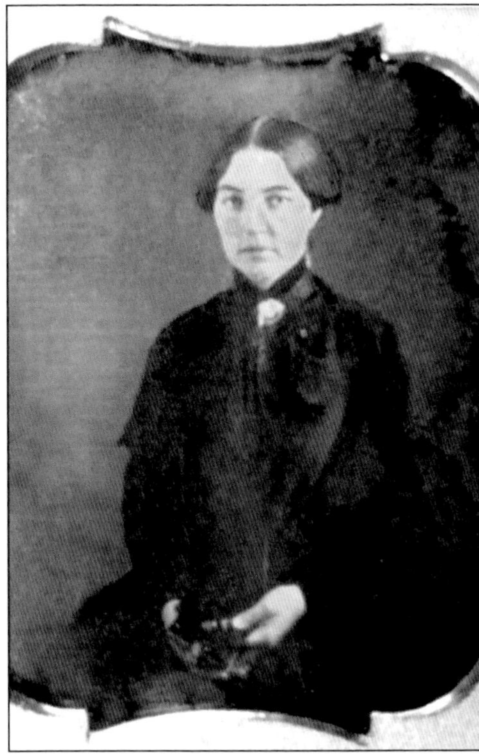

The name Harwood is familiar to nearly everyone in Wauwatosa, primarily because one of the main streets through the Village area is Harwood Avenue. Originally from New York State, Oliver Harwood and his wife, Clarissa, moved to Wauwatosa with their five children in 1852. On land he purchased from Charles Hart, Harwood built a home high on the Dewey Avenue hill, overlooking the Village growing below. Like Hart, Harwood was a miller. Like many New Englanders who moved west, Harwood brought a piano, said to be the first in Wauwatosa, with him. In his estate he provided funds for a library, and the Harwood Library and Lecture Association formed in 1886—the first library building bore his name. These rare encased daguerreotype images of the Harwoods (*c.* 1850) are the earliest depiction of Wauwatosa pioneers in the Wauwatosa Historical Society collection. Oliver (1804–1867), Clarissa (1802–1880), and son Henry are buried in Wauwatosa Cemetery. (WHS Museum Collection and WHS Photo 740 & 741.)

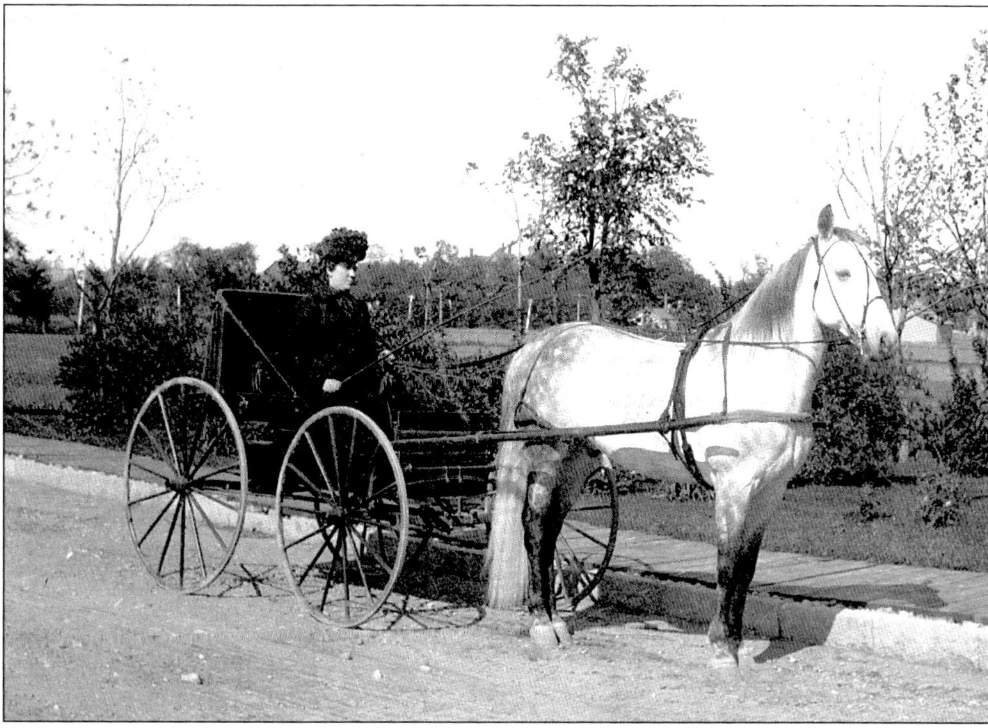

(*above*) Mrs. Charles Kieckhafer sits in her horse-drawn carriage in the 1890s. Notice the Wauwatosa limestone curb separating the dirt road from the wooden plank sidewalk. Her husband served as superintendent of the Milwaukee County almshouse until 1903, when he decided to manage the Kieckhafer Edgewood Dairy Farm at Pewaukee Lake. Ferdinand Bark replaced him at the almshouse. (WHS Photo 742.)

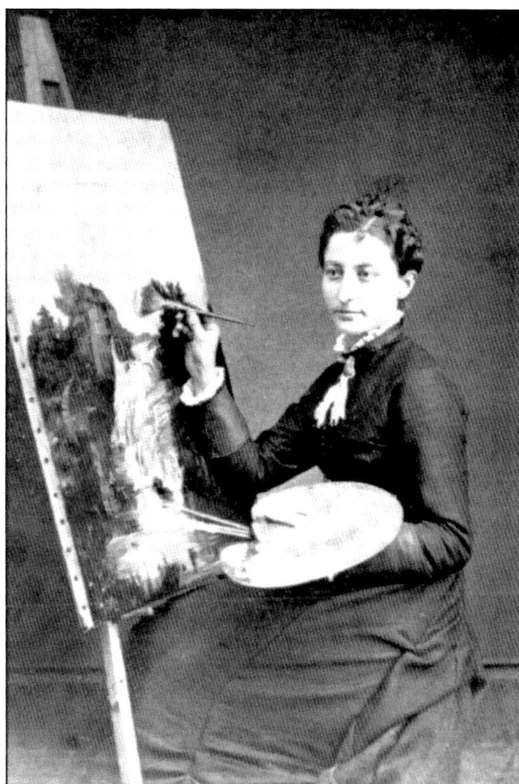

(*right*) A young Florence Holmes sits at an easel trying to put the finishing touches on her painting of a waterfall in the 1880s. Landscapes and nature were favorite subjects. Female artistic expression through painting, whether on canvas or china, was a popular pastime in the late Victorian era. Paintings could be used to decorate one's home in a tasteful manner. (WHS Photo 347.)

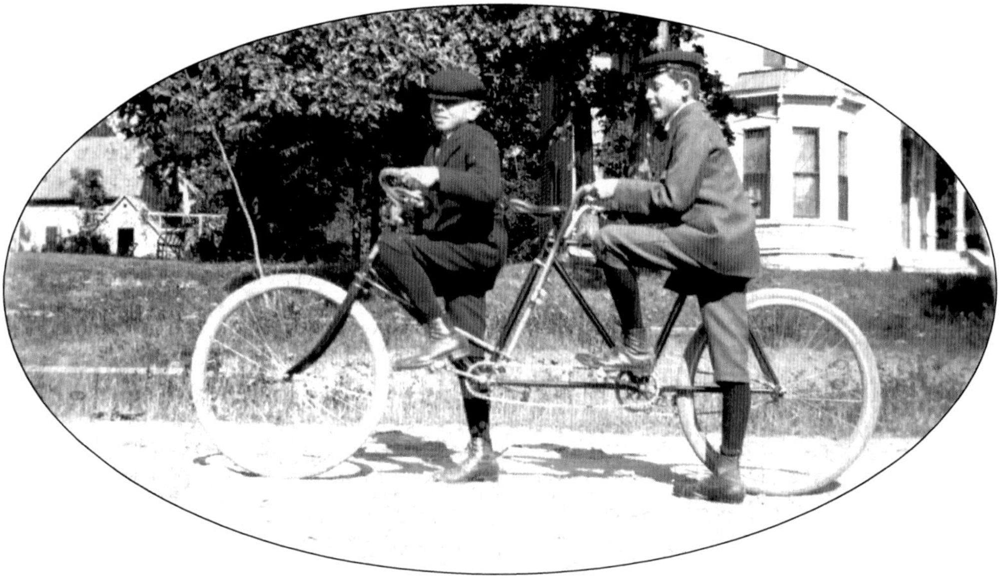

Two boys in knickers and caps climb onto a tandem bicycle to pedal their way through the streets of Wauwatosa. The boys are Arthur Blaesser and Ed Pares. The photograph was taken on Wauwatosa Avenue near Stickney Avenue, probably in the 1890s. Bicycling was a popular recreation for young and old alike. An 1895 map was published with biking routes throughout Milwaukee County, a testament to the universality of the sport. (WHS Photo 743.)

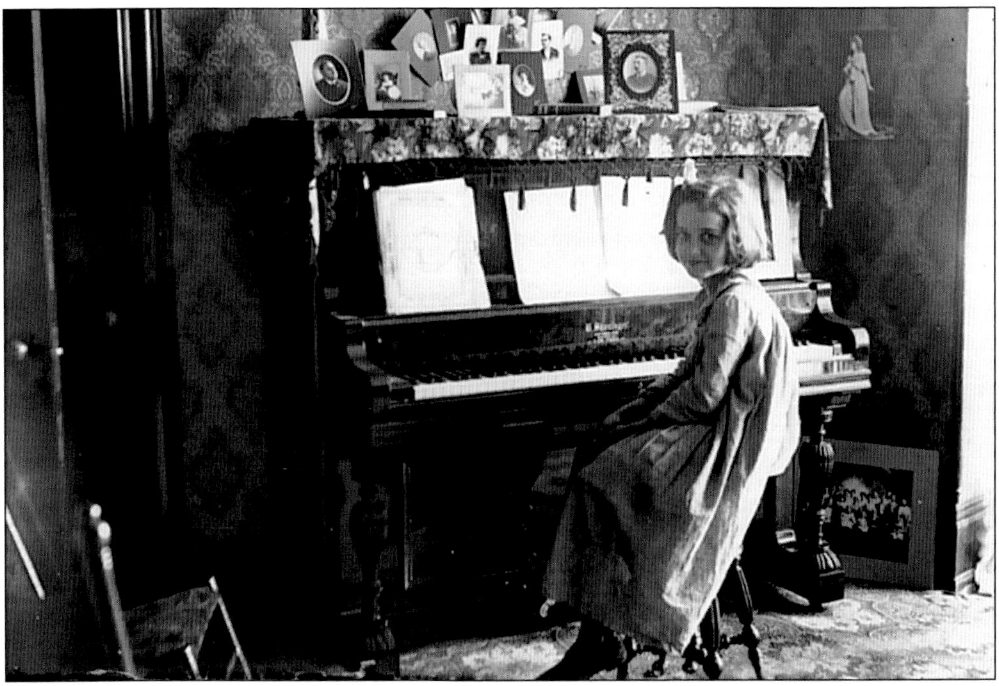

A young Ruth Arnes seems in a great mood while she takes a break from piano practice. If even for a moment she feels alone, all she has to do is glance atop the piano to the collection of family photographs keeping an eye on her. Decorative displays of photos and mementoes were typical of late nineteenth century interiors. This picture was taken on July 8, 1903. (WHS Photo LGP 246.)

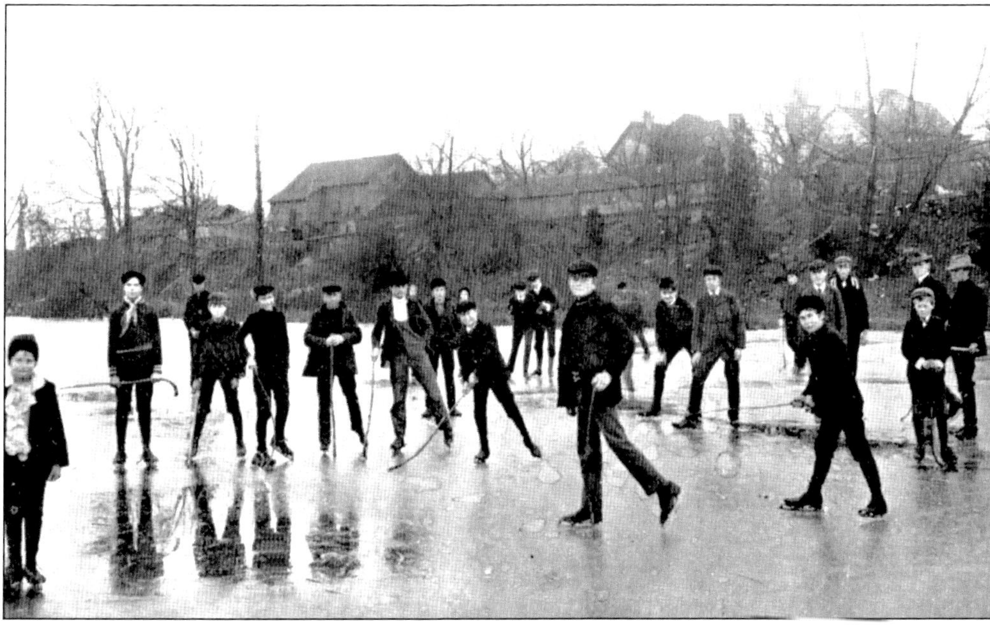

People of all ages enjoyed ice skating, wearing blades strapped onto their shoes. The frozen millpond in the Village offers a great place for local lads to play a game of hockey. Among the buildings on the hill behind them is the steeple of St. John's Evangelical Lutheran Church, faintly seen, on Harwood Avenue. (WHS Mss. 129.)

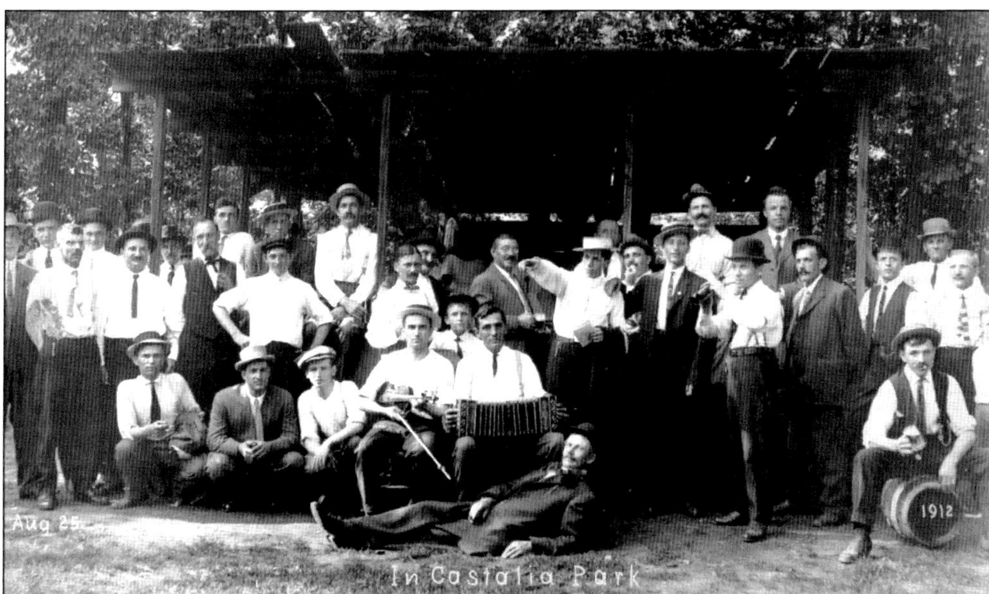

On an August day in 1912, a group of men gather in Castalia Park. Music, socializing, and beverages are in order; a gentleman is sitting on a keg of beer (far right corner). The image is undocumented as to details of the event. Castalia Park was adjacent to the Castalia Bottling Works on the west side of Hawley Road, south of the Menomonee River. The firm manufactured soda, mineral waters, lemon sour, and weiss beer, delivered in bottles, jugs, or cases. (WHS Photo 692–1.)

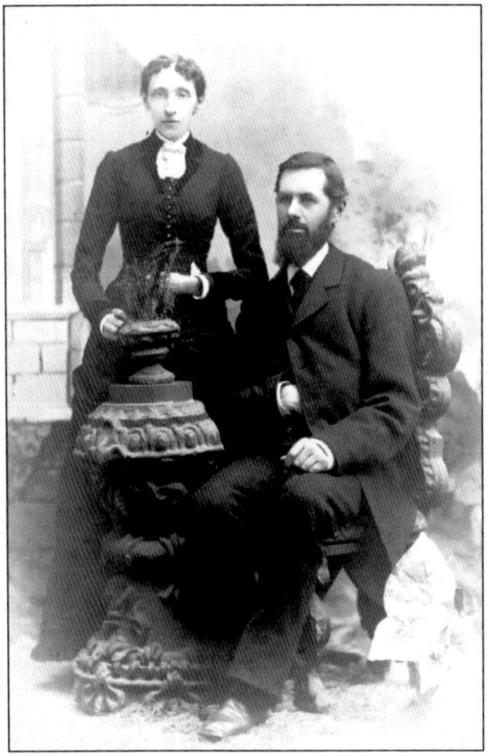

Julia Barnes Moore (1838–1923) and William H. Moore (1845–1936) sit for a typical Victorian studio portrait in 1885 (left). William was a New Salem, Massachusetts, native and he served with Company E of the 24th Wisconsin Regiment in the Civil War. William and Julia were married 55 years. (WHS Mss.112.)

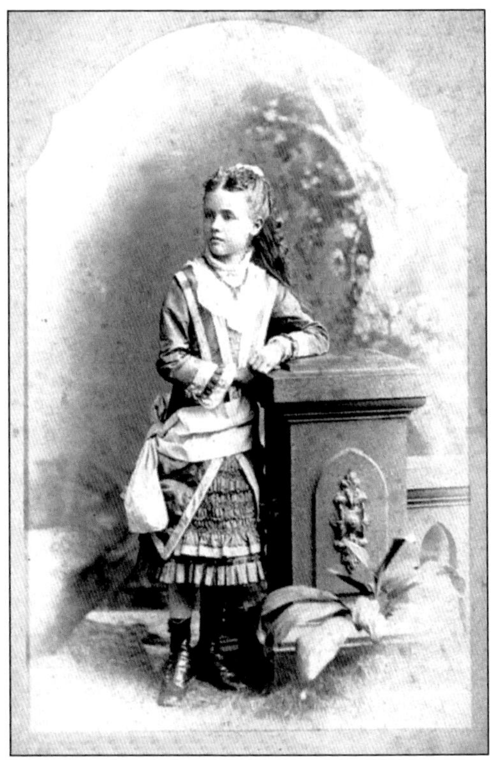

The professional photo (right) is of their daughter Estelle Moore at about 12 years of age (*c.* 1884). She wore her prettiest and very best ruffled dress and high-button shoes, with her long tresses pinned up in the back. This cabinet card, as the prints were called, is illustrative of the portraits done in this era of photography. A studious looking young lady, Estelle went on to become a kindergarten teacher (1896) and married Otto August Zillmer in 1904. Estelle died in 1964 at the age of 91. (WHS Mss.112.)

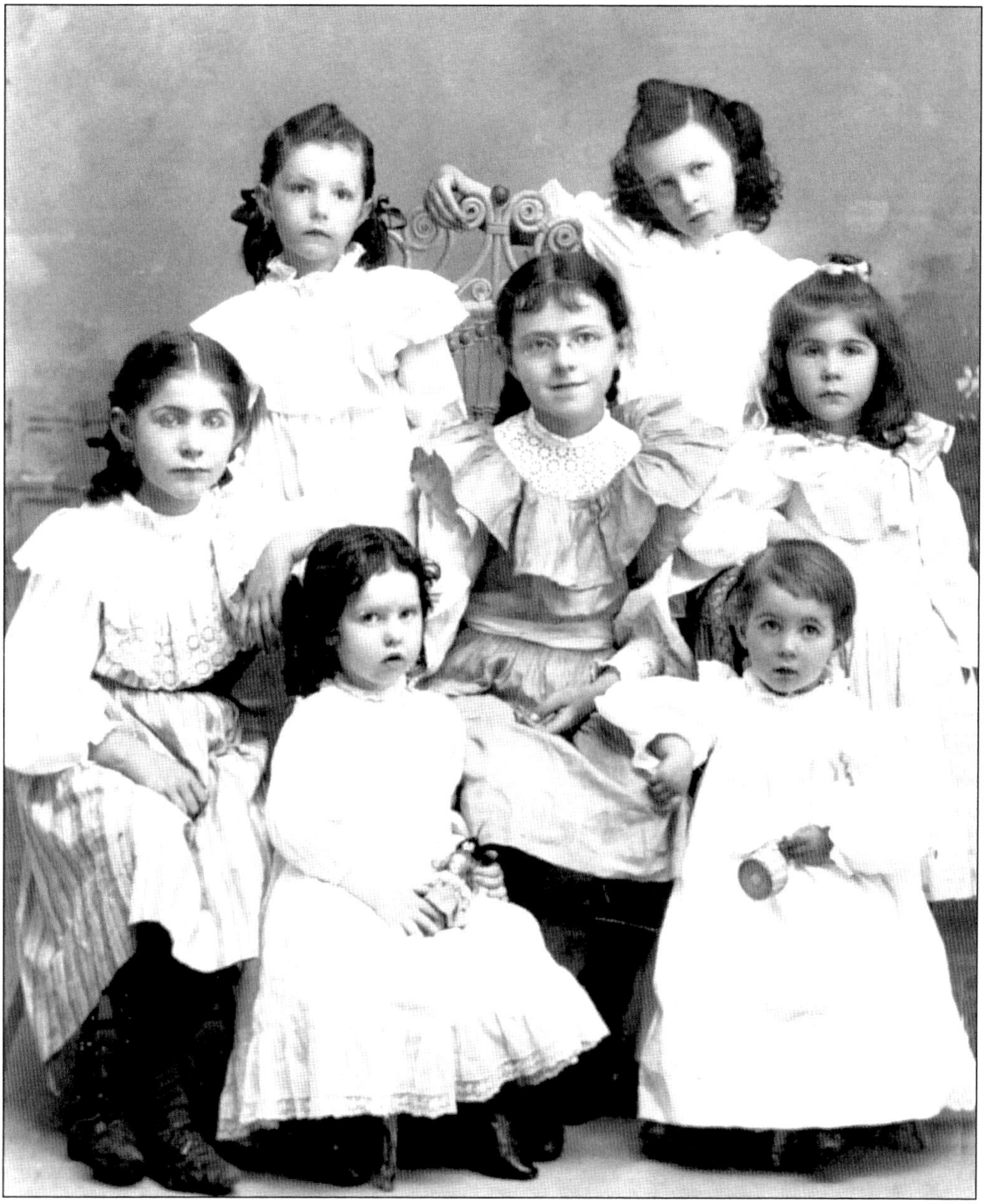

Seven Clapp family cousins sit attentively for the photographer in approximately 1898. Grandchildren of Reverend Mr. Luther Clapp and his wife, Harriet, the Clapps raised six children (see page 75). After serving as minister of the First Congregational Church for nearly 30 years, Clapp assumed other duties in 1872. He was appointed General Missionary to "care for the destitute and discouraged churches." He preached in Wisconsin and seven other states to 82 congregations, among them Congregational, Presbyterian, Methodist, Baptist, Lutheran, and to a Disciple and a Universalist group. The Clapp's daughter Sarah married the Reverend Mr. Chauncey Goodrich, D.D., and they spent nearly 45 years as missionaries in China. Their three children are in this portrait. Pictured left to right: (front row) Carol Clapp and Luther Carrington Goodrich; (middle row) Grace Goodrich, Mary Priscilla Clapp, and Dorothea Goodrich; (back row) Isabel Clapp and Grace Watner. (WHS Photo 744.)

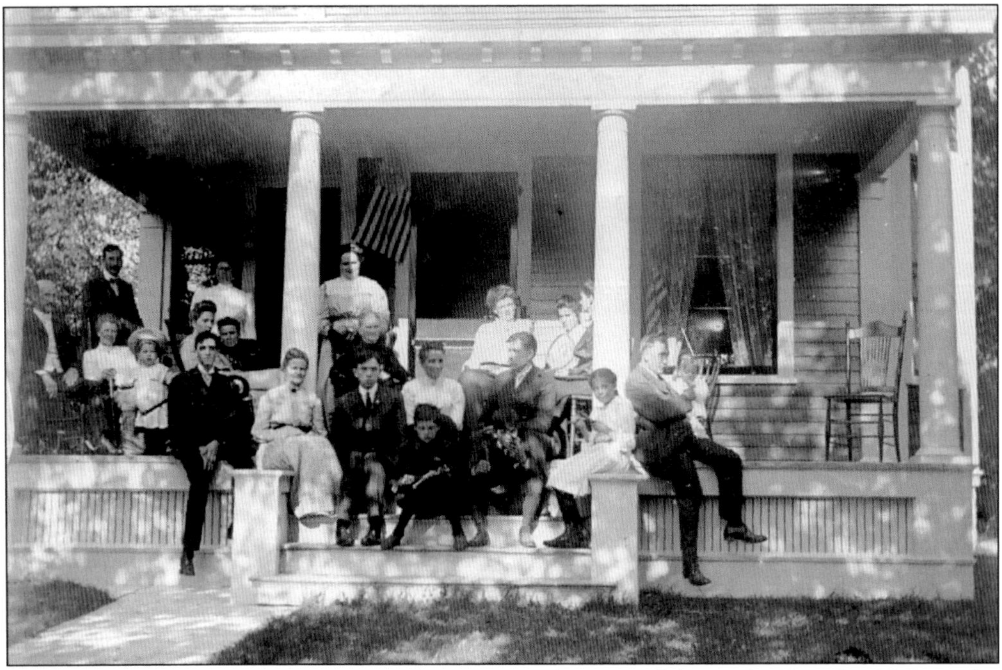

Patriotism is strong in Wauwatosa, as this group gathers to celebrate the Fourth of July in the 1890s. The flag waves proudly on the front porch as the folks sit for a relaxed candid shot at the home of George Smith, once located at 1753 Seventy-fifth Street. The site is now part of the large playing field next to Wauwatosa East High School. (WHS Mss. 133.)

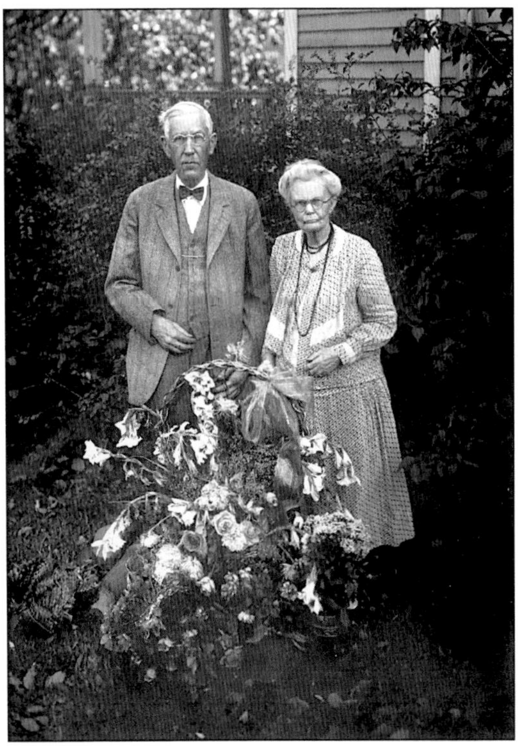

The Cornelius Lefeber family settled here in 1869, and among their five children was James. On October 1, 1878, James married Mary Courtney, a schoolteacher, in the home of O.J. Smith. The couple had seven children. On October 1, 1928, when this photo was taken, they celebrated their golden wedding anniversary with family and friends. James and his brothers Abraham and Joseph operated the Lefeber Bros. general store in the Village. (WHS Photo 745.)

Little girls a hundred years ago mimicked their mother's work. On a chilly spring day in April of 1900, an unidentified young lady hangs her dolly laundry on a line behind the house in a photo captioned "my busy day." Without the advantage of an electric clothes dryer, she has gone outside as mom would have, wearing stockings, coat, and cap to keep her warm. (WHS Photo LGP 13.)

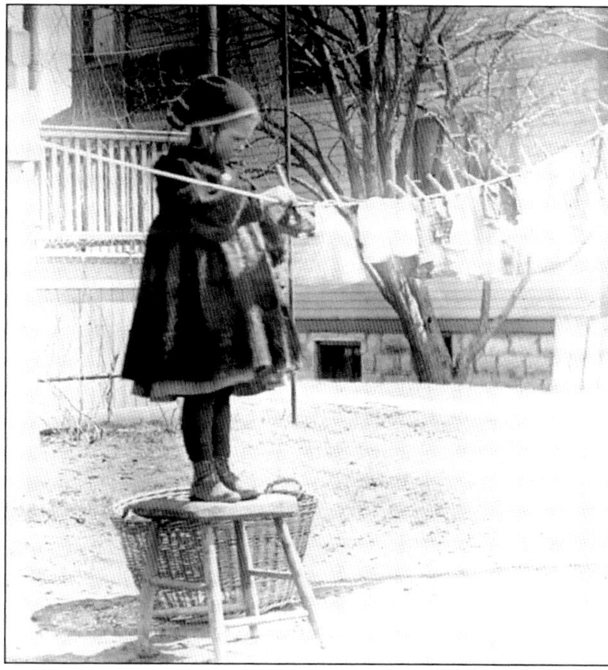

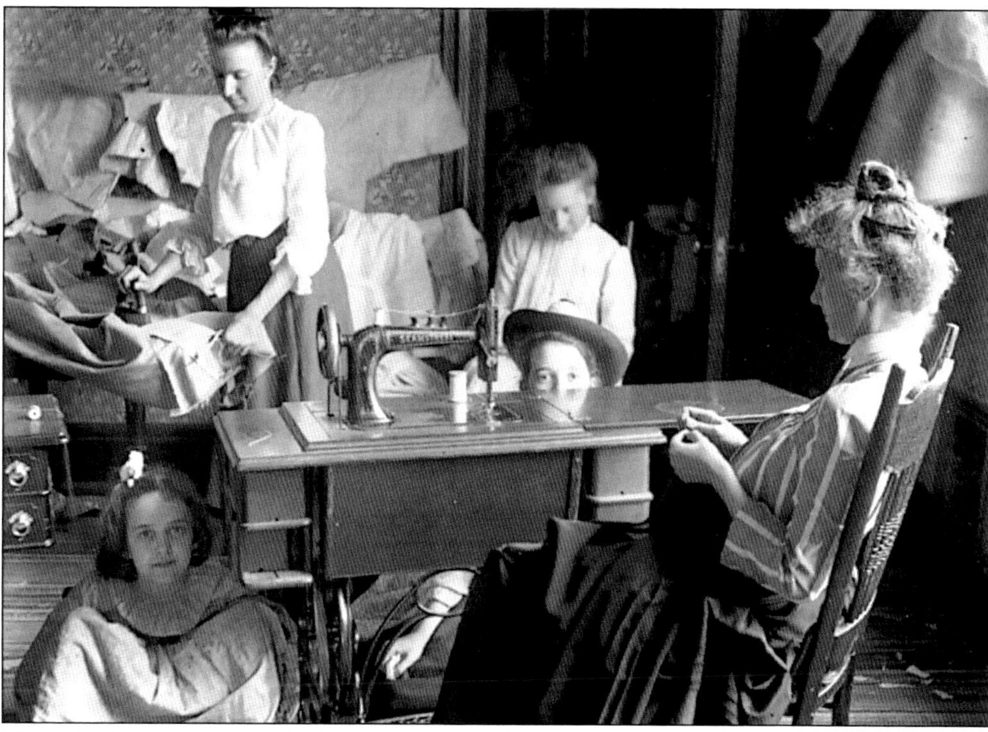

When Ruth Arnes was finished practicing piano (see page 92), she could go into the sewing room to watch other members of the household hard at work. Ruth (lower left) enjoys the company while learning about some of the women's domestic duties. The Seamstress treadle sewing machine was put to good use. Ironing was accomplished with an iron heated on a stove; they had no electric iron. The photograph was taken on July 8, 1903. (WHS Photo LGP 245.)

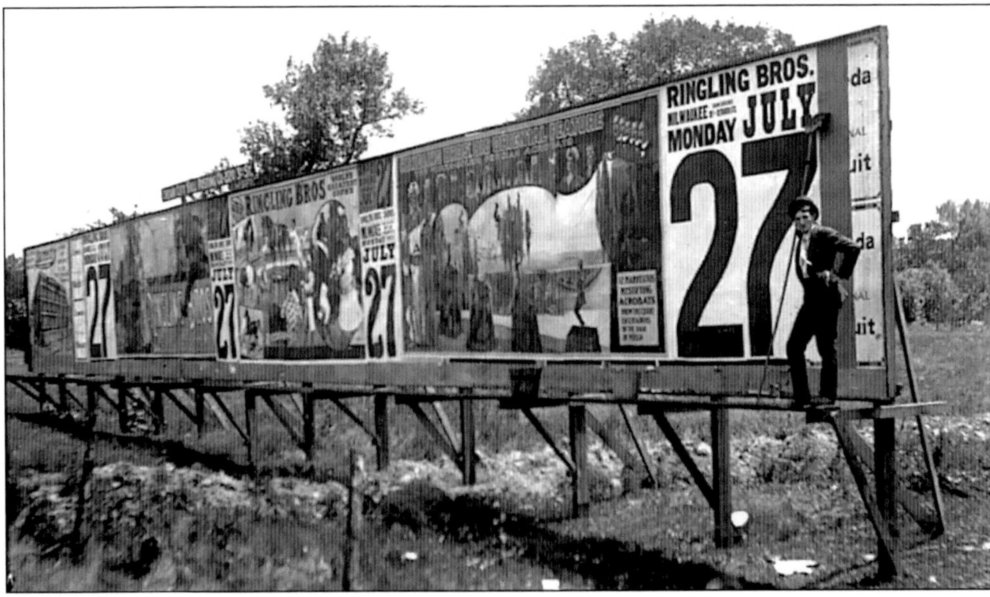

The circus is coming to town! Who could resist the allure of this billboard advertising? Ringling Bros. proudly boasts their "World's Greatest Show." See the "Oriental Feature" with 12 marvelous, mystifying acrobats! Children of all ages from Wauwatosa and beyond are invited to attend the Monday, July 27, performance in Milwaukee, only a streetcar ride away. The Cream City Bill Posting Co. in Milwaukee put up the signs (*c.* 1900). Later known as the Cream City Outdoor Advertising Co., it operated on Wisconsin Avenue just west of the Wisconsin Avenue Viaduct. (WHS Photo LGP 703.)

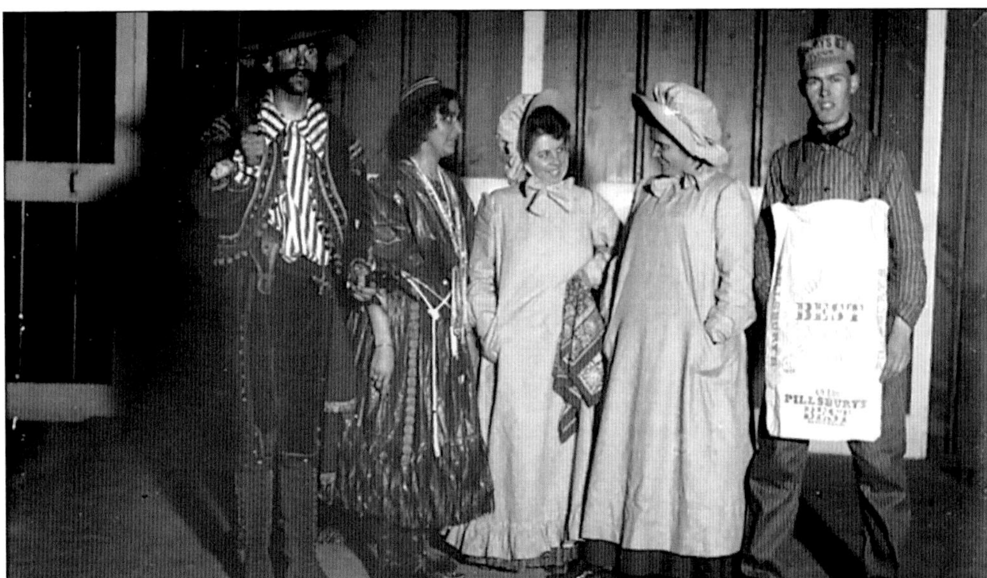

A costume party at the Watsons' caused these five friends to dress up for Halloween on October 28, 1904. They are identified as, left to right, Walter Smith, Mrs. Chamberlin, Belle Farrio, Janet Smith, and Ernest Lefeber (appropriately in a flour sack probably from the Lefeber Bros. store). (WHS Photo LGP 423.)

Abe Smith Austin Jr. (*right*, c. 1896) certainly had to be one of the cutest three-year olds in town posing in his sailor outfit, holding two impatient puppies. Abe's father, a prominent Milwaukee businessman, and his wife, Lottie, had four other children, James, Marion, Charles, and Lottie. Abe Austin Sr. purchased the Dr. Fisk H. Day home at 8000 Milwaukee Avenue in 1895. In their later years the parents moved out to live with their children, and the house stood vacant for a time before Abe Jr. returned to live there until his death in 1979. He added an enclosed porch to serve as his law office. Below is another photo from an Austin family album. Abe, now about nine years old, stands with a paddle to maneuver a rowboat, as a youngster pushes it out from the banks of the Menomonee River in Wauwatosa. Although unidentified, the other children could be Abe's siblings. (WHS Photos 734–1 & 734–2.)

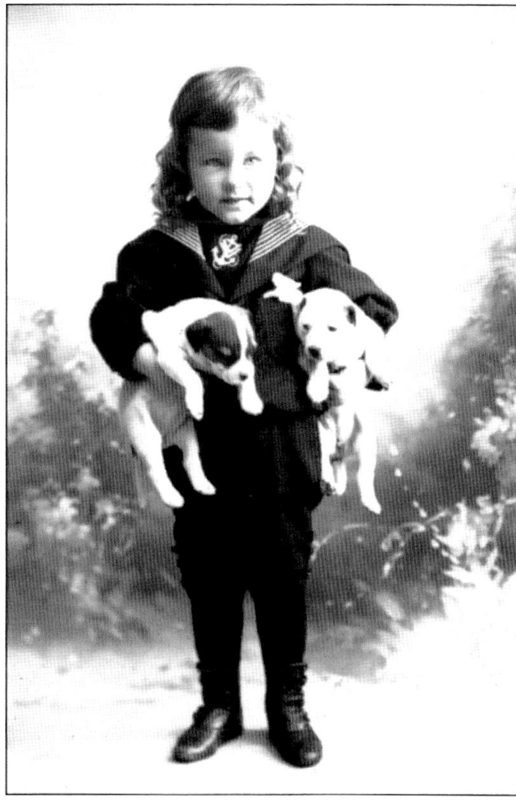

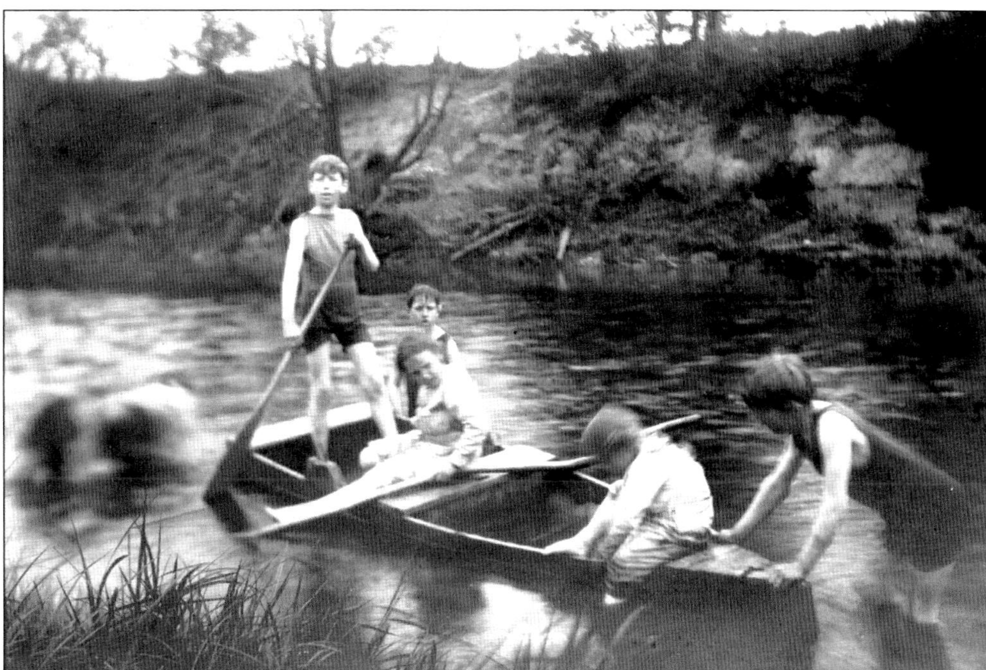

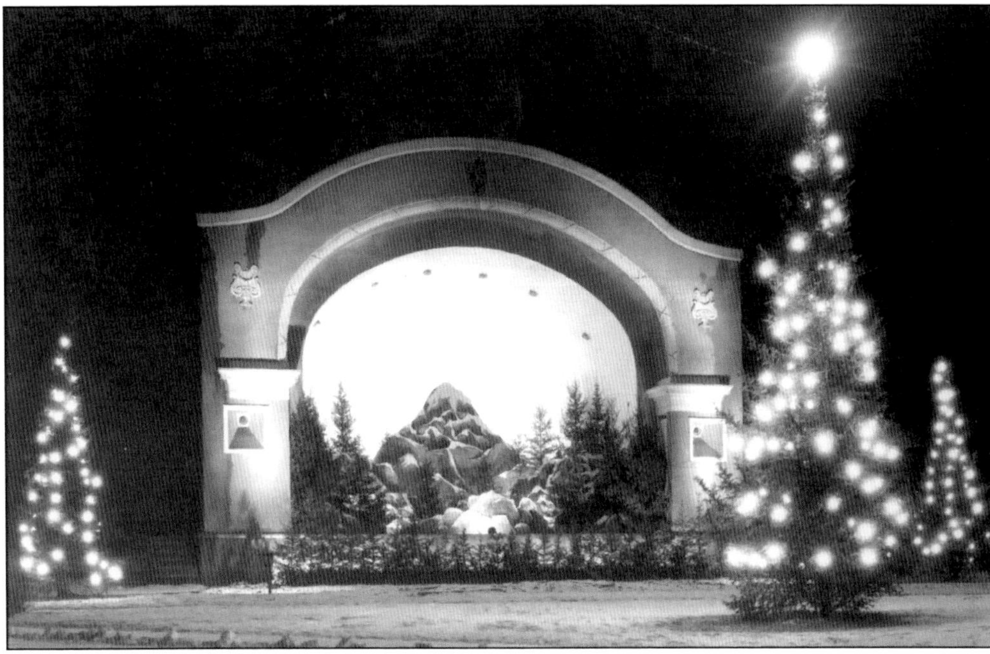

The city band shell decorated for Christmas 1929 won first prize among communities that entered a contest sponsored by the *Milwaukee Sentinel* and the Electrical League of Milwaukee. Built in 1927, the band shell became a center for civic and musical events. It was located in Root Common, the triangle formed by Wauwatosa and Harwood Avenues. The Common land, originally thought to have been donated by Oliver P. Root, was actually a generous gift of Charles Hart. (WHS Photo 755.)

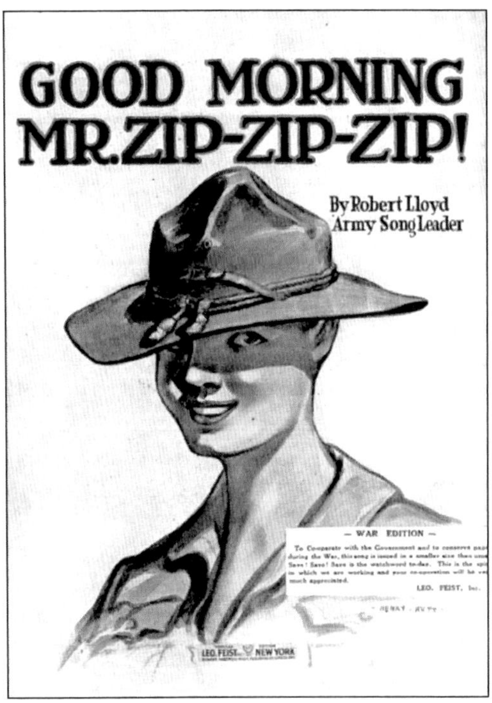

"Good Morning, Mr. Zip–Zip–Zip!" is a novelty tune dating back to World War I. This photo is of the cover of the original sheet music. The tune's name is also the title of a 2003 book written by *Time* magazine film critic and Wauwatosa native Richard Schickel. The book recounts Schickel's memories of growing up in Wauwatosa during the 1940s. (WHS Music Collection.)

Mrs. Catherine Hoyt, a church and civic leader, was the wife of Thomas Demerit Hoyt and mother of Wauwatosa's first mayor. She died in 1911. Her son, Emerson D. Hoyt, served as mayor from 1897 to 1904. He was president of the First National Bank of Wauwatosa (1907–1921). What became Hoyt Park (*below*) had its origins in 1926 as a county facility. In 1928, the City of Wauwatosa bought it from the county, purchased more land, and named the entire 34 acres Emerson D. Hoyt Park. The old park had a swimming hole in the river, and a city pool after 1931. Following the park's transfer back to the county in 1936, the Civilian Conservation Corps built this concrete pool, a giant for its time. The pool opened in 1939 and closed in 2003. The Corps also constructed the park's pedestrian suspension bridge and the automobile bridge at Swan Boulevard. (WHS Photo 746 and Postcard 667.)

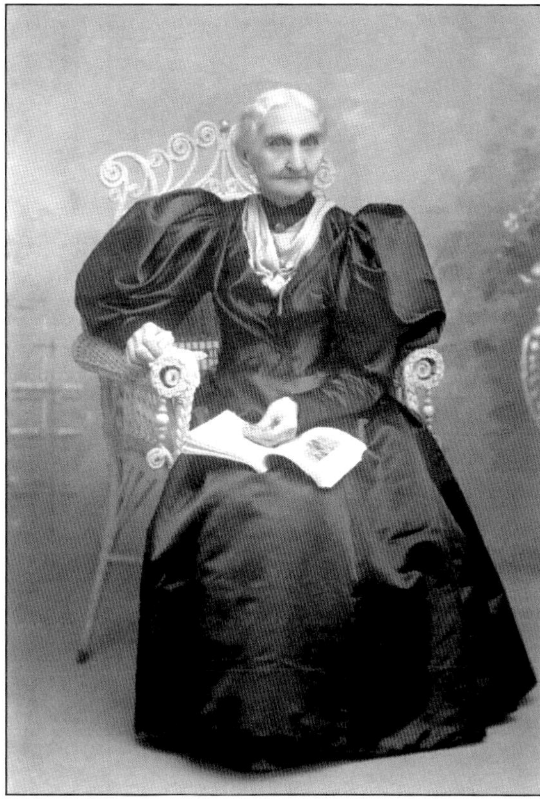

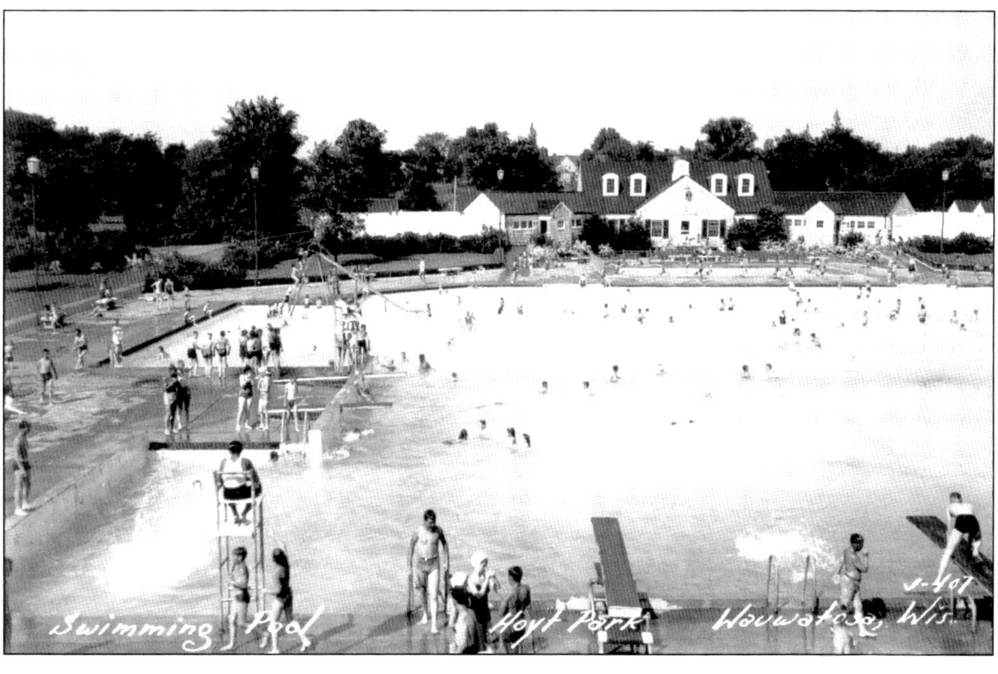

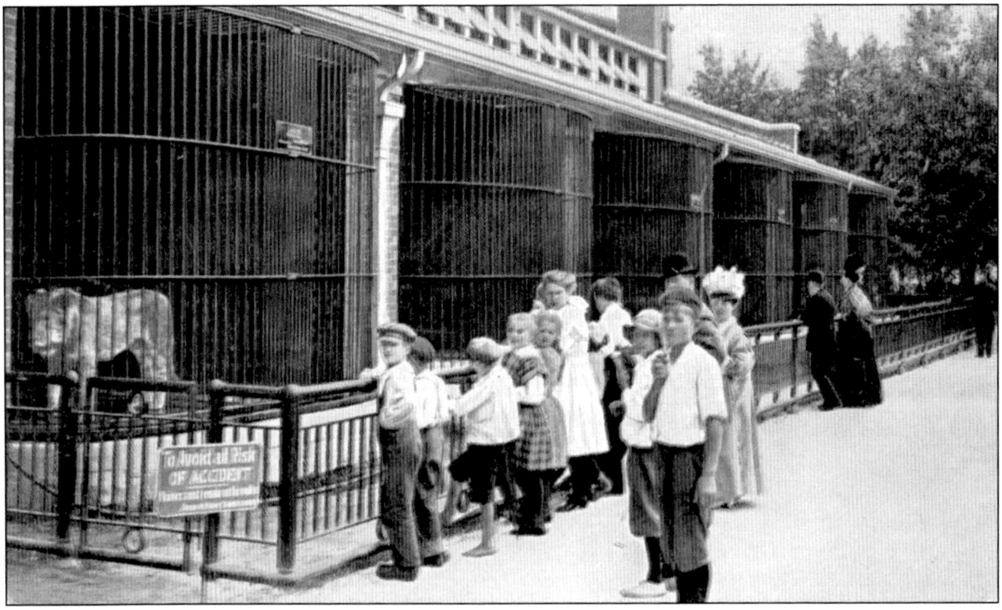

Children look at the animals in the Washington Park Zoo, initially located in the Town of Wauwatosa, about 1910. Frederick Law Olmsted, of Central Park fame, designed Washington Park and Milwaukee's Lake and Riverside Parks. In 1892 the zoo opened with just a few eagles, bears, and deer. About 1907 non-North American species, beginning with monkeys, began to appear. Cramped for space, the zoo relocated to a new site on Bluemound Road, and by 1963 the Washington Park Zoo closed. (Courtesy of Judith A. Simonsen.)

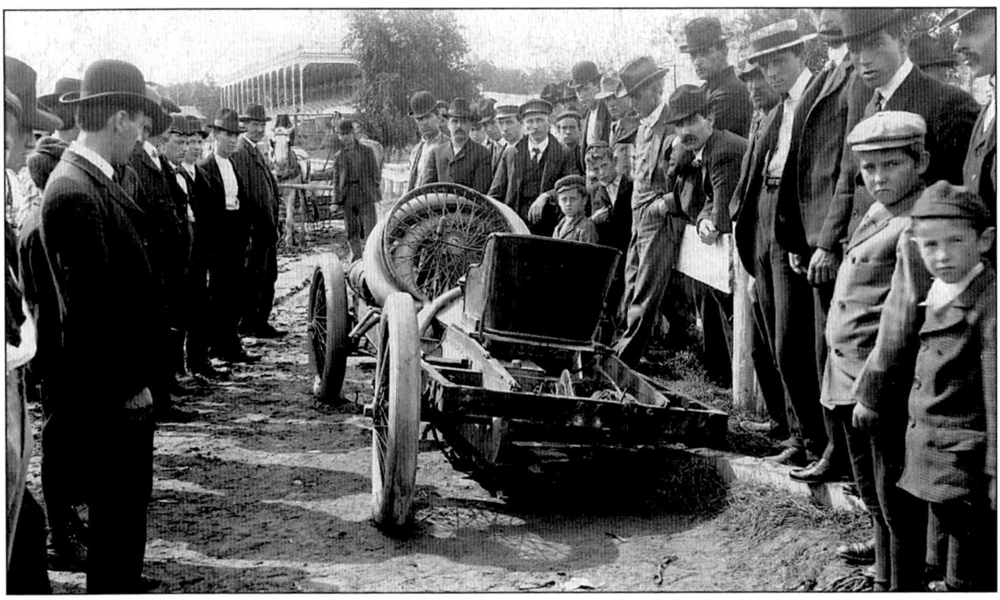

The automobile and its popular spectator sport of auto racing had early beginnings. Crowds gather to look at the racing car in which driver John Day was killed during an accident on the racetrack at the Wisconsin State Fair Park in 1903. The grandstands are in the background. In 1892 the state had decided on the permanent site of the fair grounds—originally located in the Town of Wauwatosa, today it is in the City of West Allis. (WHS Photo 524.)

Nine

A CITY OF HOMES

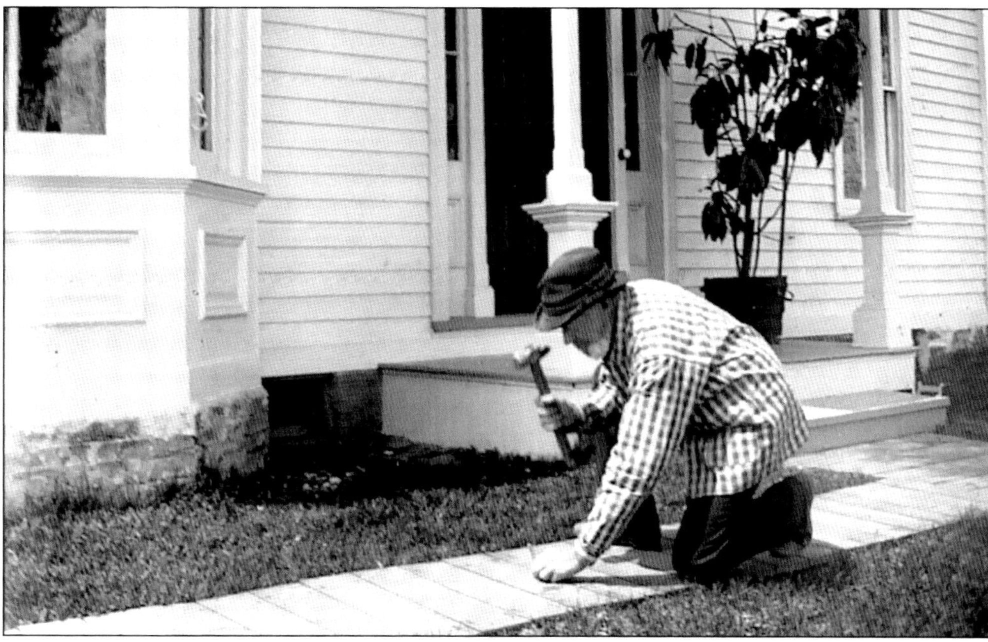

Like any homeowner at the turn of the nineteenth century, Joseph Lefeber had to make repairs to his wooden sidewalk, the precursor of concrete walks. His home once stood at 7439 Harwood Avenue. The earliest pioneers found shelter in log homes. As cut lumber became available, houses reflected the architecture of the eastern United States. Wauwatosa's oldest surviving residence is the Lowell Damon House Museum, built from 1844 to 1846. Development in the 1850s created Church Street, the community's first residential street. In addition to the railroad, two vital links between Milwaukee and Wauwatosa spurred home building in the decades before the Depression: the streetcar of the 1890s and the Grand Avenue Viaduct (Wisconsin Avenue) completed in 1911, which served increasing automobile traffic. Wauwatosa became a bedroom suburb of Milwaukee. Pride of ownership took firm root. A rich and varied housing stock from the nineteenth and twentieth centuries survives, along with strong neighborhood and preservation organizations. (WHS Photo LGP 510–1.)

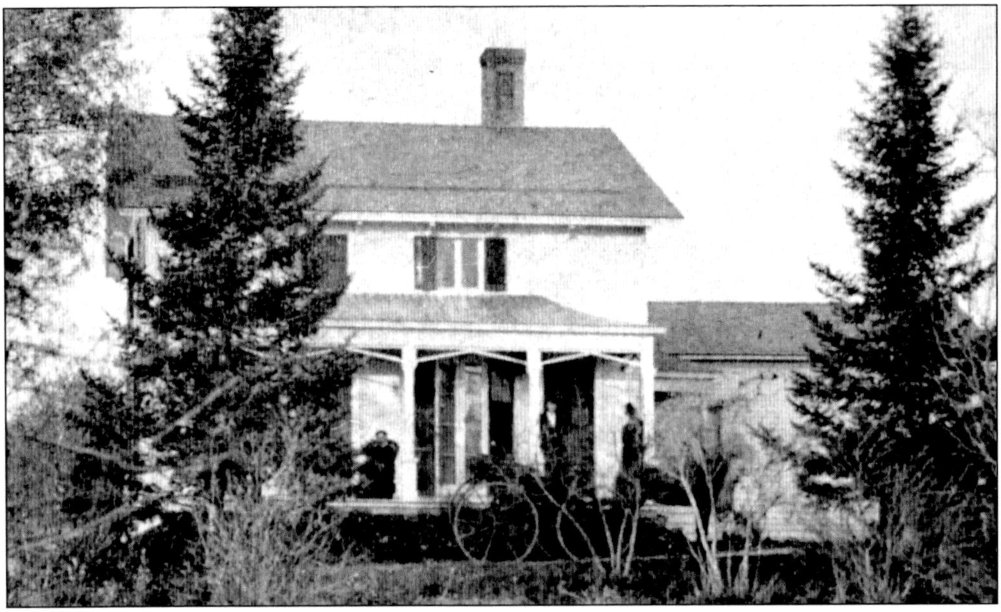

In 1856, Reverend Mr. Luther Clapp built this house near Hillcrest Drive to replace one destroyed by fire. It faced south and had French doors opening to the veranda. The carriage in front approached from Wauwatosa Avenue to the left. Later remodeling created a front door to that principal street, as well as a large addition on the east side. Scheduled for demolition, it was moved to 12323 Watertown Plank Road in 1976 and became the first city structure to receive official landmark status. (WHS Photo 520.)

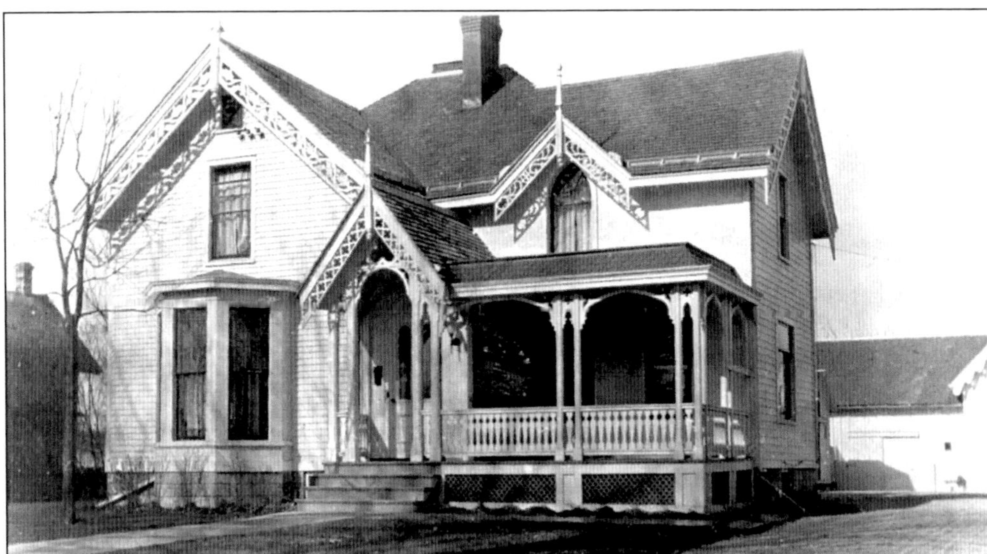

The Thomas Benjamin Hart house at 1609 Church Street is associated with the city's founding family. Charles Hart owned the land and his brother Thomas lived there from 1874 to 1885. An excellent example of Gothic Revival architecture, it displays nine pairs of bargeboards in six distinctive patterns on the house and barn. This postcard photo is from the early twentieth century. The house is believed to have been built about 1845. It has received multiple landmark designations. (Courtesy of Roy and Jo Cole.)

Dr. Fisk Holbrook Day, a local physician who arrived here in 1854, built three homes in Wauwatosa. The first, a frame dwelling called "The Bird's Nest," was for his retired parents (see page 15). The second, "Evergreen," (right) stood on what is now the Congregational Church parking lot. Razed in 1967, it was an outstanding illustration of Gothic Revival architecture, constructed of Milwaukee cream brick, with arched windows, scroll-cut bargeboards, and decorative trim. It was originally next to the Hart house (opposite page). (Photo by and courtesy of H. Russell Zimmermann.)

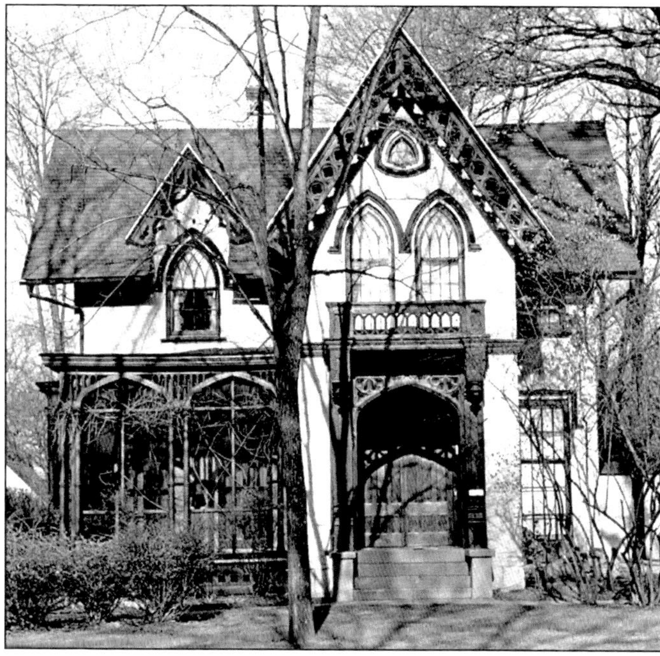

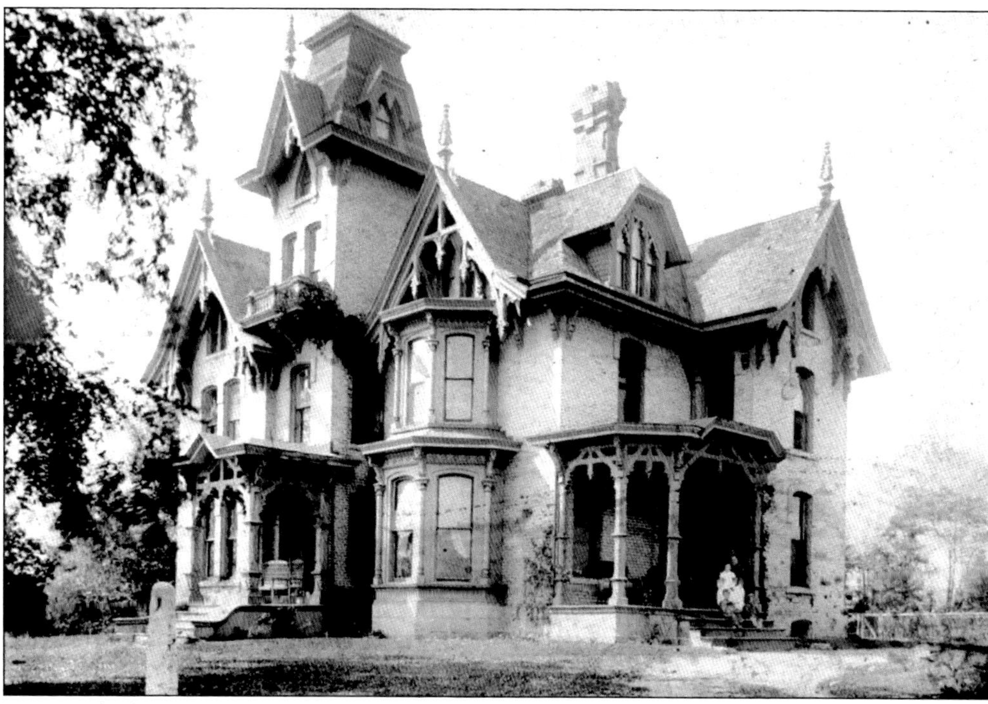

Dr. Day built "Sunnyhill" about 1874 at 8000 Milwaukee Avenue. Its extraordinary facade showcased Victorian Gothic, Italianate, and French Second Empire styles. Widower Day sold the home to Abe Austin Sr. in 1895 and Austin's family occupied it for over 80 years. In addition to other designations, it is a National Historic Landmark, in recognition of Day's avocational interests in archeology, botany, astronomy, and particularly geology. He gathered a nationally recognized fossil collection that was housed in his residence. (WHS Photo 734.)

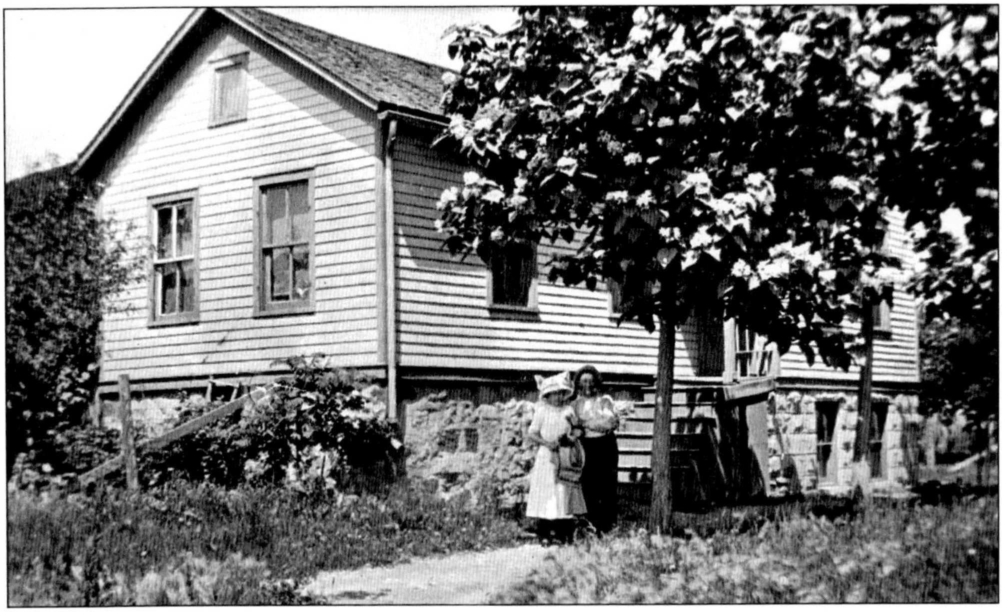

Many early dwellings, such as this house at 6622 Vista Avenue, were simple, small frame cottages with little or no architectural detailing. Its construction history is unknown, but the two types of foundations suggest that the left side, with random fieldstone, came first, and the right side, with cut limestone, was added to what would have been a very small cabin. The photo identifies the couple as "Mr. and Mrs. Charles Larsen," at the Vista address. Their clothing suggests this photo dates back to approximately 1910. (WHS Photo 521.)

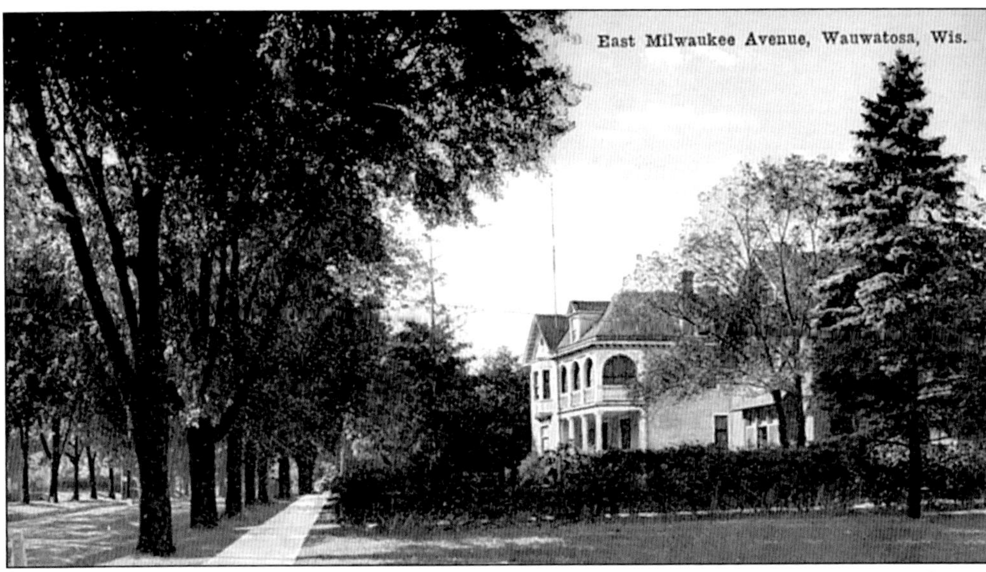

Early twentieth century postcard manufacturers helped to promote Wauwatosa as a "City of Homes" by depicting community assets, such as this fine residential street sheltered by towering elms. A major early thoroughfare, the Milwaukee and Wauwatosa Plank Road was known as East Milwaukee Street by the turn of the century and emanated a sense of quiet suburban living. The imposing residence at 7328, on the corner of Seventy-fourth Street, is essentially unchanged today. Its recessed entry and double porch remain intact. (WHS Postcard 653.)

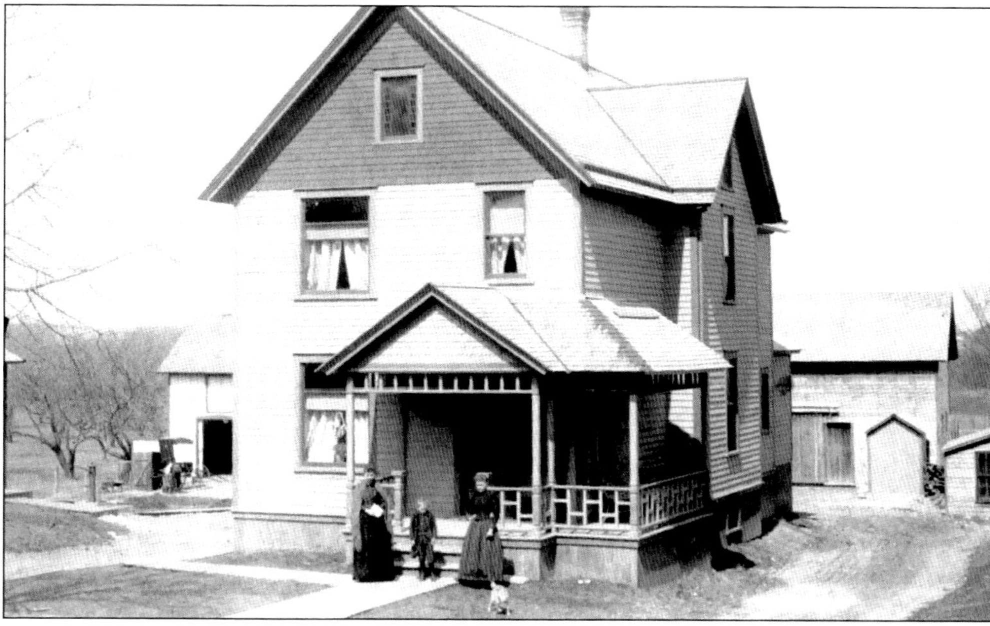

These two Queen Anne houses (*c.* 1890s) exhibit similarities in form and decoration, particularly the fretwork railings. Perhaps they shared a common builder, although stock millwork was readily available for any contractor. Both houses use shingles and decorative glass windows and display the ubiquitous Victorian lace curtains. Typically, both have carriage barns. The simpler home (*above*) was the residence of Morton and Annie Casperson, confirmed as Wauwatosa residents. However, the exact location of their house is not known; it may have stood on Dewey Avenue. Below is the Ferdinand Bark home, still standing at 1612 Church Street. The Methodist Church steeple is on the right. More sophisticated in design, it has a greater variety of surface materials and decoration, particularly the cutaway bay windows. A few plantings dress up the lawn. Each family wore their Sunday best and included their pets for the camera's eye. (WHS Photo 750 and 462.)

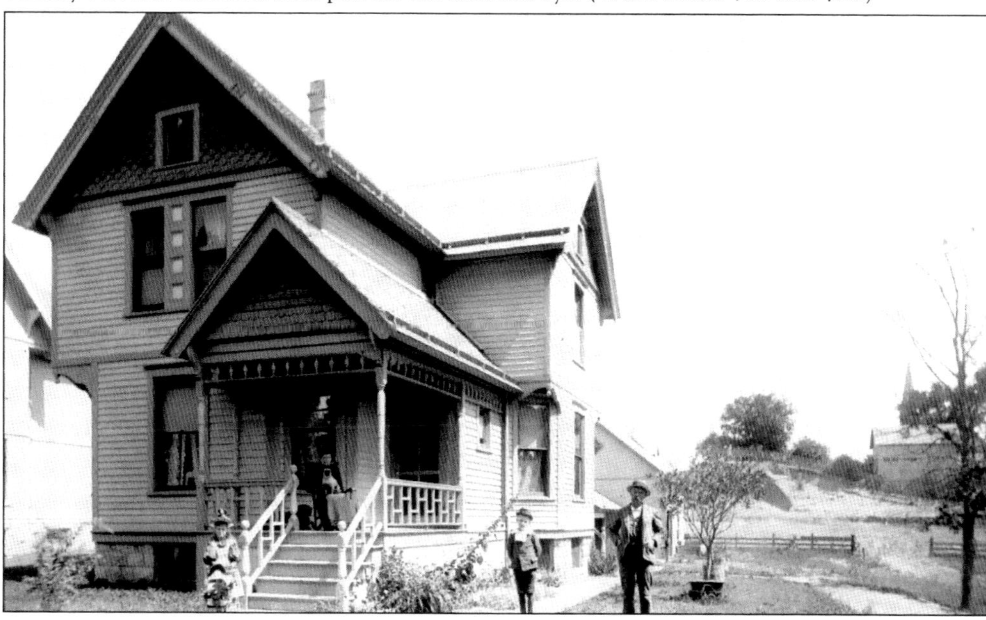

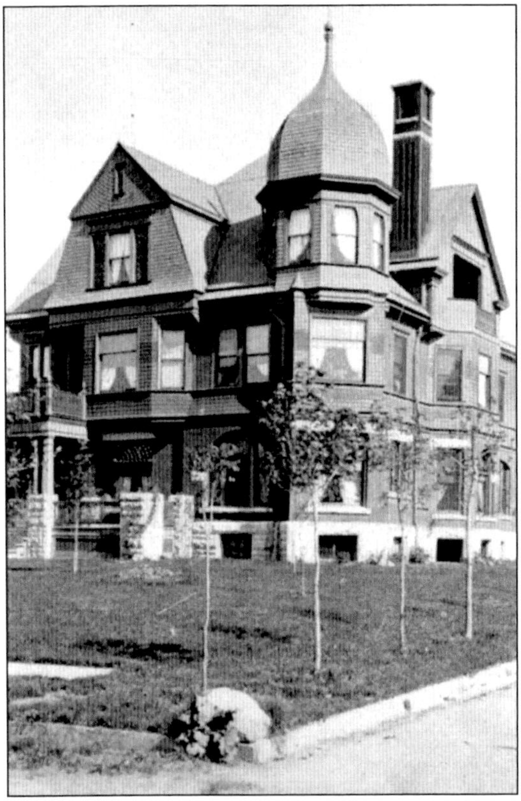

Norman Kneeland came to Wisconsin from New York State following the Civil War. He purchased farmland in the Town of Wauwatosa, and there he and his wife, Carrie, raised seven children. He sold his land to Milwaukee County (it became part of Washington Park), moved to Wauwatosa and built this elegant Queen Anne resident at 7406 Hillcrest Drive in 1890. Kneeland served as an alderman and president of the common council. The third-floor ballroom witnessed many social events. The original parcel of land remains intact, except for the house built for daughter Ella in 1893, to the west on Hillcrest. Norman died in 1900 and Carrie in 1911. This rare interior photograph of the parlor in the Kneeland home provides a glimpse of the interior decoration. Regrettably, the photo is undated and none of the people in the picture have been identified. The image has descended through the Godfrey family—Sarah Kneeland married William A. Godfrey in 1892. (WHS Photo 343 and Courtesy of William N. Godfrey.)

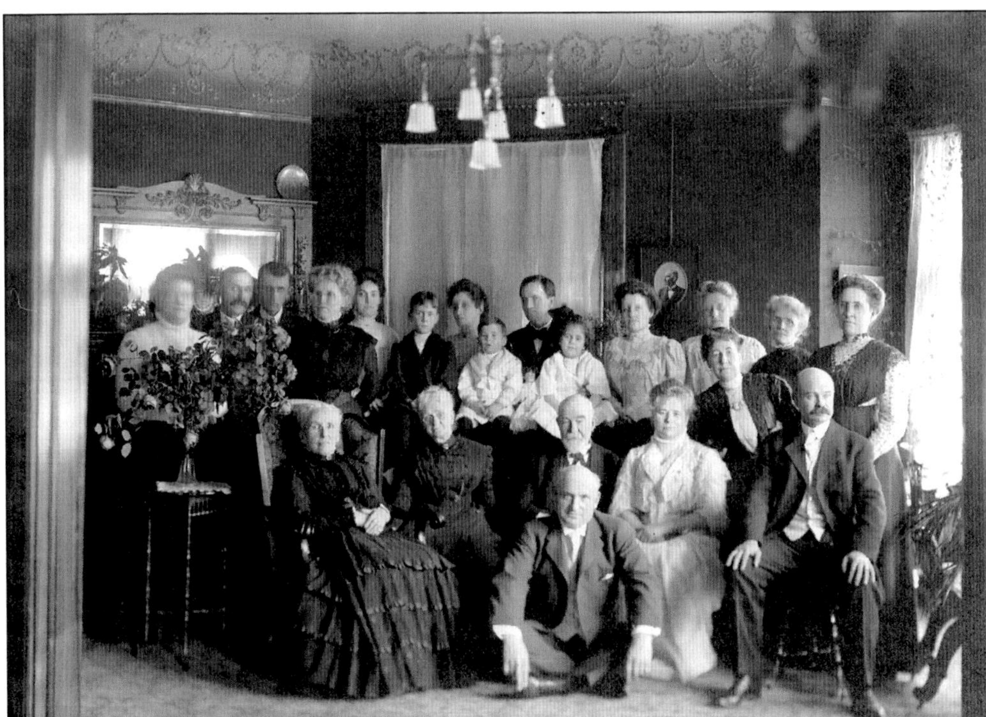

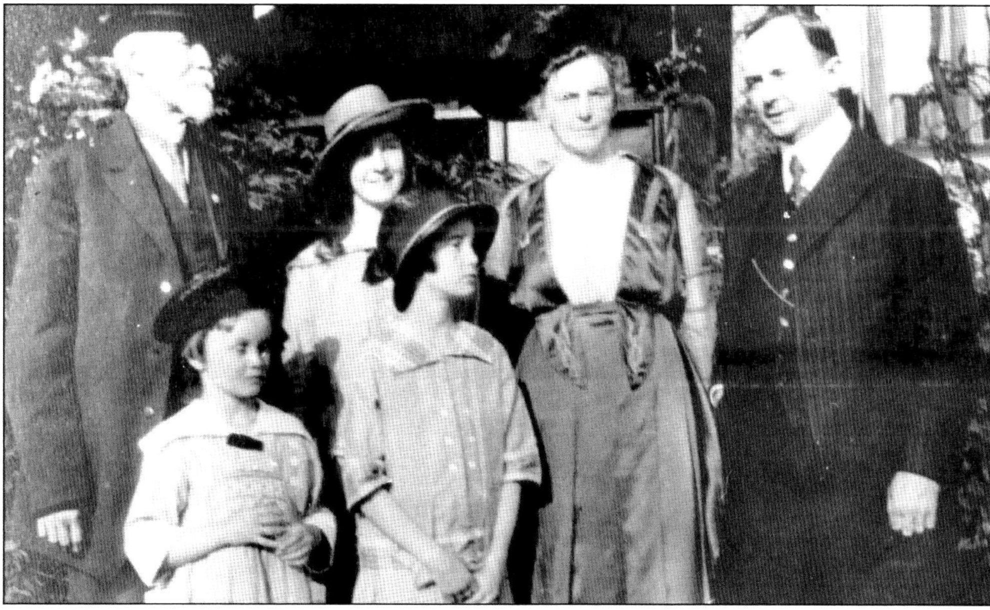

Emery L. Walker, graduate of Cornell University and vice-president of the Kieckhefer Box Company, purchased the Kneeland house in 1917. Pictured with him in this 1920 photo are, left to right, his father Jesse Marion Walker; his daughters Virginia Lou, Elizabeth, and Katharine; and his wife, Mabelle. In 1945, Maybelle died and Emery remarried in 1949. Following his death in 1967, Emery's widow, Constance, lived in the home until her death in 1985. The Wauwatosa Historical Society bought the residence from her estate in 1987 after a widely supported fund drive. (WHS Photo 752.)

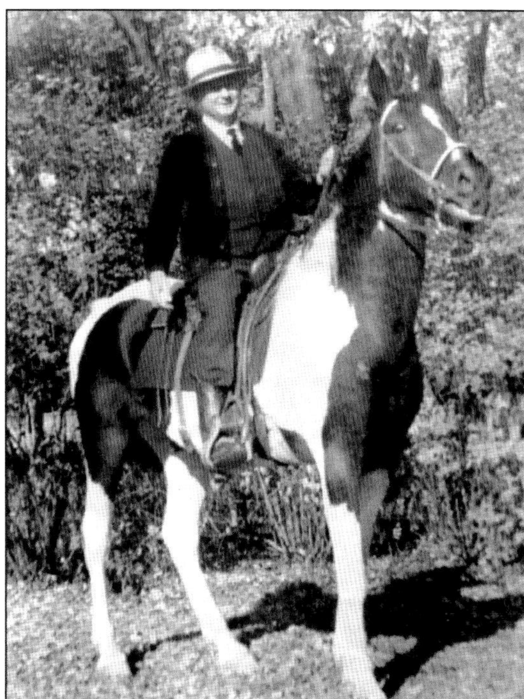

Emery Walker loved horses and maintained five over the years. Here he is on his favorite, Beau Jack, a black and white piebald gelding. Walker's modernization of the carriage barn retained the horse stalls and the large and small paddocks to the west and north. In addition to using the riding path that circled the northern section of the grounds, Walker and neighborhood children and friends rode the horses around the streets of Wauwatosa. By 1948, he retired his animals to pasture. (WHS Photo 345.)

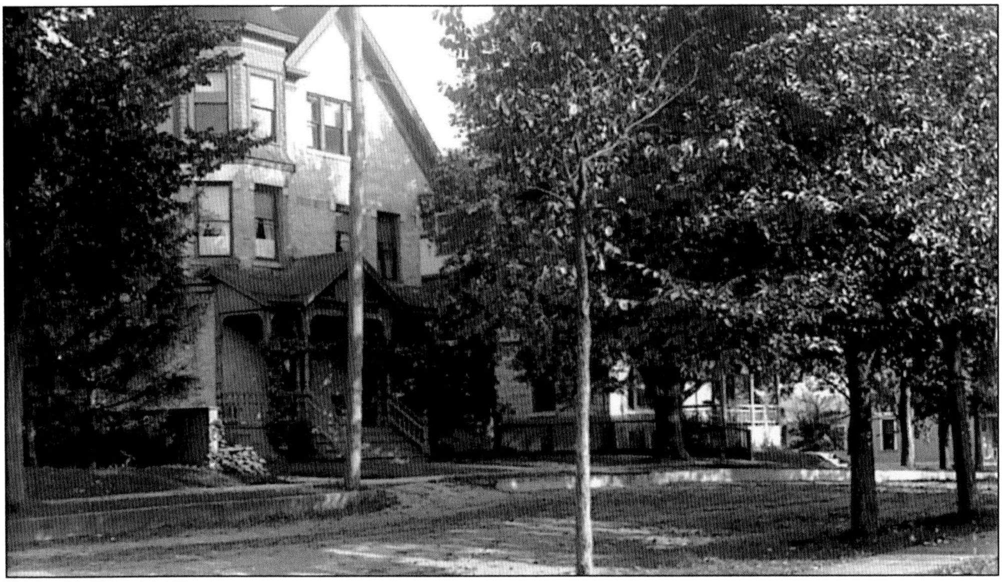

Platted in 1884, the Douglas Heights development was spearheaded by noted Milwaukee architect James Douglas. This 1904 view looks southeast down Kavanaugh Place, a street created in the subdivision, to the corner of Chestnut. The Queen Anne residence of Mr. and Mrs. Stephen Seaman, constructed of brick and stone rather than the usual wood, is on the east side. The building serves today as the administration building for the Carmelite Sisters and the Carmelite Boy's Home, established in 1917. (WHS Photo LGP 421.)

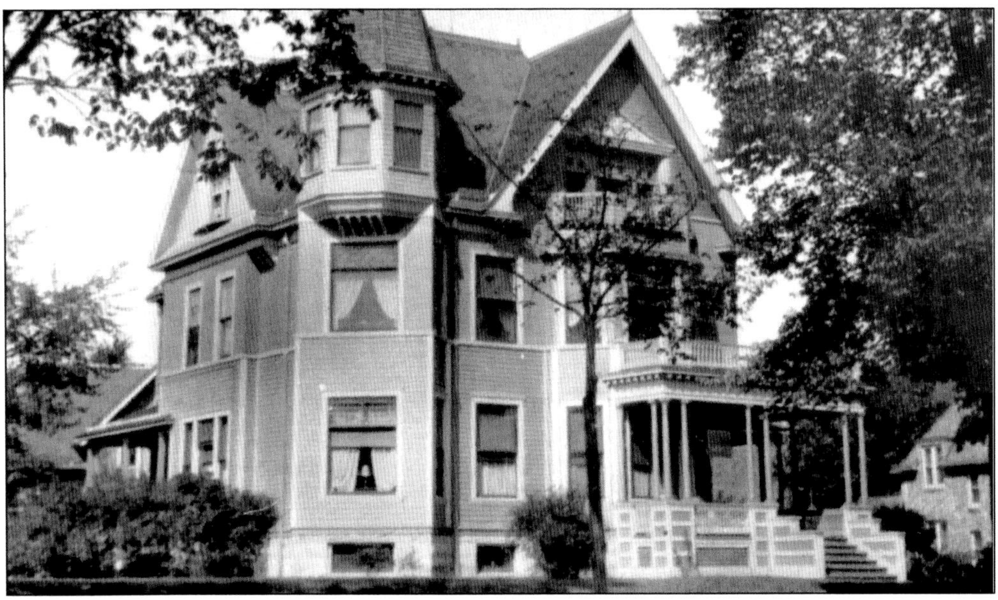

In 1889, Edwin Rice Godfrey Sr. established a family dynasty in the grocery business in Milwaukee that continued for nearly 100 years until the family sold the firm. He married Susan A. Rogers in 1863 and the family lived in Milwaukee until 1884, when Godfrey built a grand Queen Anne house (no longer extant) at 7364 Harwood Avenue. A porte cochere on the right side provided protected carriage loading. The Victorian affinity for contrasting paint colors is visible. (WHS Photo 751.)

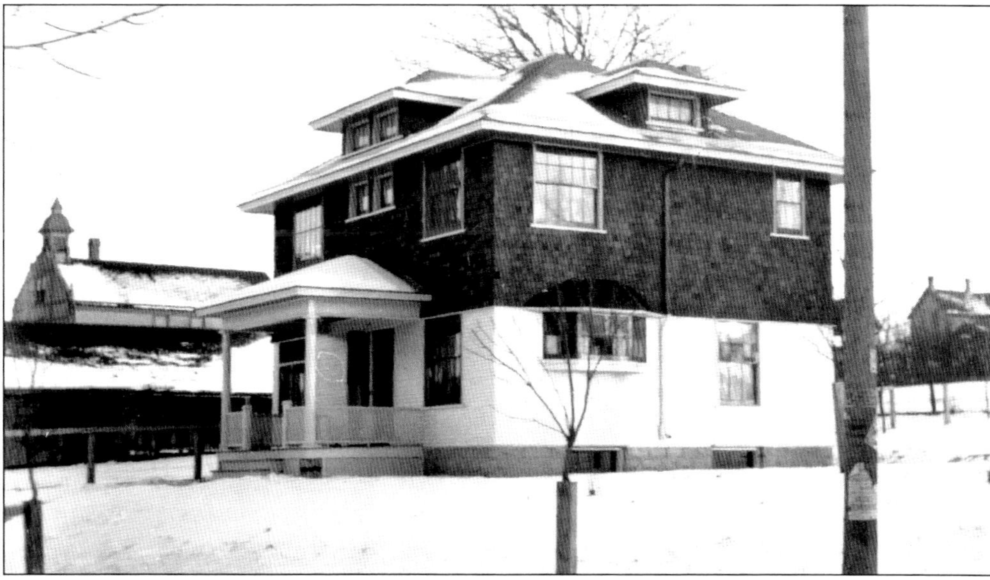

The American Foursquare house found favor in the early twentieth century, reflecting a reaction against elaborate Victorian design. Restrained Colonial Revival or Craftsman details might be added. This example at 7835 Harwood Avenue has a symmetrical facade, hip roof, and dormers, and is clad in a popular combination of clapboards and shingles. This image, dated December 1904, shows the completed home of Miss Carrie G. Warren. The building at left, with the cupola, is the school of St. John's Evangelical Lutheran Church. (WHS Photo LGP 431.)

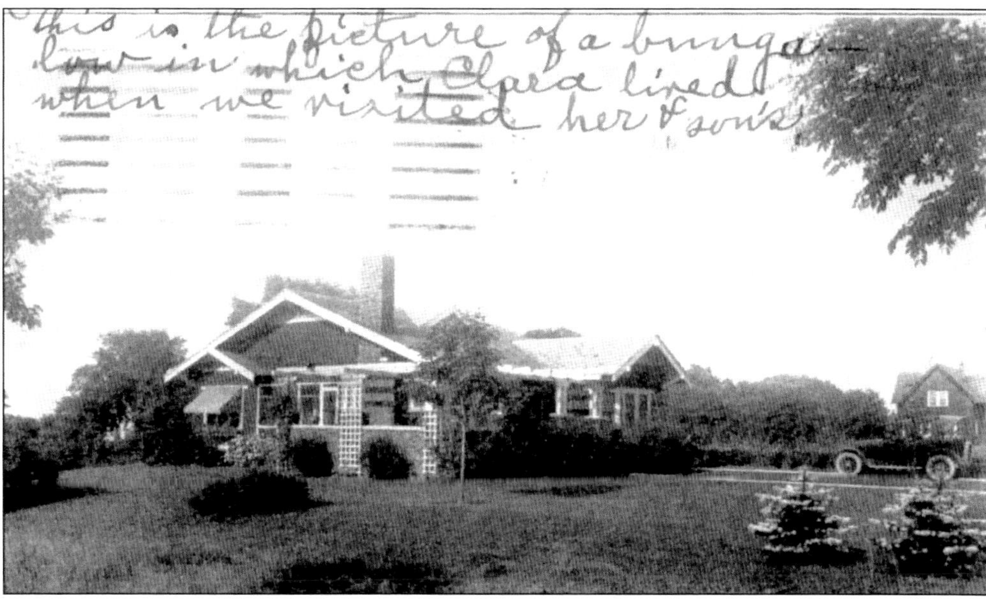

A postcard from 1923 shows a Craftsman home at 7915 Warren Avenue where "Clara lived." This very up-to-date style had its beginnings in California and was promoted in national magazines, particularly the *Craftsman*, between 1901 and 1916. The designs were artfully adapted to smaller homes and countless one-and-a-half-story bungalows, frequently with clipped gables, were constructed in Milwaukee and its suburbs. The car in the driveway proclaims the birth of suburbia. (WHS Postcard 651.)

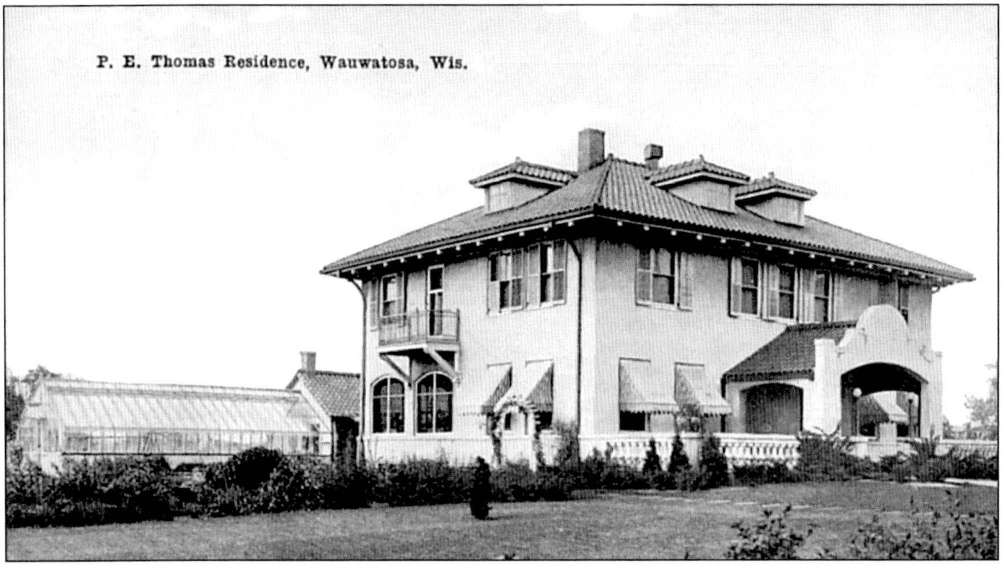

The Paul E. Thomas residence at 1945 Wauwatosa Avenue was built about 1918. Thomas was secretary-treasurer of the Kempsmith Manufacturing Co. in West Allis. A greenhouse and sunken gardens beautified the spacious corner grounds. The low-pitched roof with overhanging eaves, red barrel tile, and rectangular shape are characteristics of this Mediterranean Revival style. Variations are seen throughout Wauwatosa, often clad in Lannon stone or brown brick, rather than the stucco used here. An impressive entry greeted visitors. (WHS Postcard 650.)

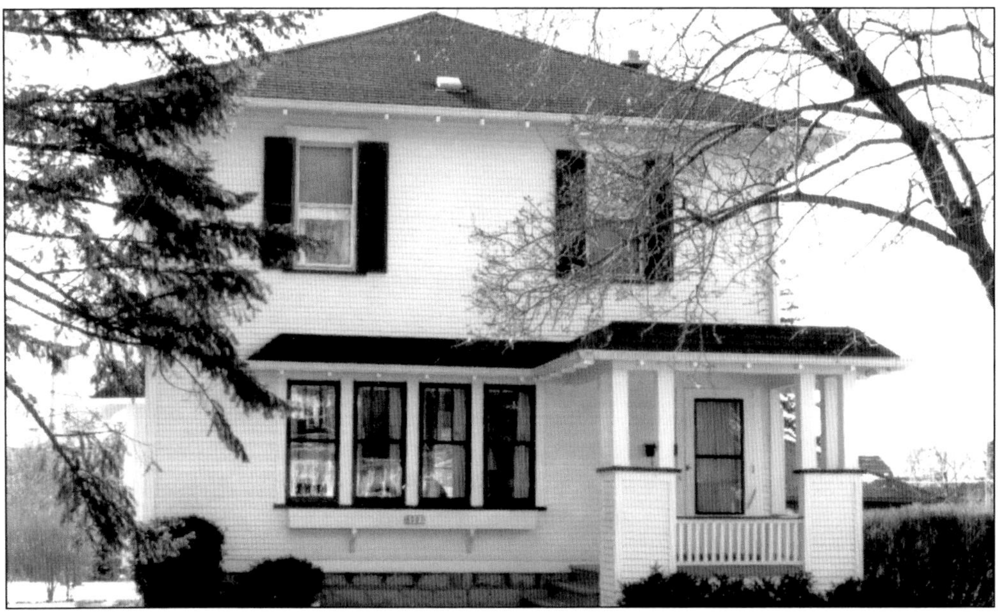

Sears, Roebuck and Company sold mail-order homes from 1908 to 1940, shipping materials by rail. The Louis Otto Stauff family built two of them on Stickney Avenue. The first, shown here and built at 8001 in 1917, is a modified Sears design. The second, which became the family homestead, was at 7933, a two-story frame colonial assembled in 1923. Louis rented 8001 to the family of his sister, Eva Stauff Schaeve, until she and her husband, Harry, built 8011, a one-story Sears stucco bungalow, in 1923. (Courtesy of Carol M. Schaeve.)

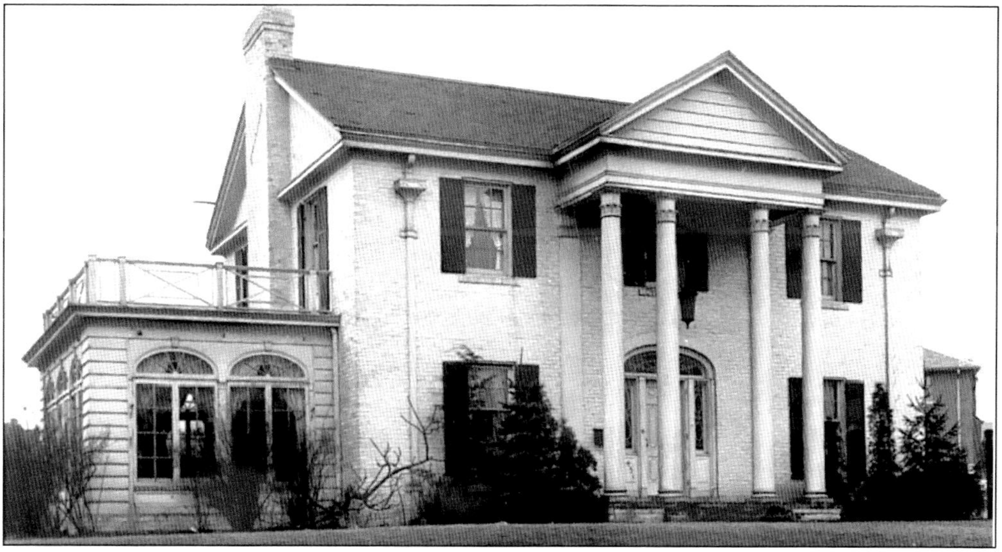

The Washington Highlands is a showcase for outstanding architect-designed residences of the 1920s and 1930s. This Colonial Revival (*above*, c. 1930s) stands at 2031 Martha Washington Drive. The unique design and topography of the Washington Highlands subdivision is most visible in an aerial view (*below*). It is bounded (clockwise) by Sixty-eighth, Lloyd, and Sixtieth Streets, and E. Milwaukee Avenue. The land was formerly part of the Pabst Brewery farm. In 1916, German city planner Werner Hegemann and landscape architect Elbert Peets developed a master plan for residential development, incorporating ideas of the English Garden City movement. The design, with curving streets and private parks, preserved the natural rolling landscape and meandering creek. A variety of plots, for small and large single-family homes and for two- and four-family flats on the perimeter, assured a mix of homeowners. The Washington Homes Association was established in 1918. Over 85 percent of the subdivision had been built by the start of World War II. (Courtesy of Milwaukee County Historical Society and photo by Clair J. Wilson, WHS Photo 749.)

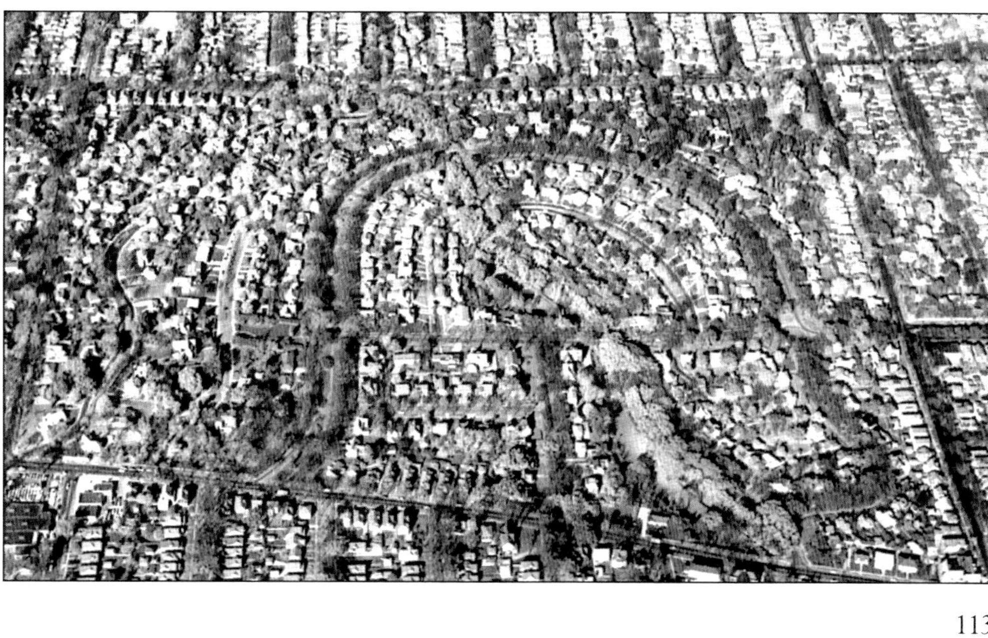

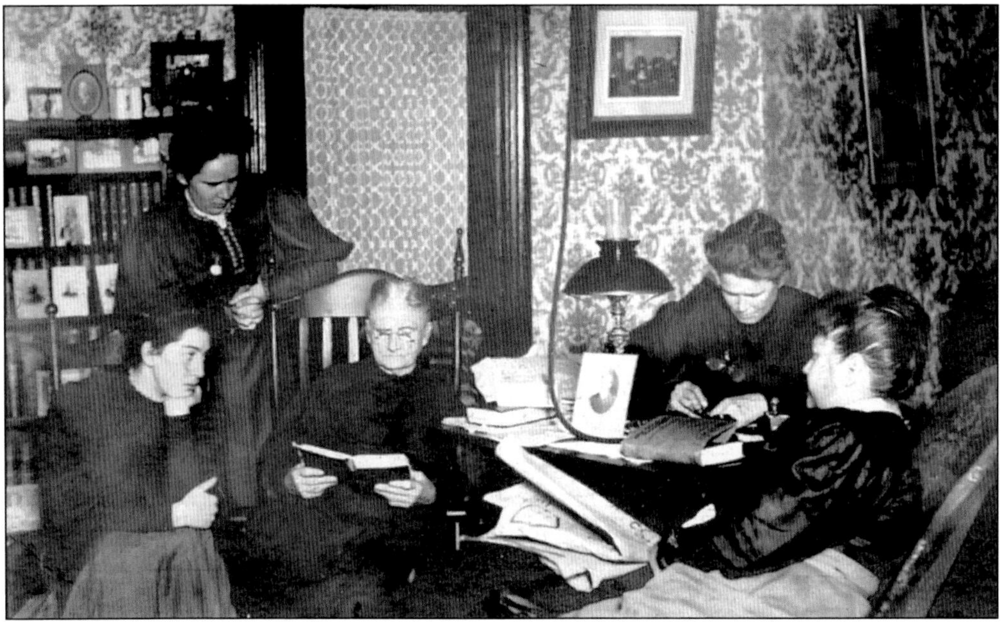

This photo of the Cairncross sitting room shows Jeanette Smith and her daughters, from left, Catherine Smith Blodgett, Janet Smith, Helen Smith Cairncross, and Jennie Smith Breese. The gas lamp is connected by a rubber tube to a gasolier mounted on the ceiling, as an effective way to create additional light from a stationary source. (WHS Mss. 133.)

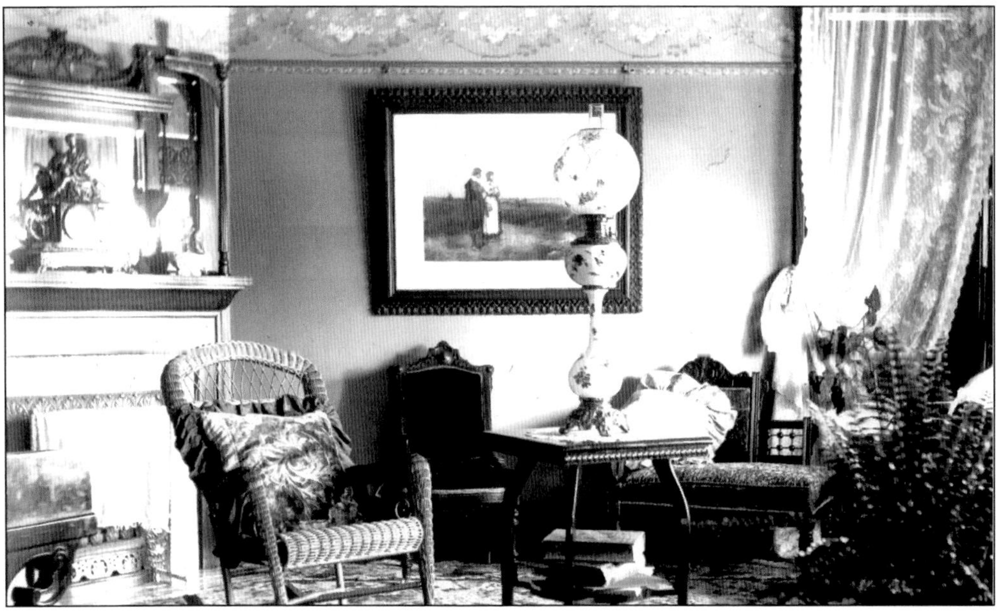

This is the parlor in the Queen Anne home of George and Sarah Wells, at 1218 Glenview Avenue, built in the 1890s. Colorful patterned wall-to-wall carpeting and two-part wall treatments were very fashionable, as were lace curtains. The fireplace and the ormolu figural clock are a focal point of the room. The fluid lamp on the center table indicates the lack of electricity. A small organ, partially seen at left, provided entertainment for family and friends. Wicker furnishings were ubiquitous in Victorian homes. (Courtesy of George Wells.)

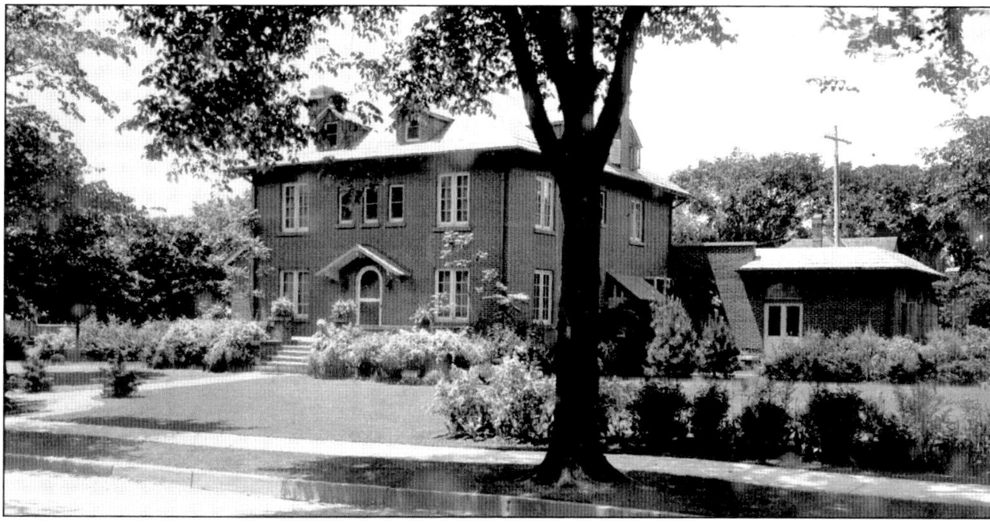

Edward J. Kearney, a founder of the Kearney and Trecker Corporation in 1898, built his home (*above*) in 1906 at 1839 North Seventy-fourth Street. In 1920, he became president of the American Exchange Bank and undertook a major remodeling of his residence that resulted in a much larger home in the Colonial Revival style. Additions included a glass-enclosed, in-ground swimming pool, measuring 55 feet by 23 feet (*below*). Lush plantings, inlaid tile, and decorative railings, crafted by master Milwaukee ironworker Cyril Colnik, enhanced this elegant space. In 1920, the household included Edward and his wife, Ella, their daughters Katherine and Alice, and a live-in servant, Della. Landscaping was equally important to the family. Kearney purchased adjacent properties, and a Victorian home on the corner of Hillcrest Drive and Seventy-fourth Street was moved to 1827 North Seventy-third Street to provide space to enhance his grounds. To the south of the house was a beautiful rose garden. (WHS Photo 801–1 and 801–2.)

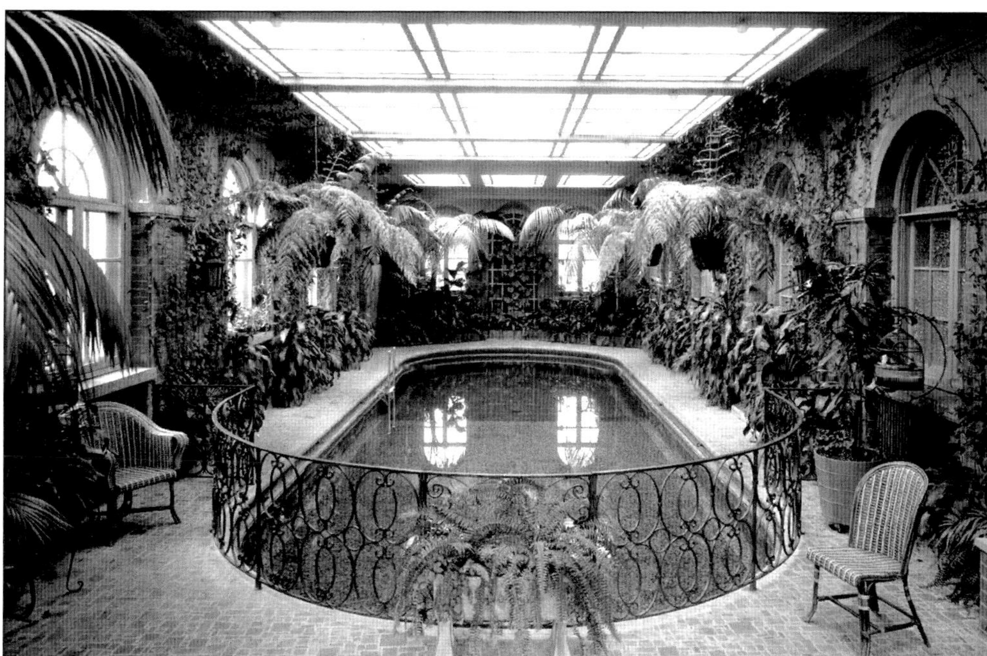

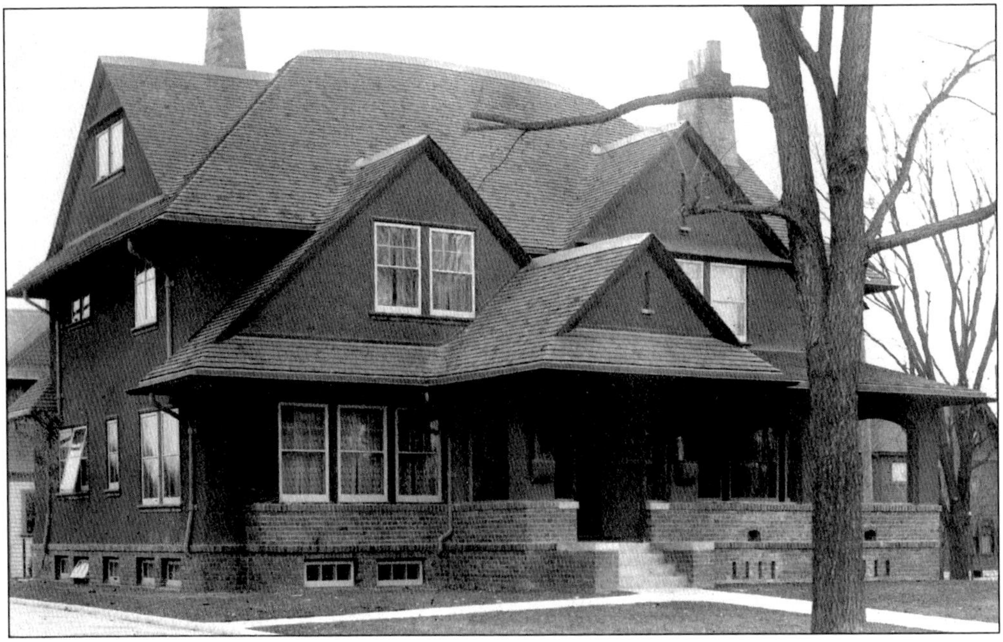

The Edgar True Craftsman home (*above*) at 7429 Hillcrest Drive exemplifies American architecture influenced by Frank Lloyd Wright's Prairie style and the Arts and Crafts movement. Designed by Milwaukee architect Frank L. Bader in 1910, it has a hip roof with intersecting gables and broad eaves. Clad in stucco, the walls slope outward slightly to meet the brick foundation that provides horizontal grounding and triangular-braced supports ornament the entry. The rain gutters empty into the basement to connect with underground sewer lines. The dining room (*below*) epitomizes the use of wood in Craftsman interiors, and the richness of the red douglas fir is found throughout the house. French doors open onto a double foyer, at right. The Tiffany-style art glass electric chandelier echoes the circular table and elaborate cloth beneath. The floral frieze was hand-painted. The home's original interior is intact today. (Courtesy of Gary Hofmeister.)

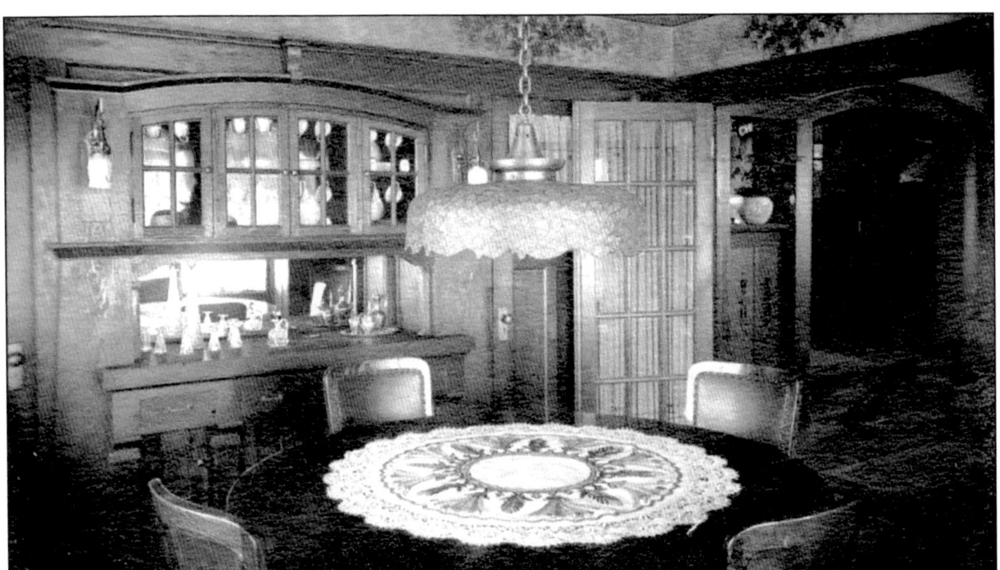

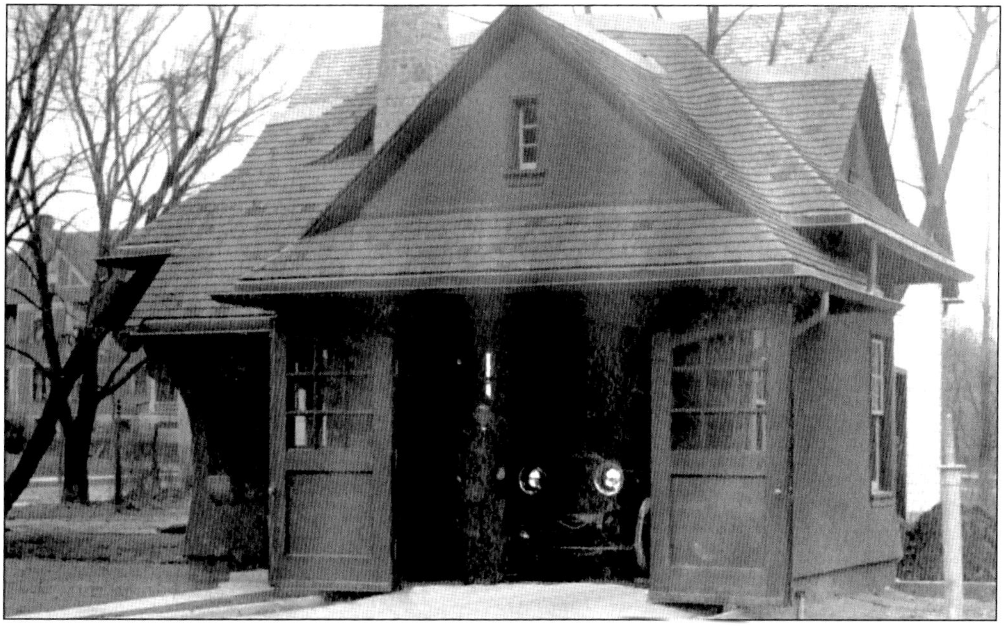

Edgar True proudly stands next to his automobile (*c.* 1920). His garage displays the same architectural details as the house. The interior is entirely finished with wood paneling. At left is a work/storage area with windows. The chimney once connected to a stove, a feature found in other Wauwatosa garages—the stove provided warmth to help start the car in Wisconsin's cold winters. The second/current owners purchased the True property in 1965. The Stick-style Victorian house at 7336 Hillcrest Drive is partly seen at left. (Courtesy of Gary Hofmeister.)

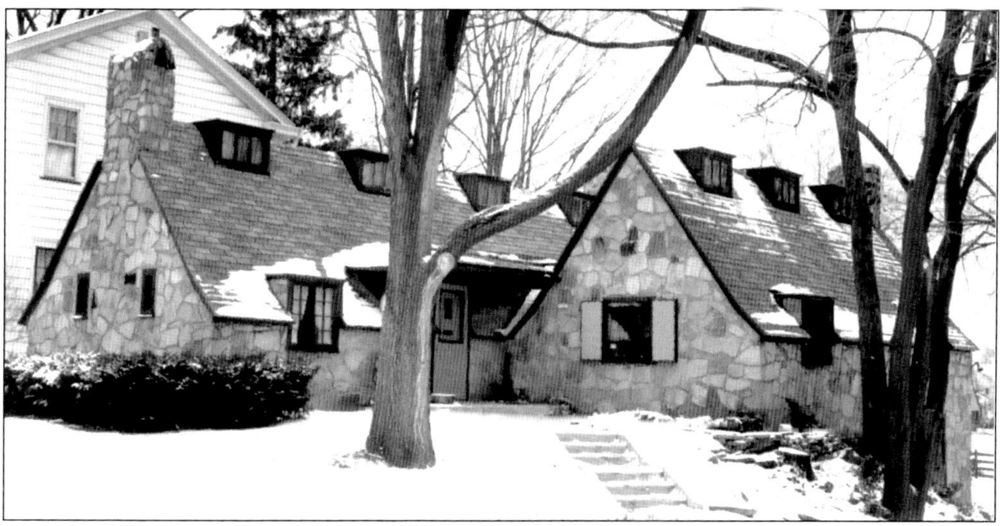

Prominent New York architect Ernest Flagg (1857–1947) designed houses based upon a modular system with standardized parts and workmanship, with design influenced by the cottages of rural Normandy. Distinctive house features are random stone construction, steeply pitched roofs, and low side-walls, as well as ridge dormers, skylights for the beamed ceilings, casement windows, and broad chimneys. The Flagg home at 7707 Stickney Avenue, constructed in 1925, is one of five such houses in Wauwatosa, all listed in the National Register of Historic Places. (Courtesy of Drexel and Charlotte Hansen.)

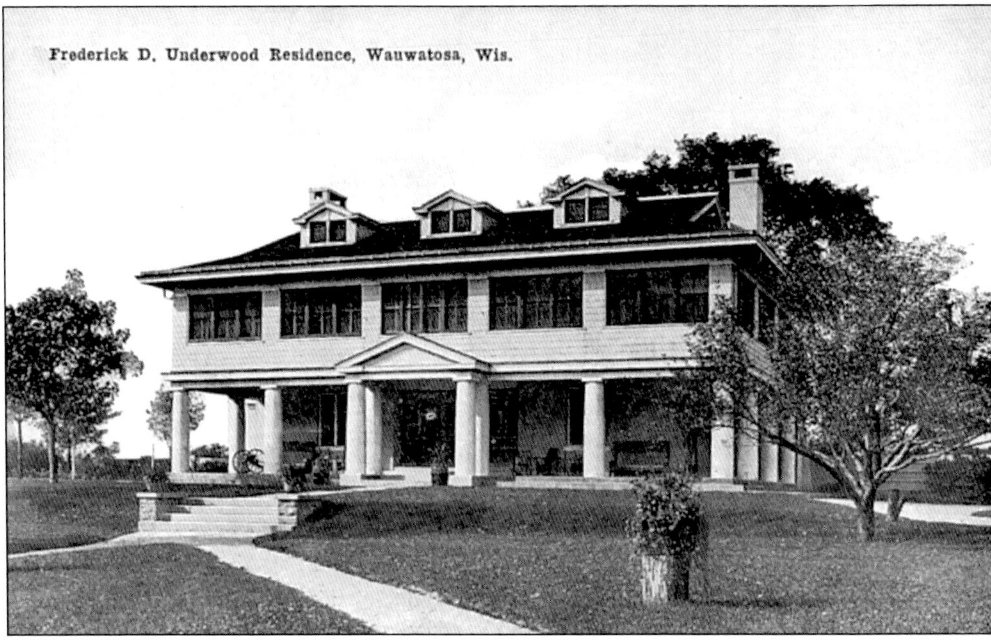

Frederick D. Underwood was born in 1849. In a world dominated by railroads, he took a job as a brakeman in 1869 and advanced to the presidency of the Erie Railroad, appointed by J.P. Morgan himself in approximately 1900. Underwood turned the beleaguered company around. Living in New York, Underwood frequently returned here in a private car named "Wauwatosa." Among his land holdings was a seven-and-one-half-acre parcel at the southwest corner of North and Wauwatosa Avenues, called "Few Acres." He built this retreat (*above*) between 1905 and 1909. A high concrete wall along North Avenue provided privacy. Underwood's ashes were strewn here after his death in 1942. The photographer climbed a tree to shoot the photo (*below*) of the empty compound in the early 1950s, prior to demolition of the house for the new Civic Center-Library. In the foreground, 7714 Stickney Avenue is visible. (WHS Postcard 649 and photo by Tom McFarland, WHS Photo 706.)

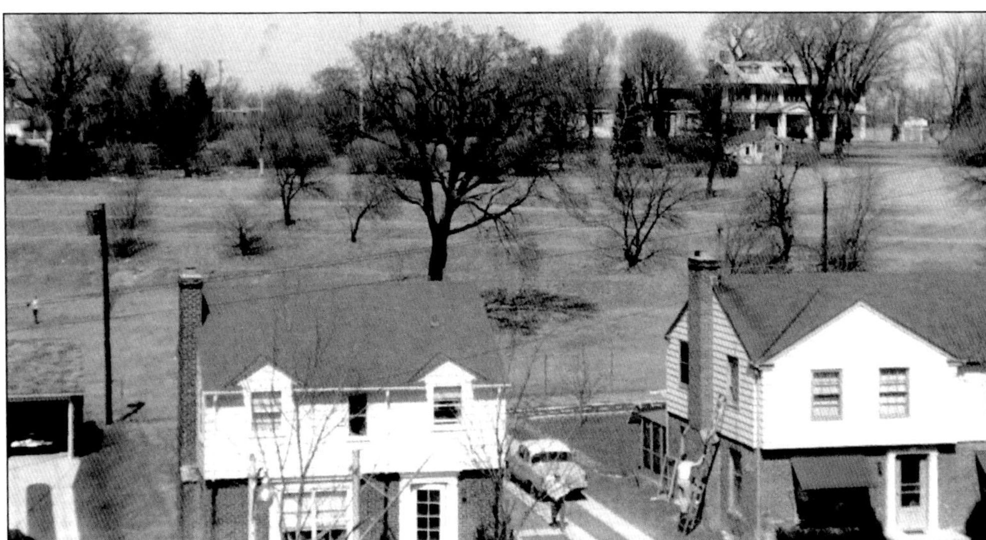

Ten

A Changing Landscape Post-World War II

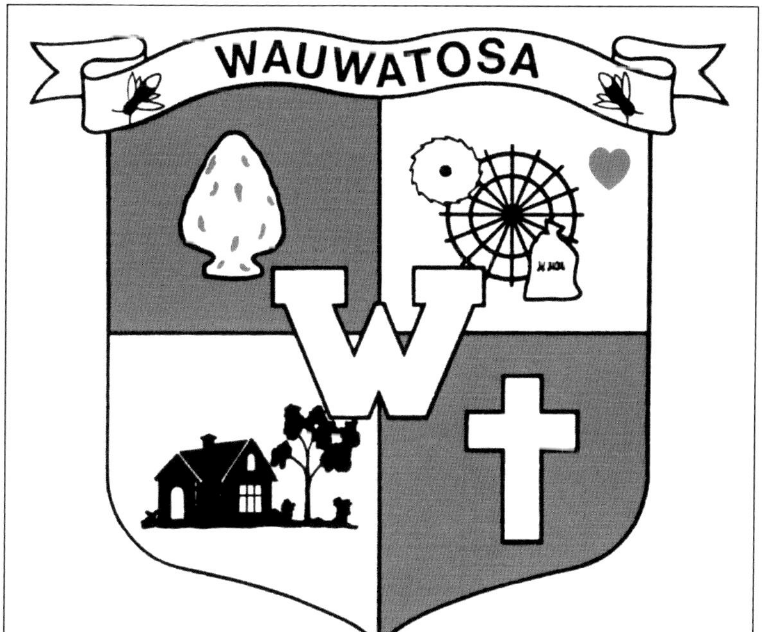

The annexations of 1952 tripled the size of Wauwatosa. The land brought new opportunities for residential, commercial, and institutional development. A major addition was the existing Harley-Davidson factory at 117th Street and Capitol Drive, today one of their largest sites. Briggs & Stratton purchased land at Burleigh and 124th Streets in 1951 and opened their plant in 1954. Annexation had its growing pains, such as water and trash disposal problems, but the city met the challenge. In 1963, the first Wauwatosa expressway segment opened and four years later the new position of planning administrator was instituted. The city adopted the mayor-city administrator form of government in 1972 and changed to a part-time mayor in 1976. In 1956, a children's design contest created a city emblem (above). In the early 1990s, threatened with an atheist's lawsuit, the Common Council voted to remove the cross and later replaced it with "In God We Trust." (WHS Mss. 79.)

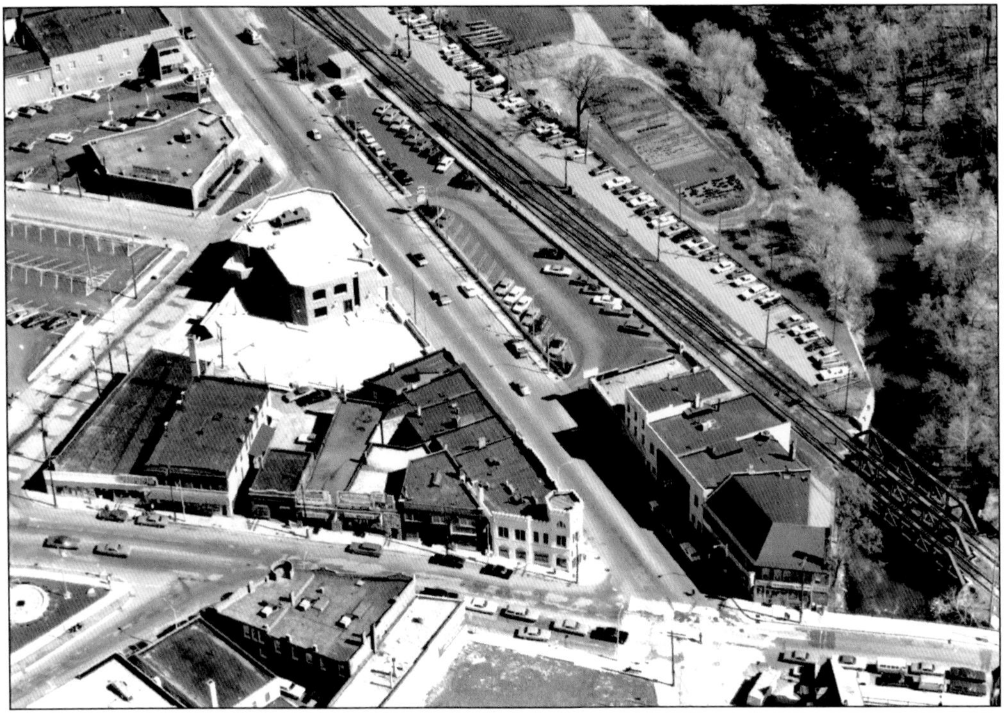

Village revitalization began after the war. A 1971 aerial photo (*above*) shows the Blanchard Street public parking lot (left center) built in 1952. In the lower left corner is the 1967 Pioneer Fountain, renovated in 1980. The large street parallel to the train tracks is State, the former train depot site has become a parking lot. At lower right are four of the five Village corners, including the Lefeber lot (vacant since 1964). In the center the new Wauwatosa Savings & Loan Golden Anniversary building is under construction at 7500 West State Street. The angular building across from the Savings & Loan is the First National Bank in Wauwatosa at 7430 West State Street. It was built in 1957 on the site of the businesses pictured below: Hickey's Shell, and Lix's Tavern, in the two-story frame building dated 1889 on the cornice. A sign to the right announces the new bank location. (Photo by Robert T. McCoy, WHS Mss. 72 and Photo 408.)

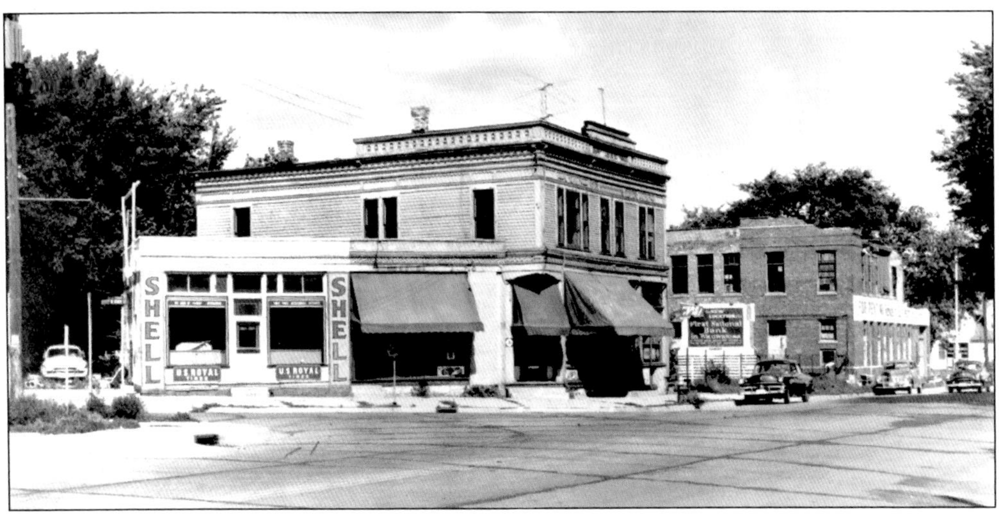

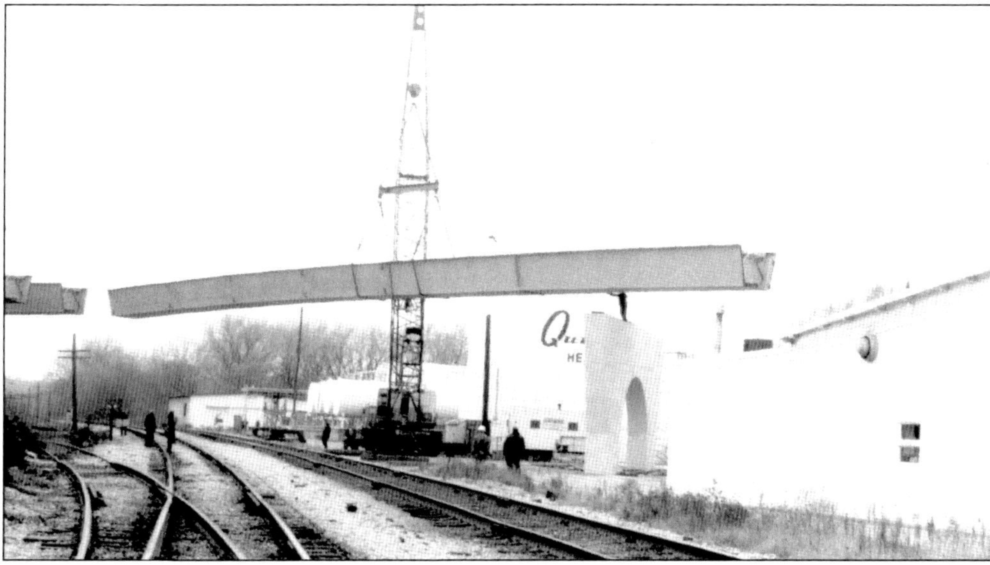

Harmonee Bridge, under construction in this photo, opened for traffic in August 1981. The bridge was designed to span the historic Village and thus eliminate the long waits and congestion at the railroad tracks on Harwood Avenue. Some feared it would be a detriment to the Village, but business activism, local government, and concerned citizen organizations sparked a rebirth. Partially visible is a storage tank for Quickflash Fuels, on the site of the former power plant (see page 12). (WHS Photo 416.)

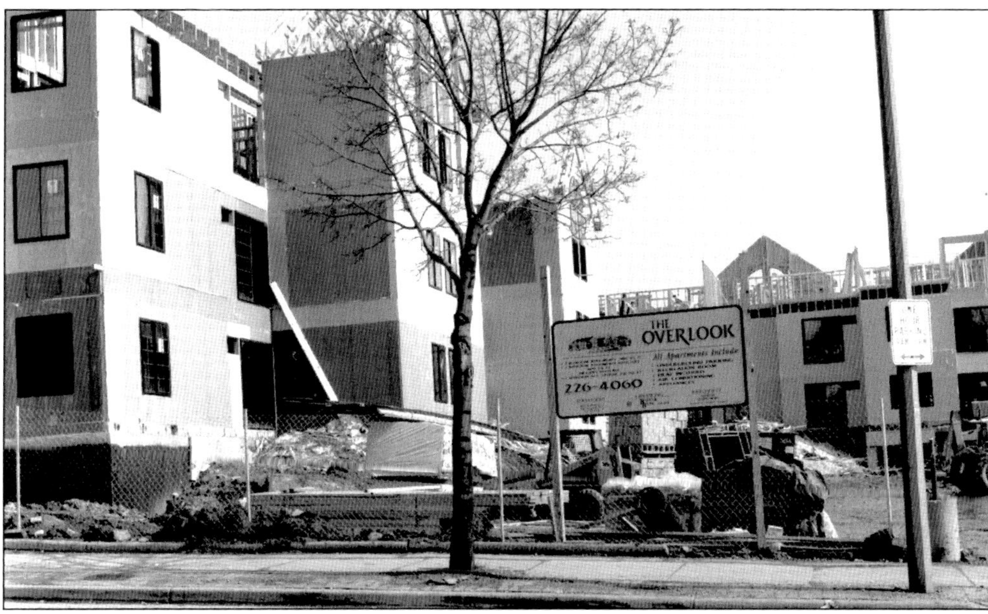

The Overlook Apartments were built at 7439 Harwood Avenue in the early 1990s. In the nineteenth century, Joseph Lefeber's home stood on the site (see page 103). In the 1960s, a food store occupied the land. Today, there is an appealing mix of eateries, banking, shops and galleries, businesses, and housing in the Village of Wauwatosa. In 2001, the 1414 Underwood building, a multi-use structure that incorporates housing, was built on the long-vacant Lefeber site. (WHS Photo 476.)

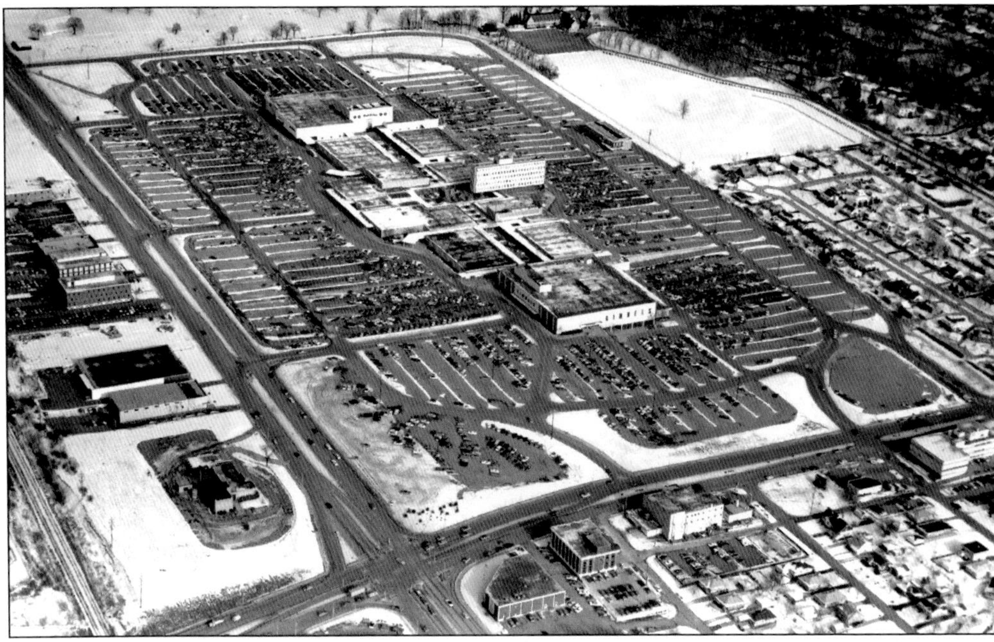

Mayfair Mall shopping center cost an estimated $20 million and transformed a rural spot into the city's commercial hub. By January 1959, both Gimbels and Marshall Fields were open. "Meet me on the Mall at Mayfair!" became a slogan. In the foreground of this 1969 photo is the intersection of North Avenue and Mayfair Road (Hy 100, formerly Lovers Lane Road and renamed Mayfair Road in Wauwatosa). Both streets were rebuilt. Fisher School is at left and Bluemound Country Club at the top. (Photo by Robert T. McCoy, WHS Photo 486.)

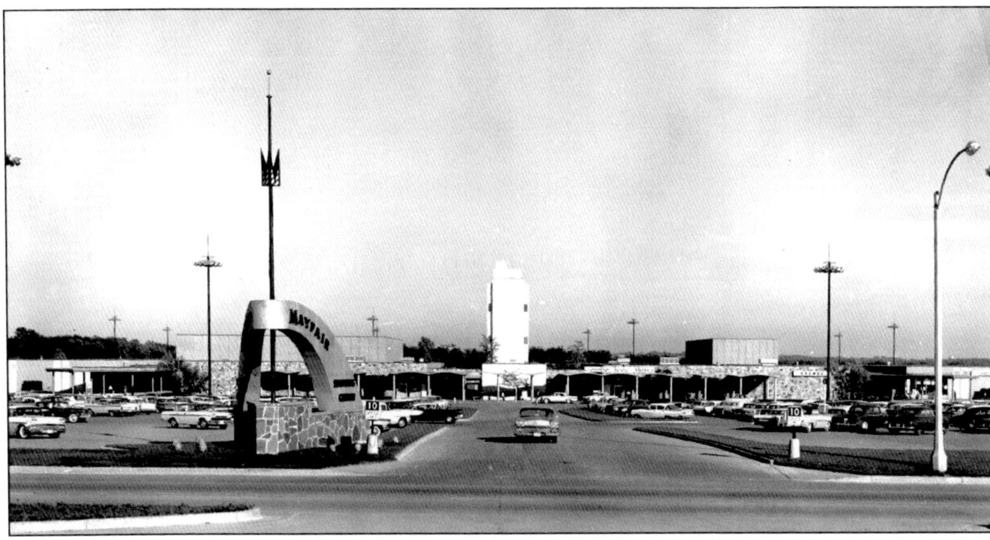

This is the west main entrance into Mayfair Mall shopping center from Mayfair Road in about 1963. The Mayfair office building rises above the low profile of the original complex. Initially an open-air mall, the center was enclosed and it has grown to include 180 stores, an 18-screen movie theater, a food court, and restaurants. The premiere mall in the metropolitan area, it attracts 16 million visitors annually. Twin office towers also rose at the north and south ends of the parcel on Mayfair Road. (Photo by Hildebrand Studio, WHS Photo 492.)

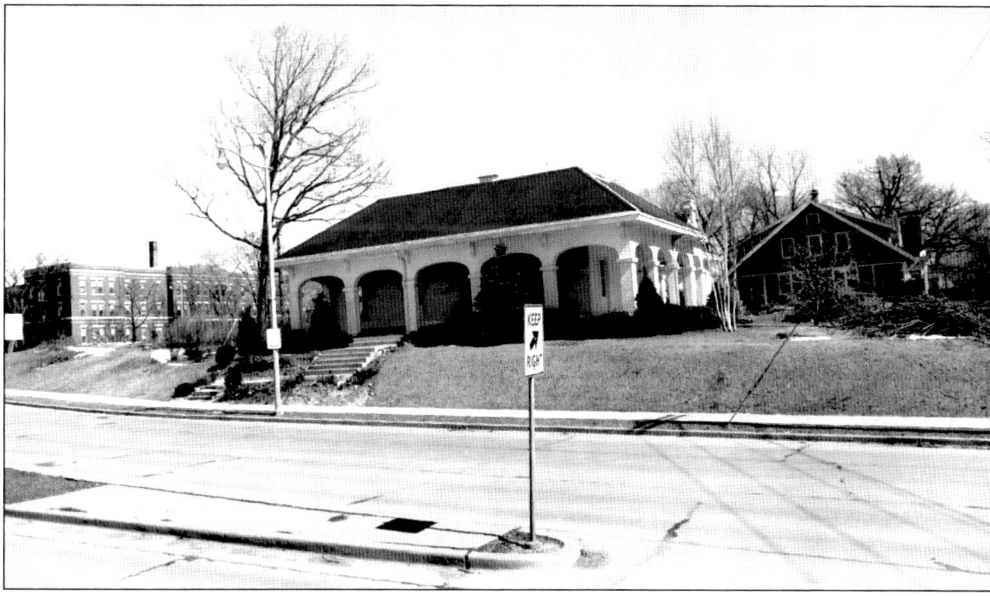

The Wauwatosa State Bank opened for business in the Village in 1920. Needing more space, the bank moved to a new building on the southeast corner of West North and Wauwatosa Avenues in 1974. Originally a residence, this white building (*above*) housed the dental office of Stanley J. Rogge before it was razed and Watson Avenue was blocked off to provide access to the bank parking lot and drive-thru service (*below*). In both views, the old building of the Lutheran Home is seen. In 1983, the bank was purchased in a stock exchange by the M & I Marshall and Ilsley Bank and operated as a unit bank until 1994, when it became a branch. In its 74-year existence, only five men served as presidents, Gilbert J. Davidson, Frank Olson, Arthur B. Kohasky (for 30 years), George A. Keller, and Paul E. Menzel. (WHS Photos Mss. 72.)

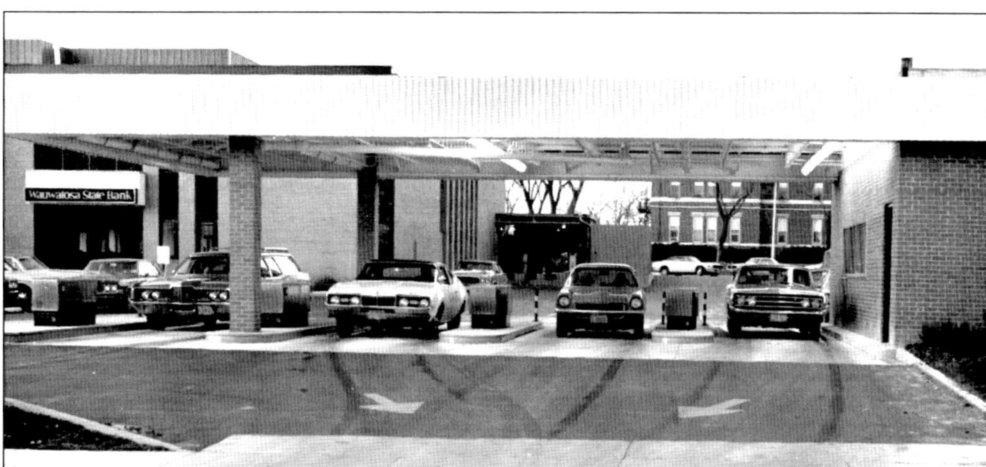

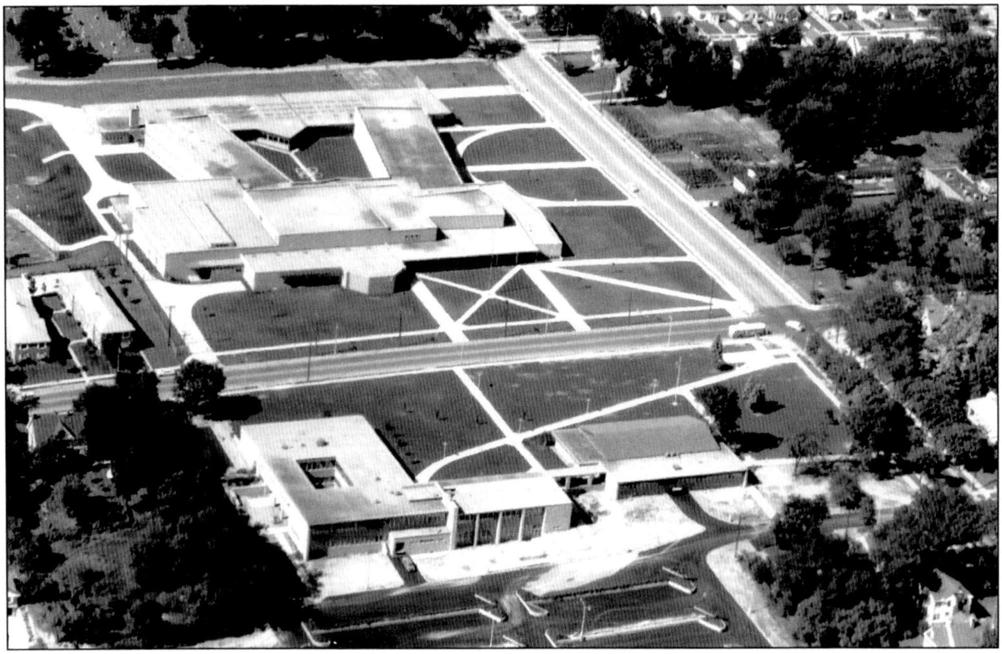

The Wauwatosa Memorial Civic Center is under construction (foreground) in April 1957. Located on the southwest corner of West North and Wauwatosa Avenues, the site of the former Underwood estate, the center was dedicated in October. The complex, comprising the city hall and the library, has meeting rooms and a memorial center to honor those Wauwatosans who died in wars and conflicts. At the very top is Wauwatosa Cemetery, with Longfellow Junior High School (opened in 1956) between it and the Civic Center. (WHS Photo 475.)

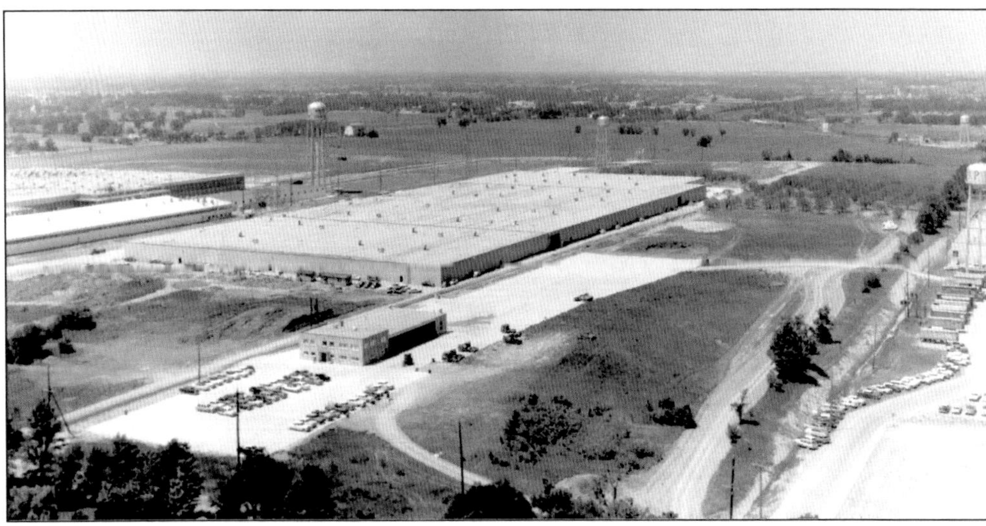

Post-annexation commercial construction included the General Merchandise Company's distribution center at 118th and Burleigh in 1958. Its "thirteen acres under one roof" (center) soon became the J.C. Penney Catalog Distribution Center, with an outlet store in the front. The smaller building in the foreground is Hillside Transit Company. Also seen are a portion of Briggs & Stratton (left) and the A & P water tower (right). A freeway exit came to the corridor a few years later. (WHS Photo 748.)

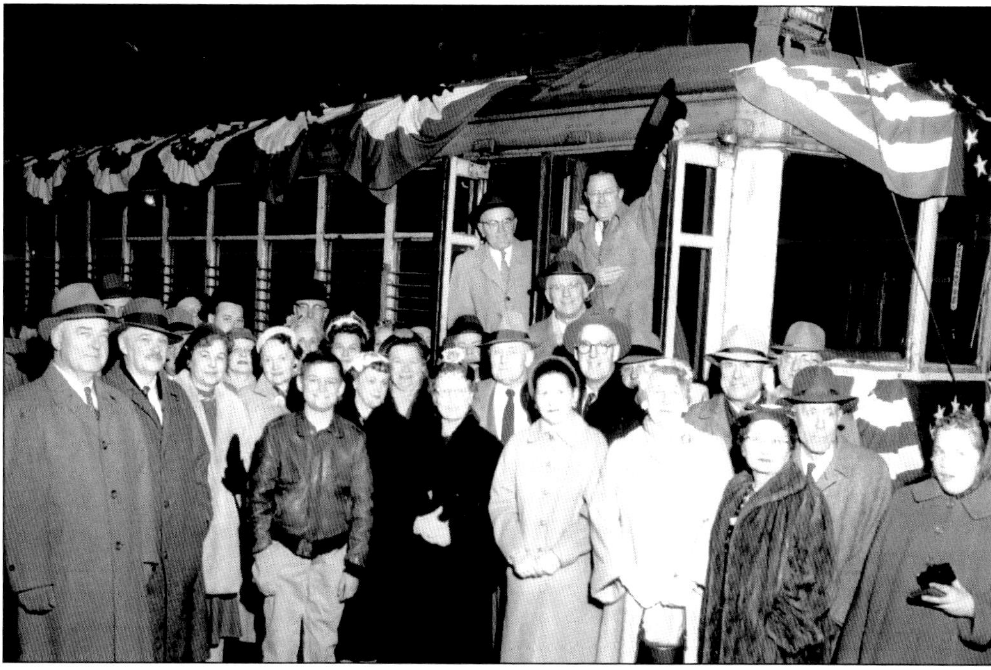

The street railway service on Wells Street to Wauwatosa began in 1897. On March 1, 1958, an era ended at the Harwood terminal in the Village with the last run of the #10 Wells/Farwell streetcar. A crowd witnesses the event. Ervin Meier, an alderman, waves from the car doorway. First elected alderman in 1937, he became mayor in 1964 and served until 1972. (WHS Photo 575.)

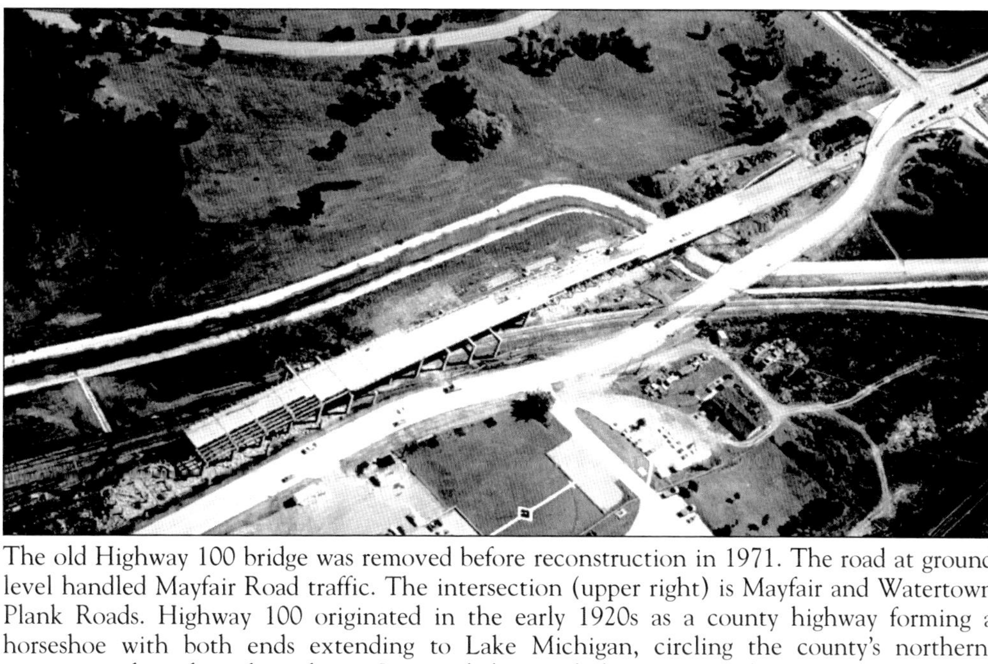

The old Highway 100 bridge was removed before reconstruction in 1971. The road at ground level handled Mayfair Road traffic. The intersection (upper right) is Mayfair and Watertown Plank Roads. Highway 100 originated in the early 1920s as a county highway forming a horseshoe with both ends extending to Lake Michigan, circling the county's northern, western, and southern boundaries. It provided an early bypass route through the county and the Waukesha county Village of Menomonee Falls. The roadway was designated a Milwaukee County Landmark in 2003. (Photo by Robert W. Baldwin, WHS Photo 477.)

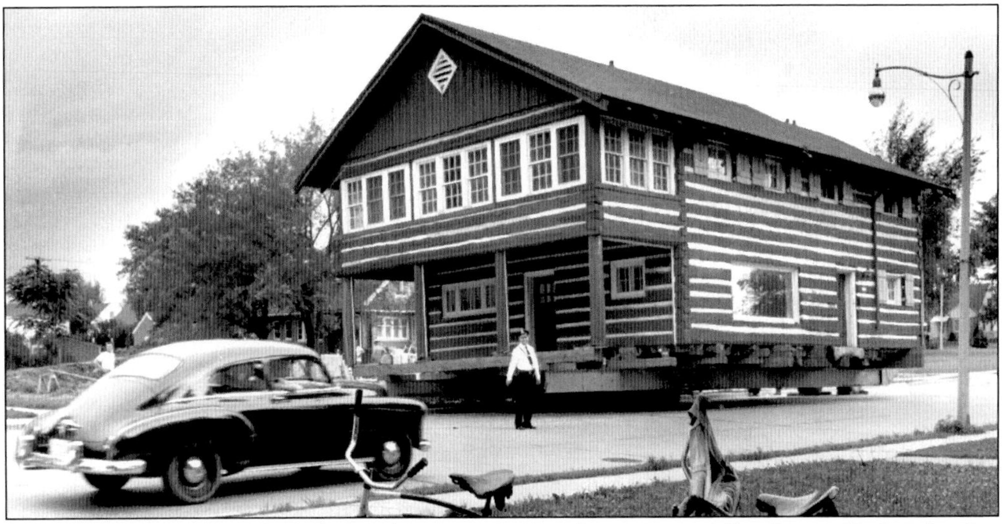

Increased numbers of students led to the construction of a new Longfellow Junior High School at Wauwatosa and North Avenues; land was cleared in 1955. In an act of early historic preservation, a log cabin built in 1880 by Frederick Underwood was moved from the site, at 7720 West North Avenue, to 2515 Wauwatosa Avenue for commercial use. It sits on the location of the former greenhouse and floral shop operated by florist John M. Dunlop. (WHS Photo 761.)

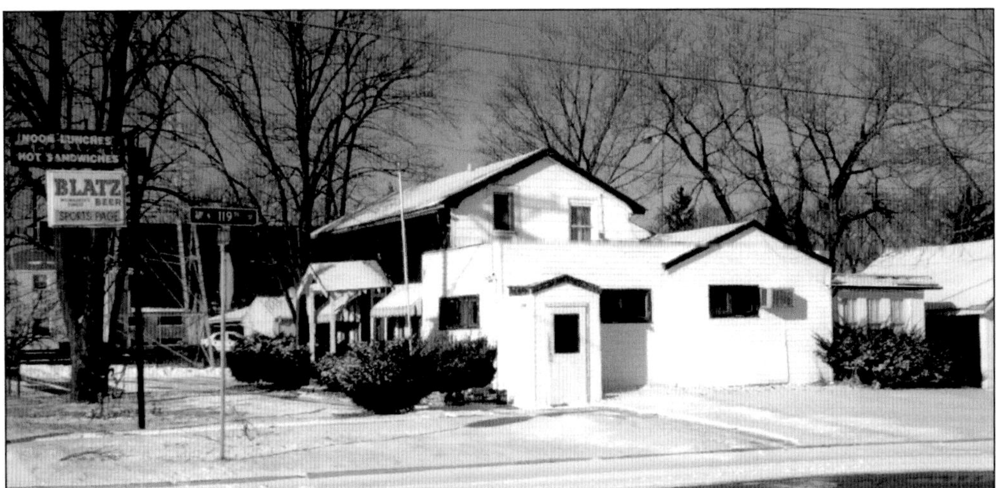

Originally a farmhouse built by Nathan Mower in the Town of Wauwatosa in the mid-1850s, 11904 West North Avenue became part of our city through annexation. Zoned commercial, it became Kay's Oak Ridge Tap in about 1950, and, in 1976, The Sports Page tavern. It was greatly altered and added to over the years; few details of its original Greek Revival style remained when it was razed in 2000. A new commercial building replaced it. (Courtesy of Earl Peychal.)

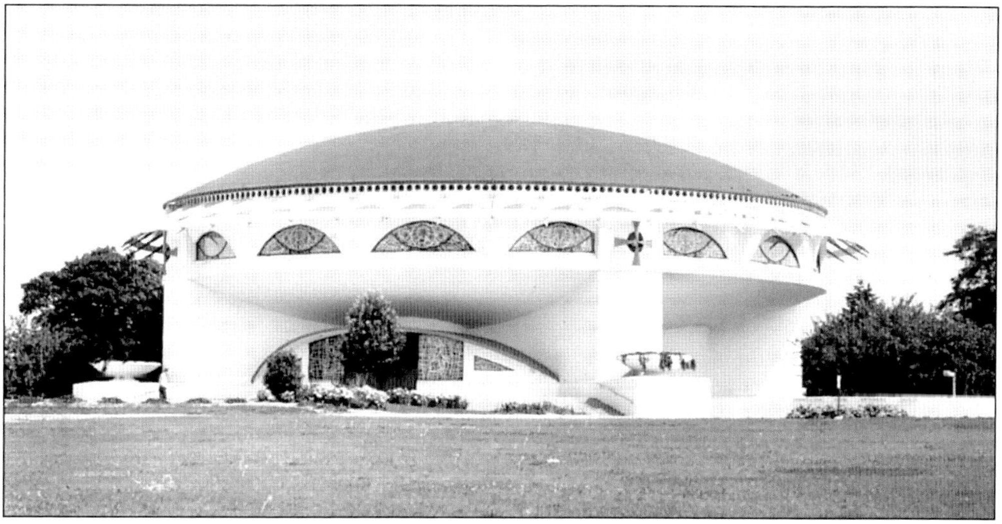

Deemed the greatest architect of the twentieth century, Wisconsin's Frank Lloyd Wright designed a religious jewel at 9400 West Congress in 1956—the Annunciation Greek Orthodox Church (photo c. 1985). Wright died in 1959, before groundbreaking, and the church was dedicated in 1961. Wright's circular plan, incorporating a domed space and based upon the Greek cross inscribed with a circle, adhered to historic elements in a radically different interpretation of traditional Byzantine church form. The Greek cross is also a prominent decorative feature in the interior. (Photo by Judith A. Simonsen, WHS Photo 749.)

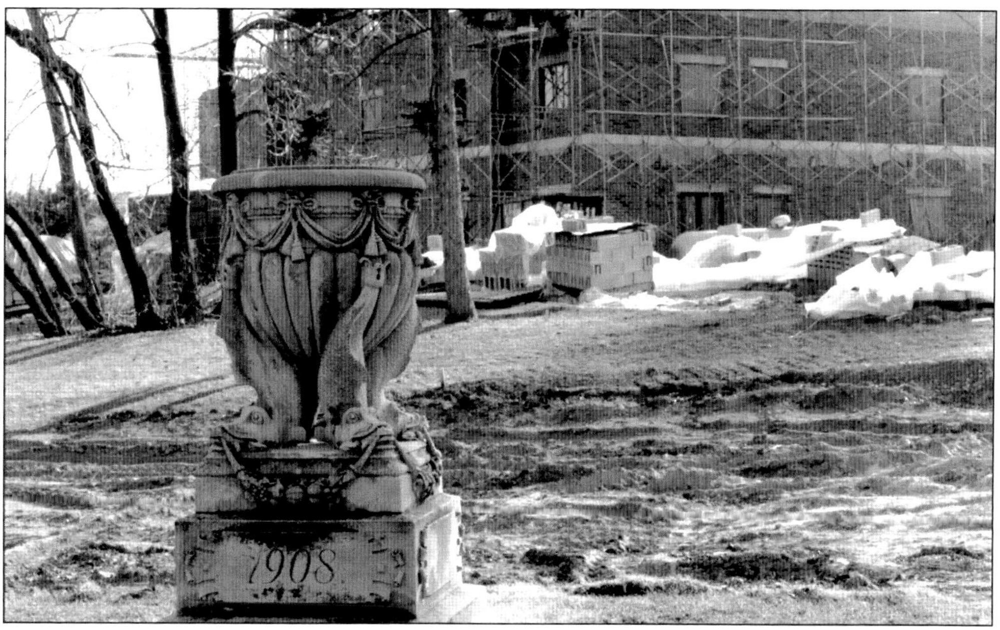

The Milwaukee County Institutions were transformed into a medical complex with modern buildings and concentration of services in the last decades of the twentieth century. In 1977, they became the Milwaukee County Regional Medical Center. The Ronald McDonald House is being built here in 1983 on the grounds. A dolphin urn, dated 1908, stands as a relic from the past. The only remaining old county buildings are that of the Children's Home Administration and four of the five Agricultural School Complex structures. (WHS Photo 511.)

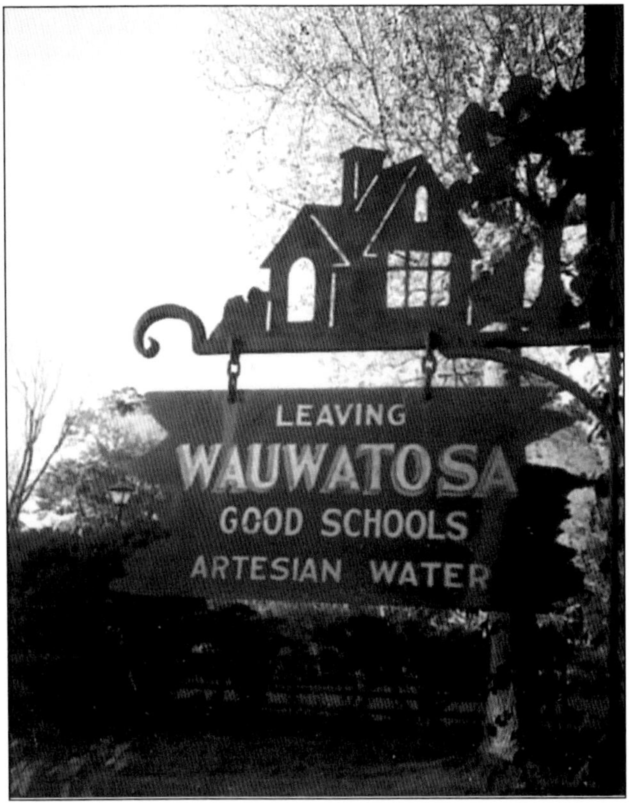

The community welcome signs had a message on both sides. This message touted the attributes of our fine city to those who were leaving it. (Photo by James Ruzicka, WHS Artifact Collection and Photo 759.)

The Honorable Mayors of Wauwatosa:

Emerson D. Hoyt 1897–1904
Edwin R. Godfrey 1904–1906
Charles B. Perry 1906–1916
Hans A. Koenig 1916–1920
Albert C. (A. C.) Hanson 1920–1934
Alfred C. Loose 1934–1943
William B. Knuese 1943–1964
Ervin A. Meier 1964–1972
Francis D. Kuckuck 1972–1976
James A. Benz 1976–1984
James A. Brundahl 1984–1992
Maricolette Walsh 1992–2000
Theresa M. Estness 2000–